GHOSTS AND SPIRITS

GHOSTS AND SPIRITS

Alan Baker

ORION

First published in 1998 by Orion Media
An imprint of Orion Books Ltd
Orion House, 5 Upper St Martin's Lane, London WC2H 9EA

A CIP catalogue record for this book is available
from the British Library.

ISBN 0-75281-766-3

Typeset by SetSystems Ltd, Saffron Walden, Essex
Printed and bound in Great Britain
by Clays Ltd, St Ives plc

CONTENTS

INTRODUCTION

According to H. P. Lovecraft, the New Englander who wrote his bizarre and astonishing short stories and novels in the early years of the twentieth century, the oldest emotion is fear, and the oldest fear is that of the unknown. To this we might add that the greatest unknowns are death; and the destiny that awaits the consciousness of every human being on Earth – indeed, of every intelligent being in the Universe. It is therefore no surprise that the concept of a connection between the worlds of the living and the dead should have endured from the earliest days of humanity, and that it should retain its power in our own cynical and materialistic age.

It has often been observed that the gradual undermining of our relationship with nature, a process that began in the furnaces of the Industrial Revolution, has resulted in a profound hunger for the wonder and mystery – the sense that the world is far stranger, far more *interesting* than everyday circumstances would seem to indicate – which our ancestors largely took for granted. And yet this underlying need extends much further back through history than the late eighteenth century. As a species, we seem to be trapped in what the British writer Colin Wilson calls the 'triviality of everydayness', the sense that there is a vast realm of experience lying beyond our mundane consciousness, to which we might gain access, if only we could shake ourselves free of the constrictions placed upon us by the very process of maintaining our familiar existence from day to day.

The concept of the ghost or spirit of the dead is as old as our awareness of death itself. Ghosts and spirits are to be found in all epochs of human history, from the early shamanic cultures of Asia, to the flight crews of modern commercial aircraft, and have been the cause of inspiration, terror or merely puzzlement for those encountering them.

While all paranormal phenomena are of immense significance in their own right, of all the mystifying events that have been recorded and investigated over the years – from clairvoyance to psychokinesis, from telepathy to precognition – by far the most significant is the set of phenomena pertaining to the survival of the human personality after physical death. In fact, there is surely no question of greater importance.

This, then, is the subject of this book. In gathering together the hundred or so cases that follow, I have attempted to present an overview of the vast amount of material that has been documented concerning the apparent return of the dead to the physical world. In providing such an overview, it is necessary to include those cases that have come to be regarded as 'classics', in addition to newer and lesser-known reports. Thus, it is hoped, the book will prove interesting both to those investigating the subject for the first time and to those with a little more experience, who will enjoy returning to some 'old favourites' as well as the newer cases.

In the Introduction to a previous book written for this series (*UFO Sightings*), I described an encounter I had with an unidentified light in the sky, and how I almost immediately realized that the 'UFO' actually had an entirely mundane cause. I would now like to describe an altogether more puzzling event that occurred in 1985, when I was twenty-one years old and living at home with my parents. I was lying in bed one night, having just switched off the light, and was preparing to go to sleep. The night outside was quiet, the house silent. Suddenly there was an almighty noise, apparently coming from the stairs just outside my bedroom door; indeed, the loud crashing sound seemed to be travelling down to the hallway, as if someone had thrown some large, heavy object down the stairs. Imagine what it would sound like if a large television were thrown down a flight of stairs: that is the kind of sound I heard.

Needless to say, I instantly sat bolt upright in bed, thinking that an intruder had managed to get in. However, what happened next forced this possibility from my mind, and I found myself suddenly oppressed by an entirely different kind of fear: the fear of the deep unknown. As soon as the loud crashing had ceased, a high-pitched voice sounded on the landing beyond my bedroom door. It was clearly a woman's voice, and, incredible as it may seem, it *sang* a single note. As if this were not bizarre enough, a couple of seconds later it was joined by another voice, this one obviously male, singing a note at a lower pitch, the two voices forming an unearthly harmony. After another couple of seconds, both voices fell silent, leaving me to wonder whether I had just dreamed these extraordinary events.

This question was quickly answered when my father came bursting into my room, and asked if I had just heard the noises. I replied that I had. My father said: 'What the hell was it?' – or something to that effect, and I replied that I had absolutely no idea. We searched the house, but found no signs of any intrusion, or any other disturbance. Everything was in its place, and no large objects had been thrown or fallen down the stairs. We retired again to our rooms, none the wiser as to the cause of the strange sounds. Perhaps surprisingly, we all slept soundly and peacefully that night.

In the morning, my father, who is an engineer, a pragmatist and total sceptic in all matters paranormal, put the sounds down to foxes crying in the garden outside. To any other sceptic reading this, that would doubtless seem a perfectly acceptable explanation (for the sounds, if not the loud crashing). There was only one problem with this: the voices we heard on the landing that night sounded *nothing* like the crying of foxes. Although they sound very eerie, fox cries are instantly recognizable as such. The voices we heard were undoubtedly *human* voices, and they definitely came from the upstairs landing, not from the garden outside.

While my father considered the mystery solved, my mother, who is as fascinated by the paranormal as I am, preferred to accept that the events of that night were simply an example of the strange things that happen to people every day, all over the world, and for which there is no easy explanation.

What had made those noises? Was it a ghost (or, rather, two) that had somehow and for some unknown reason briefly manifested in our house, only to depart into the night as soon as it had made its presence known? There were certainly no subsequent manifestations of anything that could remotely be called the 'paranormal'. The loud crashing implies some form of poltergeist activity, in which a force (whether from beyond the grave or from the subconscious of those present who are still living) acts upon physical objects, or creates noises seemingly from out of 'thin air'. There are even a few reports in the literature on ghosts of poltergeists (derived from the German, meaning 'noisy spirits') manifesting very briefly, causing a disturbance only once, before departing for ever. Perhaps this is what my family and I experienced that night (although I can imagine my father shaking his head in exasperation at the thought!).

Personally, I am inclined to agree with my mother, and file the events away in my memory under 'Interesting and Unexplained', as so many other people must do every day, when faced with such things. One thing is for certain: the sound of those voices is as clear in my mind as I write this in 1997 as it was that night in 1985.

The fact that ghostly encounters are as common today as they have ever been explains our continuing fascination with them, and I hope that the reader will share in this fascination as the story of ghosts and spirits unfolds in the following pages. Each of the first ten chapters deals with a particular type of report – ghostly encounters in past centuries, the first spiritualists, the various types of ghost (poltergeists, interactive ghosts) and so on. In Chapter 11, I shall look at some of the theories that have been put forward to account for the origin, appearance and behaviour of ghosts.

Whether you are a newcomer to this subject, would like to add to an already well-stocked paranormal bookshelf or simply require a spine-tingling read for a rainy evening, I hope you will find this book both informative and entertaining.

1

GHOSTS AND SPIRITS OF LONG AGO

THE GHOST OF EN-DOR

One of the earliest written histories of ghostly encounters is in the Bible, with the description, in the first book of Samuel, of Saul's interrogation of the ghost of the prophet Samuel at En-dor in 800 BC. At that time there was much tension between Saul, who had been proclaimed the first King of Israel by Samuel, and his comrade David, whose popularity was in no small part due to his legendary boyhood feat of slaying the Philistine giant, Goliath. As the Philistine threat grew, Saul's rage against David culminated in the King outlawing him, forcing him to retreat to the wilderness of the Negev desert, below the hills of Judaea. (Later, on Saul's death, David would seize the southern kingdom of Judah and subdue the northern kingdom of Israel, ultimately uniting the Israelites.)

Watching the advance of the Philistines, Saul prayed to God, but received no answer, 'neither by dreams, nor by Urim [an object used to divine the will of God], nor by prophets'. In desperation, Saul turned to his servants and ordered them to find a woman with a 'familiar spirit' (in other words, a witch), with whom he might consult. His servants replied that there was such a woman at En-dor, and so Saul disguised himself and went to the woman's house in the company of two bodyguards.

When Saul approached her in his disguise, the woman refused to help: since Saul had banished all witches and wizards, she suspected the stranger of laying a deadly trap for her. However, Saul assured her that no harm would result, and asked her to raise the spirit of Samuel. When she had done so, she turned to Saul and cried: 'Why hast thou deceived me? for thou art Saul.' The King asked her what she had seen, and she replied: 'An old man cometh up, and he is covered with a mantle.'

Saul then perceived the prophet who had anointed him King, and bowed down before him. The ghost of Samuel was displeased, and demanded: 'Why hast thou disquieted me, to bring me up?'

Saul replied: 'I am sore distressed; for the Philistines make war against me, and God is departed from me, and answereth me no more.' And he asked the ghost of Samuel what he should do.

Samuel replied that God would take the kingdom of Israel from his hands and give it to David, since Saul had failed to obey the voice of the Lord. The prophet also said that Israel would first fall to the Philistines, and that Saul and his sons would perish. At this announcement, Saul prostrated himself on the ground. He had not eaten for a day and a night, and his strength was gone.

After much argument, the woman finally prevailed upon the King to eat some unleavened bread. Then he took himself off into the night. The ghost had indeed spoken the truth, for three of Saul's sons subsequently died in the Battle of Gilboa. The King himself was seriously wounded in the battle, and later committed suicide.

In his commentary on this account in his book *The Catalogue of Ghost Sightings*, Brian Innes speculates as to whether Saul actually saw the ghost of Samuel, or whether the woman went into a mediumistic trance, in which she spoke with Samuel's voice. Innes draws attention to the way in which the ghost was compelled by the woman to appear, thus strictly placing it in the category of necromancy (the raising of the dead in order to elicit information from them).

THE BATTLE OF MARATHON

Another account from the pre-Christian era is supplied by a Greek author of the second century AD, named Pausanias. While writing a travel guide to Greece, Pausanias was told the story of the ghosts of Marathon, which lay 'halfway between Athens and Carystus in Euboea'. According to Pausanias:

> It was in this part of Attica that the foreign army landed, was defeated in battle, and lost some ships as it took off again. In the plain there is a grave for the Athenians, and on it there are slabs with the names of the fallen arranged according to their tribes. There is another grave for the Boeotians, one for the Plataeans, and one for the slaves, because slaves had fought there for the first time.

Pausanias goes on to relate how at this place one could hear men fighting and horses whinnying throughout the night. Anyone who went there with the intention of listening to the ghosts would suffer ill fortune, although the ghosts would 'not get angry with anyone who happens to be there against his will'.

In view of the theory that ghosts and spirits tend to return to Earth as a result of certain events that refuse to allow them to rest, or move on to join the afterlife, it is perhaps understandable that the scenes of battles are prime candidates for hauntings. Not only are these places of extreme trauma and suffering, but the dead are left without the benefit of relevant religious ceremonies. In addition, the warning against searching for the ghosts of Marathon seems to presage the modern belief that ghosts do not take kindly to being 'hunted', and that those actively looking for them will be disappointed.

THE HAUNTED HOUSE IN ATHENS

The Roman orator Pliny the Younger (who lived in the first century AD) tells us in one of his letters how a large house in Athens was the site of a haunting, in which the ghost apparently indulged in what has come to be regarded as a somewhat clichéd activity: the rattling of chains. According to Pliny, anyone brave enough to stay at the house would hear this chilling noise, which would steadily draw closer, until the ghost itself would appear, taking the form of a thin, old man with long hair and a beard.

Eventually, the house was abandoned and fell into disrepair, until the Stoic philosopher Athenodorus arrived from Tarsus, and wondered if the house's dilapidation might allow him to rent it cheaply. The rent was, indeed, remarkably low. The house's owners made no secret of its being haunted, but nevertheless Athenodorus decided to take the place.

On the evening he moved in, the philosopher went straight to work, and became so absorbed that he failed to notice when the rattling of chains began in the distance. He continued with his notes as the unearthly sounds drew nearer, until the ghost itself appeared, and Athenodorus looked up from his work to be confronted by the phantom, just as the owners of the house had described it to him. The ghost beckoned to him, entreating him to follow it. Perhaps in keeping with his vocation as a Stoic, Athenodorus decided to finish what he was doing before attending to the appeals of the ghost. Eventually, however, the rattling of the chains became so irritating that Athenodorus gave up and followed the beckoning apparition. He was led into the courtyard of the house, where he watched the ghost move to a clump of shrubs and promptly vanish.

The following day, Athenodorus paid a visit to the magistrate, suggesting that the courtyard be dug up. This was done, and a skeleton was discovered, bound hand and foot in shackles. The bones were gathered together, and were buried

9

with the appropriate rites. Thereafter, according to Pliny, the house was haunted no more.

THE HAUNTED FARMHOUSE AT BINGEN ON THE RHINE

The chronicle *Annales Fuldenses* records a German tale dating back to AD 856, in which an unnamed farmer, who lived with his family near the village of Bingen on the River Rhine, became the victim of ghostly activity. An evil spirit that tormented the family announced its arrival by throwing stones and hammering on the walls of the house. When the farmer examined the walls of his property, he found them to be undamaged. As we shall see later, this, along with stone-throwing, is a common feature of poltergeist hauntings: although the loud sounds reported would seem to indicate that a great deal of damage is being done, later inspection proves this not to be the case. In addition, even when the victims of such attacks are physically struck by objects thrown by the poltergeist, they are rarely injured.

The 'focus' of the Bingen poltergeist seemed to be the farmer himself, who would be followed around constantly by the family's tormentor, even when he visited friends and acquaintances, to the extent that he was soon no longer welcome in their homes. In such cases, the 'focus' is that person who seems to be the principal object or centre of the manifestation and who apparently unwittingly acts as a kind of catalyst for whatever mysterious agency is ultimately responsible for the occurrences.

The Bingen poltergeist displayed some particularly unpleasant traits, and apparently victimized the family in ways that were not only malicious but also pointless. For instance, it would frequently cause fires to break out, especially in crops that had just been gathered. Presently, the entity began to speak, and claimed that the farmer was the perpetrator of all manner of sins, including adultery.

Eventually, word of the haunting reached the Bishop of

Mainz, who sent several priests, armed with holy relics, to banish the otherworldly miscreant. When the priests arrived, they promptly set to work sprinkling the farmhouse with holy water. This infuriated the poltergeist, which began to throw stones at them.

Although the chronicle does not mention whether the poltergeist was exorcized (according to Colin Wilson in his book *Poltergeist: a Study in Destructive Haunting*, this implied that it was not, since the triumphs of the Church over evil were invariably recorded at every opportunity), the tale does have an intriguing twist. It seems that the poltergeist was actually a 'familiar' spirit that had attached itself to one of the priests who had been instructed to exorcize it. Apparently, the priest had committed adultery, which caused the arrival of a servant who was demonic and difficult to control.

THE PHANTOM DRUMMER OF TEDWORTH

One of the most famous of all ghostly tales concerns the phantom drummer of Tedworth (now North Tidworth) in the county of Wiltshire, England. This mid-seventeenth-century case, first chronicled by the contemporary writer, the Revd Joseph Glanvill FRS, chaplain to Charles II, in a book on witchcraft entitled *Saducismus Triumphatus* (1681), concerned a local magistrate named Mr Mompesson. In March 1661, Mompesson came upon a vagabond, William Drury, who was playing a drum loudly, begging in the streets and making a general nuisance of himself. Mompesson had the beggar committed to Gloucester gaol. Although he left Drury's drum with the bailiff at Tedworth, it was later sent to Mompesson's house, on the border of Salisbury Plain.

The magistrate had been away in London on a business trip, and when he returned on 4 May, he found his family in a state of great alarm, claiming that extraordinary noises had been plaguing them. At first, they had thought that the noises were being caused by thieves; but it became apparent that they were not and it seemed that whoever was making them was going out of his way to do so.

Three nights later, Mompesson himself heard the noises, which took the form of 'a great knocking at the doors, and at the outside of the walls', changing presently to 'a thumping and drumming on the top of the house'. Eventually, the noises faded into the night. Drawing on Joseph Glanvill's account in his 1907 book *Haunted Houses*, Charles G. Harper writes:

> It was some time before Mr Mompesson connected these disturbances with the drummer he had sentenced, but the drumming during the succeeding month became so noticeable that the suggestion became inevitable. To make the connection more certain, it [the demon] invaded the room where the drum itself had been placed, and during four or five nights in every week would beat military tattoos, from bedtime until the small hours of the morning. Later, the demon turned its attention to the children, beating their bedsteads with so much violence that everyone expected they would fall in pieces. It would then shake the children, lift them up in their beds, and scratch under the beds, as with iron talons. 'On the 5th of November it made a mighty noise; and a servant observing two boards in the children's room seeming to move, he bid it give him one of them. Upon which the board came (nothing moving it that he saw) within a yard of him. The man added, "Nay, let me have it in my hand"; upon which the spirit, devil, or drummer pushed it towards him so close that he might touch it. This,' continues Glanvill, 'was in the daytime and was seen by a whole roomful of people. That morning it left a sulphurous smell behind it, which was very offensive.'

One evening, a minister named Mr Cragg visited the house, and prayed with Mompesson and his family at their children's bedsides. While they prayed, the drummer retreated into the cockloft and waited until they had finished, whereupon it returned and proceeded to make some chairs walk around the room by themselves. 'At the same time, a bedstaff was thrown at the minister, which hit him on the leg, but so favourably that a lock of wool could not have fallen more softly.'

On another occasion, a sceptical village blacksmith asked to spend a night with the footman, so that he might also hear the strange noises. It seems that he was cured of his scepticism when 'there came a noise in the room as if one had been shoeing a horse, and somewhat came, as it were, with a pair of pincers, snipping and snapping at the blacksmith's nose the greater part of the night'.

Such was the notoriety of the case of the phantom drummer that Charles II himself sent a Royal Commission to inquire into the goings-on; however, while the Commission was there, the drummer remained silent, only to start again when it left. The drummer clearly had some aversion to officialdom, since it was perfectly prepared to perform for the hundreds of ordinary folk who came from all over the region to listen to its antics.

Up until this point, the drummer had been reluctant to show itself, but this changed: Mompesson's servant claimed to have caught sight of the thing as it stood at the foot of his bed. The servant described a creature with a large, hulking body and two red, glaring eyes, which gazed at him for some moments before disappearing. The apparition also began to widen its repertoire. 'Innumerable were the antics it played. Once it purred like a cat; beat the children's legs black and blue; put a long spike into Mr Mompesson's bed, and a knife into his mother's; filled the porringers with ashes; hid a Bible under the grate; and turned the money black in people's pockets.'

While all this mayhem was occuring, the vagabond William Drury was biding his time in Gloucester gaol. When he was visited one day by a resident of Tedworth, he asked if there was any talk of drumming in a certain gentleman's house there. When his visitor replied that there was talk of little else, Drury claimed that he was the cause, and would not cease tormenting Mompesson and his family until he had been compensated for the loss of his drum.

Drury was later tried for witchcraft at Salisbury and, although he was acquitted, was nevertheless sentenced to transportation. According to Glanvill, during his voyage, Drury raised frightful storms and managed to escape. While he had been upon the sea, the strange phenomena at Mompesson's house had ceased, and yet, so it was said, upon his return the drummings and other phenomena resumed intermittently for several years.

It would seem that there are several possible explanations for the poltergeist activity at Tedworth. Perhaps it was all a hoax, with Drury employing several accomplices to cause havoc while he sat happily in gaol. Or perhaps he was somehow able to project a form of psychokinesis (the power of causing objects to move through the action of the mind alone) from his cell to Mompesson's house. As with the vast majority of ghost reports, all we have is first- or secondhand testimony to go on, and for this reason it is extremely difficult to arrive at any satisfactory conclusion.

2

THE BIRTH OF SPIRITUALISM

THE HYDESVILLE RAPPINGS

Although our fascination with ghosts and spirits has been ever-present, the origin of the modern phase of that fascination can be traced to a small village in New York State, and to the experiences of the Fox family, who moved there in December 1847. Soon after they had settled into their new home, the family began to hear strange knocking sounds issuing from the walls. All attempts made by the family to discover the source of the noises failed, and they were kept awake for many nights.

Then, on 31 March 1848, one of the three Fox sisters, Kate, who was twelve, began to snap her fingers, asking 'Mr Splitfoot' (her name for the source of the noise and an old nickname for the Devil) to copy her. To everyone's astonishment, it complied, imitating the sounds she made. It occurred to Mrs Fox that 'Mr Splitfoot' might be made to answer questions, so she asked 'him' to rap the ages of her children. In Brian Innes's book, *The Catalogue of Ghost Sightings*, Mrs Fox described what happened next:

Instantly, each one of my children's ages was given correctly, pausing between them sufficiently long enough to individualise them until the seventh – at which a longer pause, and then three more emphatic raps were given, corresponding to the age of the little one that died, which was my youngest child. I then asked: 'Is this a human being that answers my questions correctly?' There was no rap. I asked: 'Is it a spirit? If it is, make two raps.' Two sounds were given as soon as the request was made.

Several of the Foxes' neighbours were called in to witness these happenings, and one of them, Chauncey Losey, suggested devising an alphabetical code, by which more complex questions might be put to the 'spirit'. As a result of this, they were able to learn that the 'spirit' was that of a peddler named Charles B. Rosma, who had died in the house five years earlier. Via the newly devised code, the rappings indicated that Rosma had had his throat cut in the east bedroom, and had been buried in the cellar. Although at the time the police, who were immediately informed, could find no record of a missing peddler named Rosma, and so declined to pursue a murder inquiry, in 1904 (it is alleged) a wall collapsed in the cellar, revealing a skeleton and a peddler's box. Unfortunately, this has never been substantiated.

After the noises had informed the Fox family and their neighbours of Rosma's gruesome fate, a number of new sounds were added to their repertoire. These consisted of the sounds of a frantic struggle, the gurgling of a throat being cut and the sound of a body being dragged across the floor. Eventually, the family could stand no more, and two of the sisters, Kate and Margaret (who was fifteen), were sent away briefly to stay with neighbours. The raps, however, went with them and caused havoc in the houses in which they stayed.

The rest of the family were also victimized by the 'spirit', which began to snatch off Mrs Fox's cap and pull the comb from her hair. Pins were jabbed into the family when they knelt to pray and the raps steadily increased in volume until they could be heard a mile away.

At this point it was decided that the alphabetical code should be utilized again, with the hope that the 'spirit' might be prevailed upon to leave the family alone. When this was tried, the 'spirit' sent them a message that proved to be somewhat prophetic. 'Dear friends,' it began, 'you must proclaim this truth to the world. This is the dawning of a new era.'

The Fox sisters began to display their mediumistic talents throughout the eastern United States, with the first spiritualist meeting taking place on 14 November 1849. The sisters caused a sensation wherever they went, not least because people discovered that they could reproduce the strange results in their own seances. All that was needed was a group of people to sit around a table with their fingertips touching and a certain amount of patience. Once called upon, the spirits would indicate their presence by causing the table to vibrate, or by lifting it slightly and letting it drop back to the floor.

Word of these astonishing events soon spread to Europe and beyond, and the worldwide spiritualist movement was born. The Fox sisters became professional mediums and were investigated by a number of psychical researchers, including the distinguished scientist Sir William Crookes (discoverer of thallium and inventor of the radiometer), who attended many of the seances conducted by Kate Fox and became convinced of her authenticity. As a qualified scientist, Crookes's record of attendance at seances is unsurpassed to this day.

However, many other researchers were less than impressed and maintained that the Fox sisters were merely frauds. In later years the sisters were attacked by angry crowds and succumbed to alcholism. Eventually, they confessed that they were indeed frauds, although they later retracted this confession. All three of the sisters (the third was named Leah) died soon after, Leah in 1890, Kate in 1892 and Margaret in 1893.

EUSAPIA PALLADINO

Physical mediumship is perhaps the most impressive (not to mention controversial) branch of spiritualism, the physical medium allegedly being capable of causing three-dimensional physical manifestations, such as the psychic substance known as ectoplasm. One of the most celebrated physical mediums of the nineteenth century was Eusapia Palladino, who was born in Italy in 1854. Eusapia claimed a traumatic childhood: her father was murdered by brigands when she was twelve and her mother had died giving birth to her. Alone and totally lacking in education, she was taken in by a family who were deeply interested in spiritualism. Her talents became evident from the outset, and she was apparently capable of producing materialized forms. However, the talent for which she became most famous – or notorious – was psychokinesis.

Over the course of her career, Eusapia, like the Fox sisters, was investigated by many eminent scientists, the first of whom, Ercole Chiaia, challenged his peers to examine her and put her talents to the test. Chiaia insisted that she was capable, through the action of the mind, of 'attract[ing] to her the articles of furniture which surround her, [lifting] them up' and holding them in the air. Apparently, she was able to perform these feats of psychokinesis by extending invisible 'pseudopods' from her body, which would move the objects. Over the next twenty-five years, Eusapia travelled throughout Europe, submitting to investigation after investigation. In Paris, between 1905 and 1908, she was tested by a group of scientists that included Pierre and Marie Curie, and Henri Bergson.

In his examination of psychical research, *The Hidden Power*, Brian Inglis describes what happened on these occasions.

> ... monitoring instruments were used which were designed not merely to register if physical force was applied, but which would register it in another room, so that it would make no difference if the sitters with Eusapia allowed themselves to be distracted. In these conditions she provided her stock repertoire of raps, the playing of instruments and the movements of distant objects. Playful visible hands untied the scientists' cravats and pulled their hair. A stool from outside the circle advanced to Pierre Curie, and made as if to climb up his leg. A small table floated in over his shoulder making 'a pretty curve' as it did so.

Inglis goes on to state that conjurors of the time claimed that scientists were just as gullible as the public – if not more so. After the tests in Paris, the Society for Psychical Research (SPR), which had been founded in 1882 to investigate the paranormal, sent three experts on conjuring to Naples to examine Eusapia. Wortley Baggally, Hereward Carrington and Everard Fielding were confident that they would expose her as a fake. However, they were unable to detect any trickery.

Although many scientists were utterly baffled by Eusapia's apparent abilities, others were convinced that she was somehow faking them. Some even applied the occasionally warped logic of the sceptic and stated that, although no trickery could be detected, it nevertheless must have been employed, since psychokinesis is impossible.

Brian Inglis offers an example of this logic at work, citing the case of Richard Hodgson, who in 1895 claimed to have detected Eusapia attempting to use her hands and feet in a test at Cambridge. Hodgson had concluded (even prior to attending any of her seances) that this was how she performed her trickery. Other members of the SPR, including the distinguished physicist Sir Oliver Lodge, explained to Hodgson that this could not be true and that although Eusapia invariably attempted to move her secured limbs during seances (and would actually do so if the bindings were loosened), these were merely sympathetic movements resulting from her lack of conscious control while in trance. During demonstrations of her psychokinetic ability, Lodge explained, Eusapia would 'make a little sudden push with her hand in this direction, and immediately afterwards the object [would move]'. The sceptics' response was that 'sympathetic' movements were needed because she was actually using an extremely fine thread to move the objects. This was clearly an unsatisfactory explanation, since not only would the investigators have noticed such a thread, but it could not have been used to *push* objects. Although he knew that Eusapia was wont to make such movements while in trance, Hodgson allowed Eusapia to free her feet during the Cambridge tests and then pointed to this as evidence of trickery.

In 1909, another sceptic, Hugo Munsterberg, Professor of Psychology at Harvard, Boston, also arranged to attend a seance with Eusapia. Almost immediately, the table at which they were sitting tilted sharply, the room darkened unaccountably (it had been well lit with electric lamps) and a strong breeze began to blow, causing the curtain behind Eusapia to billow out over the sitters. As with the seance at which Pierre Curie had been present, a table began to climb up from the floor to elbow height. At a loss to explain any of this, Munsterberg had an associate hide behind the curtain to discover how Eusapia's trickery was achieved. According to Inglis:

> He [Munsterberg] had allowed her an hour to give her performance ... While she was giving it he sat beside her, making sure she did not loosen her hands to make use of them. Nevertheless his arm was pinched through the curtain, as if by a thumb and fingers ... Eventually the moment he was waiting for arrived. Eusapia gave 'a wild yelling scream'. The assistant behind the curtain had seen a foot stretching out under her chair, and had caught it. 'Her scream indicated that she knew that at last she was trapped and her glory shattered.'

Munsterberg claimed that Eusapia had lifted her bare foot 'to the height of my arm when she touched me under cover of the curtain, without changing the position of her body'.

Munsterberg's account of this seance was published in the *Metropolitan Magazine*, and was read by another sceptic named Stanley L. Krebs, who was less than convinced by Munsterberg's 'exposure' of Eusapia's trickery. He pointed out that for his explanation to work, Eusapia's leg would have had to be 'articulated at the knee, upon a motionless hip, making a rotation of about 135 degrees, as well as an elongation of about double its length'. In addition, Munsterberg had been grabbed by a hand – not a foot.

Unfortunately, it seems that Krebs's analysis of Munsterberg's 'exposure' did not gain the attention it deserved; and as a result, Eusapia Palladino is still regarded with great suspicion by many parapsychologists.

THE MOST FAMOUS MEDIUM OF ALL

Daniel Dunglas Home (pronounced 'Hume') was born in 1833. His father was an illegitimate son of the 10th Earl of Home, and went to America with Daniel when the boy was nine years old, shortly before the Hydesville rappings began. Daniel was later to become the focus for many paranormal occurrences, which the British writer Peter Underwood, in his *Dictionary of the Supernatural*, summarizes as follows:

> The phenomena reported included raps and taps, inexplicable lights or jets of flame, movement of objects, levitation and elongation [of the body], xenoglossy [speaking in foreign languages of which the medium apparently has no knowledge], phantom forms, the materialisation of a disembodied hand, apports [the materialization of objects, apparently out of nowhere], the ability to handle red-hot coals, the sounds of muffled voices and various other noises, bells being rung and an accordion played.

In 1868, at 5 Buckingham Gate, London, Home performed perhaps his most famous feat. In the presence of three witnesses (Captain Charles Wynne, Lord Lindsey and Lord Adare, whose home it was), Home floated out of a third-floor window, around the corner of the building and in through another open window. Over the course of his remarkable career, Home counted many important and highly respected people among his supporters, including the Tsar Nicholas I and the Emperor Napoleon II. Many others, however, held different views, including the novelist Charles Dickens, who thought him something of a scoundrel.

Another sceptic was Sir David Brewster, an expert in the field of optics and credited as the inventor of the kaleidoscope.

Upon Home's arrival in London from the United States in 1855, Brewster made an appointment to attend one of the medium's table-turning sessions, and was apparently extremely impressed by what he witnessed. He described the table-turning as 'quite inexplicable by fraud, or by any physical laws with which they were acquainted'. However, a few months later, Brewster wrote a letter to the *Morning Advertiser* in which he dismissed what he had seen, claiming that he had not been allowed to examine the table, and suggested that Home had moved the table with his feet. A number of Brewster's acquaintances, who had heard his initial comments on the seance, were incensed that he should have so cynically reversed his opinion.

The truth of the matter finally came to light when, after his death, Brewster's daughter published a memoir, which included an account he had written at the time of the seance. In this account, he admitted that he had indeed been given every opportunity to examine Home and the contents of the room in which the sitting took place.

According to Brian Inglis in *The Hidden Power*,

It [the table] had made unaccountable movements, actually rising off the floor 'when no hand was upon it'. When a larger table was brought in, it made similar movements. A small hand-bell, placed on the carpet, rang when nothing could have touched it; it then 'came over to me and placed itself in my hand'. Disembodied hands appeared, which could be grasped, melting away under the grasp. 'We could give no explanation,' Brewster admitted, 'and could not conjecture how they could be produced by any kind of mechanism.'

As Inglis goes on to suggest, the reason for Brewster's rather unseemly and meretricious turnaround in his evaluation of what he witnessed was almost certainly fear that his reputation as the 'leading hardheaded science writer' would be threatened, should he publicly endorse Home. This illustrates, of course, one of the most frustrating difficulties facing anyone who embarks on serious paranormal research. To a certain extent, people like Brewster, who refuse to accept even the possibility that such phenomena might actually occur, can be at least partially understood, since the ridicule of one's peers (especially in the modern scientific world of departmental politics and valuable research grants) can be extremely damaging to one's career. Of course, this does not excuse the deliberate falsification of one's observations, of which Brewster was guilty.

Throughout his career, Home astounded people (many of whom had been sceptics before meeting him) with his abilities, which frequently included lifting extremely heavy objects such as dining tables without recourse to any physical means. Indeed, it would have been extremely difficult for him to move some of the items of furniture had he been allowed to wrestle with them bodily. Neither could he possibly have used any form of mechanical gadgetry, since many of his sittings were held in other people's houses, in which he had never before set foot. Unlike other mediums, Home never accepted payment for his performances, and, although he occasionally accepted gifts, not once did he ever sell or pawn them to support himself during hard times.

In the late 1850s, Home was 'taken up' by Mrs Milner-Gibson, wife of the President of the Board of Trade, and introduced to society. On one of her evenings, Alexei Tolstoy was present, and later wrote to his wife: 'The piano played with no one near it. Home was raised from the ground; and I clasped his feet while he floated in the air above our heads.'

Again and again, sceptics attended Home's sittings and came away believers. Among them was the novelist W. M. Thackeray, initially a sceptic, who later told an acquaintance who was of a similar disposition: 'Had you seen what I have witnessed, you would hold a different opinion.' At no point in his career was Home caught cheating, or doing anything that might have been construed as implying trickery.

In the early 1870s, Home travelled to Russia to submit himself to tests carried out by the scientific establishment there. It is to his credit that he should have agreed to do so, following an unfortunate experience with Michael Faraday, a British chemist and physicist, who had asked to test him, but had also insisted that Home renounce his belief in spirits prior to any experiments. Home had declined the invitation.

In Russia he was tested by Alexander von Boutlerow, Professor of Chemistry at the University of St Petersburg. During one experiment, Home increased the tension on a dynamometer (an instrument designed to measure physical force) by fifty per cent.

In spite of Home's successes in the laboratory, sceptics (that is, those who had not actually sat with him) continued to contrive ridiculous schemes by which he might have faked the phenomena described by witnesses. These included a telescopic fishing rod concealed in his jacket. As Brian Inglis notes, when compared with what was actually seen and described, such suggestions only strengthen the case in favour of Home's powers being genuine. In fact, biographers and historians have been unable to discover a single piece of evidence to cast doubt on Home's abilities.

THE SEERESS OF PREVORST

One of the first serious ghost investigations began in 1826, and was conducted by the wealthy and eccentric doctor, poet and songwriter Justinus A. C. Kerner. The results of his investigation were written up in a book entitled *The Seeress of Prevorst*, which was published in 1829 and caused a literary sensation, becoming one of the best-selling books of the nineteenth century.

Kerner, who in 1826 was practising medicine in Weinsberg, near Heilbronn in southern Germany, was contacted by the relatives of a young woman named Friederike Hauffe, who was dying of a wasting disease. At first sight, Friederike seemed to be the victim of hysterical depression, apparently

24

brought on by an unhappy marriage, at the age of nineteen, to a cousin. Since childhood, she had had the apparent ability to see and converse with spirits of the dead and to predict the future, while in trance states.

Although Kerner, as befitting a man of science, did not believe that Friederike actually saw spirits of the dead, he was intrigued by her case, not least because he discovered that she could read with her stomach. He proved this to himself by making her lie down with her eyes closed and laying documents on her bare stomach, which she was able to read without difficulty. She could also draw perfect circles in darkness, claiming that her spirit left her body and hovered above it.

Eventually, orthodox medical treatment having frailed to alleviate her condition, Kerner decided to follow Friederike's advice and try mesmerism. By placing her in a 'magnetic trance', she assured Kerner, contact with the spirits would be achieved and they would aid him in his treatment of her. It should be noted that, contrary to popular belief, mesmerism (discovered by Franz Anton Mesmer) is quite different from hypnotism, in that it seeks to influence a vital fluid said to permeate the human body, and which must flow freely if we are to remain healthy. Blockages in this fluid's movement are said to be the cause of illness, and can be relieved by stroking the body with magnets, which in turn sometimes produces a 'magnetic trance'.

Friederike entered the trance state easily, and again began to communicate with apparent spirit presences, which continued to leave Kerner unmoved. His attitude changed, however, as a result of a striking event which occurred during one of the sessions. Friederike claimed that there was the ghost of a man with a squint near by. She found him most unpleasant, and described him in such detail that Kerner was reminded of a man who had died some years earlier.

In his book *Poltergeist: a Study in Destructive Haunting*, Colin Wilson describes what happened to convince Kerner that Friederike's powers were genuine:

It seemed, according to Friederike, that the man was suffering from a guilty conscience. He had been involved in embezzlement and, after his death, another man had been blamed. Now he wanted to clear the man's name, for the sake of his widow. This could be done by means of a certain document, which would be found in a chest. The spirit 'showed' Friederike the room where the document was to be found, and a man who was working there. Her description was so good that Kerner was able to identify him as a certain Judge Heyd. In her 'vision', Friederike had seen Judge Heyd sitting in a certain place in this room, and the chest containing the document on the table. The document was apparently not in its proper numerical order, which is why it had not been found.

When Kerner told him about his patient's vision, Judge Heyd was astounded; he *had* been sitting in the position described on that particular day (Christmas Day), and the chest, contrary to regulations, had been left open on the table. When they searched, the document turned up where Friederike had said it would. The widow of the man who had been wrongly accused was able to obtain redress.

From then on, Kerner's initial scepticism began to evaporate and he accepted Friederike's assertion that we are constantly surrounded by the spirits of the dead. Colin Wilson cites another example of Friederike's supernatural powers:

Friederike provided [Kerner] with further proof of the accuracy of her visions when she succeeded in putting an end to a haunting. Kerner heard about a house where the ghost of an old man was frightening the inhabitants. He brought one of them, a woman, along to see Friederike; the seeress went into a trance and explained that the ghost was that of a man called Bellon, who was an 'earth-bound spirit' as a result of defrauding two orphans. Kerner made inquiries, but no one had ever heard of a man called Bellon. But since the ghost claimed that he had been a Burgomeister, it seemed probable that some record existed. He claimed he had been a Burgomeister in the year 1700, and had died at the age of seventy-nine. Armed with this information, Kerner asked the present mayor to check the legal documents; they soon found that in the year 1700, a man called Bellon had been Burgomeister and director of the local orphanage. He had died in 1740 ... After 'confessing', the spirit took its departure.

Friederike was also the focus for some impressive poltergeist phenomena, including sundry unexplained noises, flying gravel and the movement of various household objects. Wilson sees a connection between these psychic activities and Friederike's decline and eventual death in 1829 at the age of twenty-eight, making the interesting speculation that ghost and poltergeist phenomena might actually draw the energy required for their physical manifestations from living people.

Kerner himself was attacked by the contemporary sceptics, including the researcher E. J. Dingwall, who suggested that if Kerner had treated Friederike as a case of hysteria (which, it should be noted, he did do initially), her life might have been prolonged. As a result, Kerner's book *The Seeress of Prevorst* (Prevorst being the Swabian village where Friederike was born) has been relegated to the position of little-known literary curiosity. However, in view of Kerner's initial scepticism, and his accounts of how it was shaken and ultimately destroyed as a result of his investigations, it seems that history has treated him harshly.

THE CROSS-CORRESPONDENCES

However much we might wish to believe in the survival of some aspect of our beings after bodily death, it has to be admitted that the vast majority of evidence for the afterlife is anecdotal at best. Spiritualism was and is no exception. By the first decade of the twentieth century, many respected men of science (including Cesare Lombroso, Italy's leading psychiatrist and the founder of criminology) had investigated psychic phenomena and come away convinced that there was something to them; but many others had done likewise, and remained unconvinced.

In his book *Poltergeist: a Study in Destructive Haunting* Colin Wilson illustrates the problem faced by psychical research, with reference to two books on the subject – Robert Dale Owen's *Footfalls on the Boundary of Another World* (1860) and Lombroso's *After Death – What?* (1909) – which, in spite of the fifty years separating them, 'might both have been written at exactly the same time'.

> Lombroso offers some 'scientific evidence', by way of a few experiments in telepathy; otherwise, he presents just the same kind of evidence that Robert Dale Owen had presented. There was plenty of evidence for ghosts, for poltergeists, for telepathy, for precognition, for 'out of the body experiences', and a dozen other varieties of 'paranormal' experience. But the evidence seemed to lead nowhere.

However, evidence of a much more impressive and verifiable kind was to come in the form of the so-called 'cross-correspondences'. These were sets of communications, received at roughly the same time through mediums who had no contact with each other, which carried allusions to the same topic. A particularly impressive cross-correspondence occurred after the deaths of three of the founders of the Society for Psychical Research, Henry Sidgwick, F. W. H. Myers and Edmund Gurney. Myers had stated while living that he would make every effort to communicate after his death, and indeed, the very idea of the cross-correspondences seems to have originated with Myers *after* his death.

The Myers correspondences began in 1903, when a woman named Mrs Holland (who was the sister of Rudyard Kipling) began to receive messages through automatic writing, in which alleged communications from the spirit world are physically written down by the medium while in a trance state. Usually, these messages are rambling and incoherent, but the ones received by Mrs Holland were of a higher quality. The following year, two more psychics – a classics lecturer at Newnham College, Oxford, named Mrs Verrall and her daughter, Helen Verrall – began to receive messages via automatic writing. One of these messages was: 'Record the bits, and when fitted they will make the whole.'

It soon emerged that whoever was sending these messages claimed to be the spirits of the three founders of the SPR, Myers, Sidgwick and Gurney. It was also clear that they were attempting to communicate such information in such a way that it would be impossible to dismiss it as fraud or unconscious telepathy on the part of the medium. The information was transmitted to a large number of mediums, including Mrs Coombe-Tennant, a British delegate to the Assembly of the League of Nations, Mrs Flemming, Mrs Forbes and the famous American medium Leonora Piper (more of whom later). The result was an incredibly complex interlocking puzzle, a small part of which was transmitted to each medium, so that when all the components were eventually put together, the answer would prove the existence of a source (or sources) in the afterlife.

Colin Wilson provides us with an example:

In 1906, Mrs Flemming produced a script containing the words Dawn, Evening and Morning, a reference to bay leaves, and the name Laurence. Six weeks later, Mrs Verall wrote out a message mentioning 'laurel' and a library. Mrs Piper came out of a trance speaking of laurel, 'nigger', and a phrase that sounded like 'more head'. Mrs Flemming produced more scripts referring to Night and Day, Evening and Morning, and also a reference to Alexander's tomb with laurel leaves. And eventually, all these clues pointed to the tomb of the Medicis in the Church of San Lorenzo in Florence. It had been designed by Michelangelo, and contained his sculpture of Night and Day, Evening and Morning. Lorenzo de Medici's emblem was the laurel, and near the tomb is the Laurentian Library. Alexander (or Alessandro) de Medici was half Negro; after his murder, his body was hidden in the tomb Giuliano. 'More head' was actually 'Moor head' – the head of a Negro. This conundrum was solved only four years after the first 'clue', and there could be no question of telepathy between the mediums, since they did not understand what it was all about. Altogether, the case of the cross-correspondences is one of the most impressive – perhaps the most impressive – in the history of psychical research. It is true that the various 'clues' are so complicated that few people have ever taken the trouble to study the case. Yet the sheer complexity of the code at least indicates that it originated on a far higher level of intelligence than most spirit messages. In addition to which, it effectively disposes of the objection that spirits never have anything interesting to say.

However, the cross-correspondences have had their critics, who point to the fact that Mrs Verrall was a classical scholar, and thus might have been able – wittingly or unwittingly – to transmit fragments of classical information to the other mediums, via telepathy (conscious or unconscious). This criticism would seem to be valid, until one remembers that the classically oriented cross-correspondence information continued to be received by mediums after Mrs Verrall died. Indeed, one can be forgiven for wondering whether, if Mrs Verrall *had* been transmitting the information, she continued to do so from the afterlife . . .

LEONORA PIPER

Born in 1857, Boston housewife Leonora Piper secured for herself a prominent place in the history of spiritualism entirely by accident. While consulting a blind healing medium named J. R. Cocke in 1884, she inadvertently slipped into a trance and wrote out a message for one of the other sitters, a judge, which apparently came from his deceased son.

From that day on, Mrs Piper held hundreds of sittings in her own home, and became the channel for messages from numerous famous historical personages, such as J. S. Bach and Henry Wadsworth Longfellow, as well as the deceased relatives of local people. She also had a number of spirit 'controls' (a control is a kind of otherworld master of ceremonies, who co-ordinates the communications from the dead), the first of whom was a native American girl with the rather implausible name of Chlorine. Mrs Piper's next control was a French doctor named Phinuit who, equally oddly, could speak little French and didn't know a great deal about medicine either. It seems probable that these controls were lying and were not who they claimed to be, which for some reason seems to be a common trait among discarnate entities. However, the information they volunteered for the benefit of Mrs Piper's clients usually proved to be accurate.

Mrs Piper was what is known as a mental medium (as opposed to a physical medium); in other words, her particular gift was for providing information, rather than producing physical phenomena such as table tilting, noises or ectoplasmic objects. Like the other successful mediums of the time, she was repeatedly investigated by both the British and American Societies for Psychical Research. In Mrs Piper's case, the investigators engaged private detectives to watch her closely, in order to ensure that she did not do any research on the backgrounds of her sitters, many of whom were introduced to her anonymously anyway.

In 1892, a new control introduced himself, claiming to be the spirit of one of her earlier sitters who had died. The control's name was George Pellew, and on many occasions 'he' conducted intimate conversations with other anonymous sitters who had known him in life.

Between 1897 and 1905, Mrs Piper turned her attention to automatic writing and received communications from a number of historical figures who, for some reason, declined to give their real names, preferring to go under pseudonyms such as 'Imperitor', 'Rector' and 'Doctor'. By 1911, her trance mediumship had been completely replaced by automatic writing, and in 1915, she received a message from Richard

Hodgson, the secretary of the American SPR, who had died in 1905 and became one of her controls. The message was for the distinguished physicist Sir Oliver Lodge, and it informed him of the impending death of his son, Raymond, in the First World War (an event that indeed came to pass).

In spite of the precautions taken during investigations of her powers, Mrs Piper was never found to have been involved in fraud of any kind. However, commentators both contemporary and later suggested that her powers might conceivably have been telepathic, rather than genuinely spiritualistic, in nature, with her sitters themselves supplying information that Mrs Piper sensed, before transmitting it back to them.

THE SCHNEIDER BROTHERS

Harry Price (1881–1948) was a colourful and well-known investigator of psychic phenomena, whose outspokenness made him as many enemies as friends during his lifelong struggle to bring the paranormal to serious scientific attention. His range of interests was extremely wide, including mediumship, fire-walking, ritual magic, stigmata, psychic photography and the case of Borley Rectory (see pp. 117–121), an investigation that lasted for twenty years. While he never hesitated to expose fake mediums whenever he discovered them, neither did he fail to proclaim as genuine those who impressed him; and, since he had a considerable knowledge of conjuring and sleight of hand, it was not easy to gain his endorsement.

One of Harry Price's investigations centred on the physical mediumship of the Schneider brothers, Willi (1903–71) and Rudi (1908–57). Like Leonora Piper, Willi Schneider discovered his psychic talents by accident, while his family were holding a seance for amusement. It seems that the seance succeeded in calling up an entity that called itself 'Olga', which subsequently claimed to be Lola Montez, the mistress of Ludwig, King of Bavaria.

From then on, Willi gained the ability to perform psycho-kinesis, to produce raps and other noises, and to materialize hand-like forms while in a self-induced trance. These feats were witnessed by representatives of the Psychological Institute of the University of Munich and the Society for Psychical Research.

As with Daniel Dunglas Home, who claimed that his powers deserted him from time to time, Willi Schneider's ability later seemed to diminish. At a seance held after this lessening of mediumistic powers had begun, 'Olga' insisted that Willi's brother Rudi be brought into the room. The boy's mother strongly demurred, but Rudi, who was eleven at the time, walked into the room nevertheless, apparently in a trance state. He sat down next to Willi and began to speak to 'Olga', while Willi later developed – or discovered – another control name 'Mina'.

In his highly informative *Dictionary of the Supernatural*, Peter Underwood writes that 'Rudi was probably the most exhaustively investigated and carefully controlled physical medium of all time.' He continues:

Perhaps the most important investigations were carried out by Dr Eugene Osty in Paris in 1930–31 when it was established scientifically that 'an invisible substance' was shown to interfere with infrared beams and to set off alarms bells and photographic flash-lights, although nothing was ever discovered to account for the triggering off of the experimental and observed systems: such demonstrations took place on demand and were repeated later in London.

The Schneider brothers, like Home, were never discovered to have faked any of the phenomena associated with them, in spite of attempts by Harry Price to expose them as frauds. The meticulousness of the tests applied to them by respected scientists and psychiatrists (among them Dr Eric Dingwall and Dr E. Holub) only lends weight to the assertion that their powers – whatever their ultimate origin – were genuine.

ROSALIE

In December 1937, Harry Price began what was to be first the most celebrated and later the most notorious case of his career. On 8 December, Price was contacted by an acquaintance of his, a lady who invited him to attend a private seance which would be held in her house, which Price described as being in one of the 'better-class' suburbs of London. She told Price that the seance was held every Wednesday, and that the spirit of a little girl named Rosalie almost always appeared. Price, however, was to tell no one the identity of the family, for fear that any publicity at all would frighten the spirit away. Price accordingly referred to them as Mr and Mrs X.

On 15 December, Price went to the house of Mr and Mrs X, at which he met their seventeen-year-old daughter and a French lady whom he called Mme Z. The story they told Price was a tragic one. Mme Z had met and married an officer in the British Army, who was killed in the First World War, leaving behind his wife and their daughter, Rosalie. Five years later, in 1921, Rosalie contracted diphtheria and died.

Another five years on, Mme Z began to sense that Rosalie had returned to her. Eventually, the child spoke to her mother and even appeared before her. Mme Z told her friends Mr and Mrs X about this, and, since they were interested in spiritualism, they suggested to her that seances should be held at their London home. The only sitters at these seances were Mr and Mrs X, their daughter and Mme Z, although very occasionally an 'outsider' was allowed to participate. Price heard this curious tale over dinner, after which he was introduced to a young man he called 'Jim', who would also take part in the seance that evening.

Price, of course, was well aware that many people faked seance phenomena, and so, in spite of the fact that he knew Mr and Mrs X, he set about taking elaborate precautions in the room in which the seance was to be held. These included sprinkling fine powder around the door and fireplace, which would be disturbed if anyone surreptitiously entered while the seance was in progress. He also locked the door and sealed it and the windows with tape, which he then initialled. He then examined every object in the room, and the clothing of Mr X and Jim. The ladies were spared these examinations, for reasons of decorum.

At 9.00 p.m., the seance began, with the six sitters occupying a circle of chairs at the centre of the room. Presently, Mrs X told Price in a whisper that Rosalie had arrived in the room. Price heard the sound of soft footfalls and felt something touch his hand. He could not see what it was, however, because the room was in total darkness. Price asked if he could touch Rosalie; Mrs X said that he could. He reached out and touched what was evidently the naked figure of a young girl. He then checked her pulse and heartbeat; she seemed normal in every way.

Price had brought along some plaques covered in a phosphorescent substance, and he asked if he might uncover them, so that their glow might illuminate the scene just a little. He was again given permission, and when he uncovered the plaques, an exquisitely beautiful child was revealed in their faint, green glow. Both Mrs X and Mme Z began to sob heavily at this point and the seance soon came to an end. It was 11.00 p.m. when the lights were turned on again and Price inspected his precautions against trickery. None of them had been disturbed in any way.

Oddly, Price's report on the case did not appear for two years, finally being published in 1939. In it he declared his conviction that the phenomena he had witnessed were entirely genuine, pointing to the family's desire to remain anonymous as additional evidence. For their part, the sceptics found it difficult to gainsay Price's convictions, until it occurred to them that the seance might not have taken place at all.

The case caused a sensation, and Price was constantly regaled with requests for more information about Mr and Mrs X and Mme Z; he refused, however, to give any such information, insisting that their wishes for privacy should be respected. Subsequently, he claimed that the X family had gone on a motoring holiday through France with Mme Z and had been caught there when the Second World War broke out. Mme Z had been separated from them and had not been heard of since.

This all sounded rather too convenient to the sceptics, who questioned the sanity of anyone who would decide to go on holiday to France when the threat of a war in Europe loomed large. In spite of efforts to locate them, none of the other guests at the Wednesday night seances was ever tracked down, including Jim.

The sceptics then turned their attention to the affairs of Harry Price himself. It was well known that in 1937, he was in serious financial trouble (his National Laboratory of Psychical Research had already been shut down for lack of funds). The Rosalie case certainly revived his career, as did the Borley Rectory haunting with which he also became involved in 1939.

Although he never admitted as much, psychical researchers have come to the conclusion that Harry Price fabricated the whole Rosalie case, including the mysterious X family and Mme Z.

3

PSYCHIC RECORDINGS

THE GHOST PLANE AND THE POSTMAN

As the case of Athenodorus shows, the popular image of the traditional ghost as a chain-rattling, shrouded figure which appears to terrified witnesses, moaning and wailing about some ancient injustice committed against it, is sometimes accurate, but it is far from typical. Indeed, ghostly encounters are actually as diverse as the millions of people all over the world who claim to have experienced them. There are a number of theories on what ghosts actually are, and in this part of the book, we shall explore some ghost sightings that support what is known as the 'psychic recording' theory, according to which certain events, usually of a violent or traumatic nature, can in certain circumstances become 'imprinted' upon the very atmosphere.

Our first example is quite recent, having occurred in 1994. On Friday 5 May, Tony Ingle, a 51-year-old postman, was holidaying with his wife, Susan, in their caravan at Laneside, Hope, on the Derbyshire moors, in the north Midlands of England. On that Friday the weather was fine, and Tony Ingle decided to walk his dog, an eight-year-old retriever called Ben. At approximately 4.40 p.m., they were walking along Aston Lane, when suddenly Ingle saw a large aeroplane flying over the moors. The aircraft was banking sharply to the left, no more than sixty feet about the ground, and was apparently in trouble.

In an interview with the *Sheffield Journal* Ingle said:

I was so convinced it was going to crash, I raced 100 yards up the lane to a gateway and the plane went out of sight. I expected to see the wreckage, but there was nothing, just an eerie silence and the sheep grazing. Then I realised as I calmed down a bit that although I had seen the propellers turning, the plane had been absolutely silent.

Ingle was shown various pictures of aircraft by journalists at the *Sheffield Journal* and was able to identify the plane he had seen as a Douglas DC3 Dakota. The staff at the newspaper conducted further research and discovered that in July 1945, a US Army Air Force Dakota had crashed in heavy mist only fifty yards from where Ingle had seen the mysterious plane. All seven of the crew were killed. The postman was (and is) completely baffled by the incident and, like many witnesses to paranormal phenomena, had no previous interest in the subject. Nor was he particularly happy that this had happened to him: 'I don't believe in ghosts,' he said. 'I am just not that type. I can't explain what I saw and I find it very disturbing. Since it happened, the dog will not go up the lane.'

The Dakota was not the only aircraft to crash in the area: a few weeks earlier, on 18 May 1945, a Royal Canadian Air Force Lancaster bomber had crashed near the same spot, killing all six of its crew. Over the last thirty years, many people have reported seeing ghostly aircraft in this area, and in late June 1995, a plaque commemorating the airmen who died in the crashes was unveiled on Bleaklow Moor.

Cases like this present us with a serious problem, for if we accept that it is possible for some aspect of the human personality to survive physical death, then the question remains: how can an inanimate object like an aircraft also survive its own destruction, to reappear decades later? Can a plane really become a ghost? And if so, how? It is this fundamental question that has led to the theory of psychic recordings. The obvious analogy is with tape recordings, in which electrical impulses are stored on magnetic tape, to be repeatedly played back later. Of course, this is all highly speculative and no one is at all sure how this might be achieved with regard to ghost sightings such as Tony Ingle's spectral Dakota. And yet it is an interesting hypothesis, especially with regard to encounters in which the 'ghost' appears to be unaware of the percipient. If there is any truth to the psychic recording theory, then this is exactly what we would expect (after all, the musicians who recorded the songs in your record collection are not aware of your presence when you play them). Violent and traumatic events such as plane crashes, murders and so on could conceivably leave some kind of record, in the form of an 'imprint' in the physical fabric of a house, or the atmosphere around a lonely moor . . .

This sounds remarkably similar to the so-called 'Akashic Records', which in occult circles are believed to contain an impression of every event, thought and action that has taken place since the beginning of the Universe, and to which psychics can occasionally gain access. The word 'Akashic' derives from the Sanskrit word *akasha*, defined as the fundamental etheric substance pervading all of space. Here we find ourselves in the realm of magic and the occult, which will be dealt with in greater detail later in the book; so we shall limit ourselves to a brief speculation on the possibility that certain ghosts may actually be relics of distant times that have been for ever preserved in the Akashic Records (or something similiar), and to which people with no apparent psychic gifts may occasionally gain involuntary access.

JACK THE RIPPER'S GHOST

If violent or traumatic events can somehow leave impressions on the 'ether' (for want of a better term), to be activated later by the psyches of unwitting percipients, then we might expect the events that occurred in the East End of London in 1888 to leave a lasting impression. Indeed, the gruesome exploits of the man known as Jack the Ripper fit rather well into the 'violent and traumatic' category!

The Whitechapel murders took place between August and November 1888. Five prostitutes were brutally killed and mutilated in the most horrible way by a man who became known as Jack the Ripper, whose true identity (despite many theories) remains shrouded in mystery.

In Commercial Street stands the Ten Bells public house, which was once called the Jack the Ripper, in dubious honour of the long-dead murderer. Inside, the walls are decorated with newspaper cuttings of the Whitechapel killings; the tiles show a variety of macabre scenes. According to researcher Andy Ellis, writing in the October 1995 issue of *Fate* magazine, the Ten Bells pub is one of the few buildings still standing that existed in Jack the Ripper's time, and this is perhaps the reason that his ghost now haunts it.

A resident of Dorset Street, Joseph Ogrowski, had an unnerving experience, in which he saw a figure walking along the road:

The entire street was quiet when suddenly this figure appeared. It walked slowly down the street and it really caught my attention because of the way it was dressed. It had on some type of felt cap and a long brown coat that covered its body from tip to toe. Even the collar was turned up, so that none of his – or maybe her – features could be seen. It was carrying a small parcel under one arm. When it drew closer to number 13, it stopped, looked around, and walked straight through the hoardings that blocked the entrance.

At first I thought I must be seeing things, or perhaps the shadows had been playing tricks on me. I went outside, crossed the road, and peered through a crack in the boards. It was too dark inside to see anything, but the boards were nailed firmly to the building and I decided that I must be mistaken. But the incident bothered me, so I decided to watch again the following night.

Nothing happened for a week. Then, exactly one week later, the same figure, dressed exactly the same way, walked down the street and again disappeared through the hoardings. This time I was sure of what I had seen. Two days later, work began on knocking down the old houses and I have never seen the figure since.

As Andy Ellis points out, Joseph Ogrowski's experience seems to be historically relevant, in that the house into which the figure disappeared was the one in which Mary Kelly, the Ripper's final victim, had been murdered. In addition, the description given by Ogrowski of the figure he saw matches exactly that of a contemporary witness, who saw a man carrying a parcel walking with Kelly on the night she was murdered.

In his article, Ellis implies that this putative ghost of Jack the Ripper might be haunting the two buildings mentioned because they existed in his own time, and thus are recognizable to his restless shade. This in turn implies that the 'ghost' (if such it be) is possessed of some form of consciousness, enabling it to 'decide' to return to the sites of the Ripper's atrocities. However, this need not necessarily be so: as mentioned earlier, there is some evidence to suggest that violent events can leave a psychic imprint on their surroundings, and this may account for the appearance of the strange figure which, it will be recalled, performed exactly the same action on the two occasions it was seen by Ogrowski. This militates in favour of a psychic recording explanation, for it is hard to imagine why the ghost would wish to walk down a street and enter a house again and again for no apparent reason.

Among the other phenomena experienced in the Ten Bells pub are unexplained cold spots, malfunctioning lights, disappearing plates, knocking sounds and moans apparently coming from the attic. The sceptical response to these and other such 'haunted house' phenomena is obvious, and is certainly worth considering. For instance, cold spots are not uncommon in old buildings, in which antiquated heating systems can be temperamental to say the least; the same goes for wiring, which can result in lights that apparently switch on and off by themselves. As any victim of theft knows, it

41

doesn't necessarily take a ghost for household objects to go missing; and as for strange knocking sounds and 'moans', old water pipes can produce some truly hideous noises . . .

This is all well and good, and doubtless the vast majority of allegedly haunted houses are actually nothing of the kind. However, the case of the Ten Bells has some intriguing aspects that deserve a little closer inspection. Yvonne Ostrowski, the landlady of the Ten Bells, reported her experiences:

> There have been many times when I have been woken up in the middle of the night by footsteps in the attic, which is unused. The first time it happened I thought that perhaps we were being burgled and went downstairs to have a look. When I arrived in the bar area, all the lights were on and several decorative glasses were missing. I knew I had turned the lights off, and I always wash up before I retire to bed.
>
> About three weeks later I was again woken up by noises. The lights were back on and the glasses had been returned, except they weren't hanging up in the normal place, but were neatly stacked on the bar.

Ellis concludes his article with the opinion that Jack the Ripper is being punished by a 'higher justice' which has condemned him to linger in the streets where he committed his unspeakable crimes, perhaps for eternity. But if we accept the validity of the psychic recording theory, it seems more likely that it is actually a mindless, moving picture of the Ripper that haunts those ancient streets, and that the soul of the Ripper himself has been consigned to an altogether different fate . . .

THE FIGURE-EIGHT GIRLS

When the wealthy New York banker Norden Van der Voort married Netje Schermerhorn in the latter years of the last century, his greatest hope was for a son and heir – indeed, that had been the very reason for the marriage. So, when his wife bore him two daughters, and her doctor subsequently informed the couple that Netje would be able to have no more children, the already loveless union took a profound turn for the worse. Norden Van der Voort retreated to one of the family estates, where he devoted himself to horses and other women.

When her husband was killed in a riding accident, Netje sold all of their properties except a single New York townhouse, which she moved into with her two daughters, Janet, sixteen, and Rosetta, fourteen. The sisters would walk the streets of Manhattan arm in arm, disdainful of all suitors, living only for the winter when they would spend every available hour ice skating in Central Park. So proficient were they that they quickly earned the nickname 'the Figure-Eight Girls'.

As the years passed, Janet and Rosetta gradually grew apart from their mother, who married a wealthy financier and moved with him to France when the girls were in their late twenties. When her second husband died a few years later, Netje married again, this time a French count. Although she invited them to her wedding, her daughters declined, preferring to skate in their beloved Central Park.

When Netje herself died some years later, Janet and Rosetta were informed that the Van der Voort fortune was virtually exhausted. However, this depressing news did not stop the sisters from organizing a huge ice carnival to celebrate Janet's birthday. So lavish was this affair that the catering bill swallowed up the meagre remains of the sisters' money, and they were left with the townhouse as their only asset. From then on, they became virtual recluses, only venturing rarely on to the streets of Manhattan, and never again skating in Central Park.

Janet and Rosetta died within three months of each other in their decaying house. Not long afterwards, a soldier who was passing by the ice rink saw the sisters skating. Their arms were entwined, and their clothes out of fashion. After cutting a perfect figure eight, they skated off into the distance.

This case is interesting because the sisters' ghosts were seen only once, soon after their deaths. As they merely repeated the activities they had pursued in life rather than interacting with their surroundings, we can place them in the category of psychic recordings. And yet the single sighting does not square with the cyclic nature of such hauntings. Perhaps the sisters wanted to skate in Central Park one last time before departing forever from this world . . .

THE BABY

Not all 'ghosts' are of the dead; on rare occasions, living people take part in 'hauntings' alongside the apparent shades of people who have actually died, which provides further evidence that the psychic recording theory can be used successfully to explain certain ghostly events. The case that follows was investigated by the Institute for Psychical Research, which concluded that a psychic recording may have been responsible for the unnerving events described by the percipients.

A woman given the pseudonym 'Sally Rawlinson' moved into a house in the north of England, and spent several months refurbishing the place, which had fallen into some decay, the reason apparently being that it had been on the market for an unusually long time. This was rather surprising to Sally, given the low asking price.

All seemed well, and she was very happy to have finally finished the decorating. However, things began to change for the worse when she found herself waking up suddenly one night for no apparent reason. Lying in bed wondering what could have caused her to snap awake like that, Sally became aware of voices coming from somewhere in her bedroom, although there was clearly no one there. In increasing alarm and confusion, she listened to the loud and heavy creaking of floorboards, which should have been impossible, since she had put new, thick carpets down throughout the house. The voices, apparently belonging to a man and woman, continued. Sally could also hear the crying of a baby.

The footsteps moved out of the bedroom, on to the landing and towards the stairs. At this point there was a loud crashing sound, as if someone were falling down the stairs. The baby began to scream, and then all the voices fell silent.

Now completely terrified, Sally jumped out of bed and dashed to the kitchen, where she made herself a cup of tea and tried to calm down enough to return to bed. This proved impossible; she was too unnerved by her experience even to contemplate returning to the bedroom.

Although she was able to return to her bed the following night, it was some weeks before she again felt comfortable there. In the intervening time, there had been no further disturbances, and Sally had begun to suspect that she had been the victim of some strange nightmare. However, when she returned home one evening after going out with some friends, she again heard the sounds of voices, the creaking of floorboards, the apparent fall down the stairs and the scream-ing of the baby, followed by that awful silence.

As many people do, when faced with phenomena of this kind, Sally called in the local priest and asked him to bless the house. It was at this point that she discovered not only the reason for the low asking price of the house, but also the reason it had remained unoccupied for so long. The priest told her that he had attempted to rid the house of its ghostly manifestations on a number of previous occasions, but had been unsuccessful. It was thus with no particular optimism that he undertook, once again, to bless the place.

The noises stopped for several weeks, and returned only when Sally had a friend named Carol staying with her. This time, as Sally fled the bedroom in terror, she was met in the kitchen by Carol, who had also heard the voices, the foot-steps, the fall downstairs and the dreadful screaming of the child.

At this point, the Institute for Psychical Research became involved, and discovered that over the preceding twenty years the house had had no less than fourteen owners. Evidently, it was not a place that encouraged lengthy occupation. The

Institute also managed to track down a woman (to whom it referred only as 'Mrs T') who provided what appeared to be the explanation for the ghostly sounds.

Mrs T's story was tragic in the extreme. She told the Institute for Psychical Research that twenty years previously she had moved into the house when eight months pregnant, later giving birth to a boy. It seemed that the baby was extremely demanding, requiring attention throughout each night. On one particularly bad night, Mrs T's husband got up for the third time to prepare a bottle for the ten-week-old baby, who also needed cleaning and changing. The exasperated and exhausted husband took the child from its cot and was about to take it downstairs when he tripped at the top of the stairs and fell. The unfortunate infant died almost instantly.

Mrs T's husband, driven to breaking point by remorse, committed suicide a year later. Unable to stay in the house after this double tragedy, Mrs T moved away.

As British investigators John and Anne Spencer note in their *Encyclopedia of Ghosts and Spirits*, the psychic recording theory is particularly strongly indicated in this case, since Sally Rawlinson heard a conversation taking place between Mrs T and her husband, even though Mrs T was alive at the time. The fact that her husband had died nearly two decades earlier seems to be irrelevant in terms of the manifestations, and it is most unlikely that he had returned to the house as a genuine ghost (that is, a discarnate spirit). If we accept that what is alleged to have happened to Sally Rawlinson did indeed happen, then it is far more prudent to suggest that the tragic events of twenty years earlier somehow imprinted themselves into the very fabric of the house, to be 'replayed' at intermittent intervals, perhaps unwittingly activated by the presence of an occupant such as Sally Rawlinson.

THE ROCKING CHAIR

As we saw in the previous case, apparently 'ghostly' phenomena are not always visible to percipients: they can manifest through most of the human senses, as unusual smells or sounds, as well as unseen hands touching the body and more traditional visible apparitions. These phenomena can also cause the movement of objects. Although this usually occurs in poltergeist cases, it can also happen when no poltergeist seems to be present, as the following case from 1947 demonstrates.

The percipients were two middle-aged ladies who were holidaying in Perranporth, Cornwall, England. At 11.30 p.m. on their first evening in their chalet, they decided to retire, but were soon disturbed by the sounds of footsteps outside and the growling of a dog. They looked out of the windows, searching for whoever might be wandering around, but they could see no one.

Presently, the two ladies heard the door of the chalet, which they had previously bolted, opening and closing, and footsteps moving across the living room. They then heard what sounded like the pages of a newspaper being rustled, followed by an obviously good-natured chuckling, as if whoever was reading the paper was amused by what he was reading.

Now feeling some considerable concern, the ladies left their beds and moved gingerly to the bedroom door. After pausing to gather their courage, they threw open the door, fully expecting to confront the intruder face to face. However, there was no one in the living room – at least, no one who could be seen; but the wicker rocking chair was moving steadily back and forth.

As John and Anne Spencer state:

The picture therefore seemed very clear. The ladies were hearing someone who had come into the room (after having settled his dog down?), picked up his newspaper and was

47

enjoying reading it, sitting in the wicker chair and chuckling at whatever humorous passages were in it. At one point they [thought] they hear the sound of an invisible dog.

Understandably enough, the following day the two ladies requested that they be moved to another chalet in the holiday village. On hearing their story, the owner of the village admitted that other guests had reported similar events. Since whoever had sat in the rocking chair (the 'ghost' has never been identified) was obviously perfectly happy, we cannot put the manifestations down to some violent or traumatic event in the past, which begs the question: can moments of extreme contentment also imprint themselves on the atmosphere?

THE BIG GREY MAN OF BEN MACDHUI

There have been countless legends associated with remote, lonely and isolated places far beyond the familiar urban sprawl of humankind, where the forces of nature retain their hegemony, and in which the solitary traveller can encounter all manner of strangeness. One such place is a mountain called Ben MacDhui, at 4,296 feet the highest in the Cairngorms of Scotland. The mountain is said to be haunted by an eerie and terrifying presence, known locally as Am Fear Liath Mor, or the Big Grey Man.

In 1891, the noted mountain climber Professor Norman Collie encountered the Big Grey Man while descending from Ben MacDhui's summit. He related his experience at the Annual General Meeting of the Cairngorm Club in Aberdeen in December 1925. He was making his way through a heavy mist when he became aware of another presence near by.

I began to think I heard something else than merely the noise of my own footsteps. For every few steps I took I heard a crunch, and then another crunch as if someone was walking after me but taking steps three or four times the length of my

48

own ... I was seized with terror and took to my heels, staggering blindly among the boulders for four or five miles.

Professor Collie's audience was somewhat bemused by this story, but he remained adamant that he would never again dare to scale the mountain alone. As is often the case with paranormal encounters, the newspapers swiftly got wind of the story and it soon became widely known that, in Collie's words, there was 'something very queer about the top of Ben MacDhui'.

As news of Collie's frightening encounter spread, other mountaineers came forward with their own tales of strange noises and sudden terror which caused them to dash headlong away from the mountain's haunted summit. Some claimed to have seen a huge, mist-shrouded, humanoid figure; others heard strains of ghostly music and sinister laughter carried by the chill winds. All experienced the feeling that some dreadful, malign thing was warning them, in no uncertain terms, to stay away from the mountain's peak.

According to the highly respected researcher Dr Karl Shuker, there have been a number of possible explanations put forward for the Big Grey Man of Ben MacDhui: 'They range from a yeti-like man-beast, a mystical holy man, a geological holograph ... an optical illusion ... a marooned extraterrestrial, a visitor-induced energy trace image, an electromagnetic phantom, and a hallucination engendered by oxygen deficiency.'

Shuker goes on to suggest another, yet more intriguing possibility, and one which reminds us of the elements of the mystery of 50 Berkeley Square:

In view of the vast variety of unexplained phenomena reported from Ben MacDhui over the years, could this mountain be a 'window' area – an interface between different dimensions or alternate worlds? If so, there is a good chance that such a significant portal would have a guardian, to deter would-be intruders or trespassers. Is it just coincidence that this is the precise effect so successfully accomplished by Ben MacDhui's Big Grey Man?

THE PRESIDENT WHO LINGERS

There are a number of ghost reports associated with famous people, which is perhaps unsurprising given our fascination with celebrity. They tend to be of variable quality and are frequently to be found in the splendidly hilarious pages of the tabloid newspapers. There is, however, the occasional story that demands closer inspection, and one of particular interest involves the alleged ghost of Abraham Lincoln, which is said to haunt the White House in Washington DC.

There have been a number of sightings of Lincoln over the many decades since his death, the first of which was reported by Grace Coolidge, wife of Calvin Coolidge, who was elected thirtieth president in 1923. Mrs Coolidge allegedly saw Lincoln standing in the window of the Oval Office, gazing out, perhaps towards the distant battlefields of Virginia.

During a stay at the White House as the guest of President Franklin D. Roosevelt (elected in 1933), Queen Wilhelmina of The Netherlands heard a knock at the door to her room. Upon opening it, she found herself standing face to face with a top-hatted Abraham Lincoln. Queen Wilhelmina later told Roosevelt of her astonishing encounter; he replied matter-of-factly that she happened to be staying in the Lincoln Room, and that the sixteenth president had often been seen in that part of the building. Apparently, one of Roosevelt's secretaries had seen the ghost in the Lincoln Room, sitting on the bed and pulling on a pair of boots.

There is an associated story concerning the train that carried Lincoln's body back to Illinois for burial. John and Anne Spencer describe the journey as 'an extraordinary form of mobile lying-in-state', during which thousands of people watched the train pass. It is said that a ghost train, manned by skeletons, follows the route every year. The Spencers go on to quote the description of the apparition given in the *Albany Times*:

> It passes noiselessly. If it is moonlight, clouds cover over the moon as the phantom train goes by. After the pilot engine passes, the funeral train itself with flags and streamers rushes past. The track seems covered with black carpet and the coffin is seen in the centre of the car, while about it in the air and on the train behind are vast numbers of blue-coated men, some with coffins on their backs, others leaning upon them.

This is, of course, an intriguing and darkly romantic legend; but one is forced to wonder (as with all 'anniversary apparitions') why, if the phantom train rushes through the landscape of the Midwest with such frequency, no television cameras have been deployed to capture the spectacle as irrefutable proof of the existence of ghosts.

One of the intriguing aspects of this case is the apparently synchronicitous connections between the assassination of Lincoln at Ford's Theatre, Washington, in April 1865, and that of John F. Kennedy at Dealey Plaza in Dallas, Texas, in November 1963. These striking connections have been cited by American ghost researcher Hazel M. Denning as tentative evidence of 'a soul connection that could be a continuous expression of a soul whose destiny was to emancipate the oppressed'.

The so-called 'Lincoln-Kennedy Correspondences' were summarized in *Fortean Times*, Number 72, from three main sources: the Wallace family's *Book of Lists No. 3* (1983), an article by Larry King in *USA Today* (21 November 1988), and one by E. Randall Floyd in the *San Antonio Express-News* (Texas) of 16 July 1991. They are as follows:

- Abraham Lincoln studied law, was elected a Congressman in 1846 and President on 6 November 1860. John F.

Kennedy studied law, was elected a Congressman in 1946 and President on 8 November 1960. Both were civil rights campaigners.

- Two of Lincoln's sons were named Edward and Robert. Edward died at the age of three, Robert lived on. Two of Kennedy's brothers were named Robert and Edward. Robert was assassinated, Edward lived on.
- Lincoln was succeeded by Andrew Johnson, who was born in 1808. Kennedy was succeeded by Lyndon Johnson, who was born in 1908. Both Johnsons served in the US Senate.
- Mary Lincoln and Jackie Kennedy both had children who died while their husbands were in the White House.
- Both presidents were shot on a Friday in the back of the head with their wives present. Both men had expressed anxiety about possible assassination earlier in the day.
- Lincoln's assassin, John Wilkes Booth, and Kennedy's alleged assassin, Lee Harvey Oswald, were both southerners in their twenties. (Booth was born in 1838 and Oswald in 1939.)
- Lincoln's secretary, John Kennedy, advised him not to go to the theatre. Kennedy's secretary, Evelyn Lincoln, advised him not to go to Dallas.
- Booth shot Lincoln in a theatre and hid in a warehouse. Kennedy was shot from a warehouse; Oswald was found sitting in a theatre. Lincoln was killed in Ford's Theatre. Kennedy was killed in a Ford Lincoln convertible. Booth and Oswald were both killed before they could be tried in court.
- Lincoln was shot with a pistol and his assassin with a rifle; Kennedy with a rifle and his putative assassin with a pistol.
- The names Lincoln and Kennedy each contain seven letters. Andrew Johnson and Lyndon Johnson each have thirteen letters, and John Wilkes Booth and Lee Harvey Oswald each total fifteen letters.

Hazel Denning reports that President and Mrs Lincoln held at least five seances in the White House. 'Although Lincoln was skeptical of metaphysics, his attitude changed when certain predictions concerning the Civil War proved to be accurate.'

So what of the strange correspondences between the lives and deaths of Lincoln and Kennedy? Is Hazel Denning correct in her inference of something akin to reincarnation at work in these apparently *meaningful* coincidences? While it would seem that the sightings of Lincoln's ghost in the White House over the years imply a psychic recording of the President going about his daily business, the correspondences (if not merely random coincidences) suggest some profound yet unexplained connection between the two men, stretching through the century separating their deaths. Is it possible that the transmigration of a soul (if this is indeed what happened) can influence the events surrounding its subsequent incarnation?

SOLDIERS AND BATTLES

If events of an extremely violent or traumatic nature can leave psychic impressions of themselves upon the fabric of houses, or even the very atmosphere of outdoor locations, it is not surprising that, as we have observed, theatres of war are particularly redolent with the heady scent of the paranormal. Even a cursory glance at the literature of war yields hundreds of cases of historic battles being fought again and again by ghostly armies.

Peter Underwood, the redoubtable seeker after the unexplained, has investigated many of these reports, including the famous haunting of the even more famous Culloden Moor, near Inverness, Scotland, site of the last battle fought on British soil, which took place in 1746. This savage, sixty-eight minute battle was fought between the Jacobite forces of Charles Edward Stuart (Bonnie Prince Charlie) and the English army commanded by the Duke of Cumberland. The battle was to mark the final defeat of the Jacobites and heralded a period of dreadful repression by the English in the Scottish Highlands. Bonnie Prince Charlie commanded 5,000 Highlanders; Cumberland had 9,000 troops. The Highlanders were utterly routed, and the English, having lost only about fifty men, killed their wounded prisoners.

According to Peter Underwood:

> ... on occasions, and especially at dusk, the dim form of a battle-worn Highlander has been observed in the vicinity of the cairn [marking the scene of the battle] and one visitor, while looking closely at the Highlanders' graves, lifted a square of Stuart tartan which had blown down from the stone of the grave-mound and distinctly saw the body of a handsome, dark-haired Highlander, lying full length on top of the mound.
>
> The visitor began to sense that the figure she was looking at was not of this world; his clothes were dirty, muddy and of old-fashioned cut and material; his face had an unnatural pallor – and as she fully realised that she was seeing something of a paranormal character, she turned and fled from that field of memories.

The Treasurer's House at York Minster, England, was the site of some very unnerving apparitions in the 1950s and 60s, which have been extensively investigated by the British author Ian Wilson. When it comes to ghost reports, Wilson is not easily impressed, and is an extremely diligent and demanding researcher. As a consequence, when he suggests that a ghostly encounter is more than likely genuine, we are obliged to sit up and take notice.

One witness to the apparition, a retired policeman named Harry Martindale, was in February 1953 an eighteen-year-old apprentice plumber helping to install central heating pipes in the warren-like cellars of the Treasurer's House. Suddenly, he heard the sound of a trumpet, apparently coming from the wall. He was then flabbergasted to see a soldier's helmet emerged from the brickwork. Martindale promptly fell off the ladder on which he had been standing, and retreated rapidly to a corner of the cellar, as a Roman soldier, carrying a trumpet, walked from one side of the cellar to the other, disappearing into the opposite wall. The soldier was immediately followed by a large cart-horse and approximately twenty more men, walking in double file. Interestingly, Martindale was unable to see below the soldiers' knees, except when they walked across a section of the cellar floor that had been dug away.

Fleeing from the cellar, Martindale found the curator of the Treasurer's House. Before he could say anything, the curator noted his expression and said: 'By the look of you, you've see the Romans, haven't you?'

According to Ian Wilson in his book *In Search of Ghosts*:

> The soldiers were nothing like the Roman soldiers as portrayed in the films of the 1950s that Harry had seen. In stature they seemed surprisingly small: 'Not much more than five feet' in height. Their helmets were decorated with bedraggled, undyed plumes of feathers and their kilts dyed a streaky green. Although they seemed to have little armour, there was at least one round, bulbous shield and their weapons included spears and short daggerlike swords. They walked rather than marched, no more than two abreast, and not in any proper formation, and appeared to be 'extremely tired', dishevelled and unshaven.

The curator showed Martindale several reports from previous years, in which people claimed to have seen the phantom soldiers; these included the previous curator, who had had the experience in 1946, and an American professor in the 1930s. There was also a story from yet further back, when the Treasurer's House was privately owned. It seems that during a fancy dress party, a young lady went down to the cellars and discovered a Roman soldier standing in the passage, barring her way. Assuming the 'soldier' to be one of the guests, the young lady went back upstairs to enquire who he was. She was told that no one had come to the party dressed as a Roman soldier.

Ian Wilson also tells us that, besides Harry Martindale, there is at least one other witness to the phantom soldiers who is still living. Mrs Joan Mawson lived and worked in the Treasurer's House with her first husband, Tom Morcum, in the late 1950s, a few years after Martindale's encounter. At weekends, since the maintenance man was only available during the week, the couple had to attend to the boilers themselves, in order to heat the house.

At 5.00 p.m. on a Sunday in the winter of 1957, Joan went down to the cellar with the couple's bull terrier. When she was only a few steps down, the dog started to howl and fled back up the stairs, while Joan became aware of the sound of horses, accompanied by an unseen presence behind her. Suddenly terrified, she backed up against the wall and watched in disbelief as a troop of Roman soldiers marched past. Like Martindale, she was unable to see the lower parts of their legs. The soldiers and their horses, however, were completely solid and looked tired and dishevelled, as if they had been on a particularly long and arduous journey.

Interestingly, the apparitions were carrying round shields, which did not correspond to the equipment carried by Roman infantry, which did not include round shields. However, 'it was discovered that about the time that the Sixth Legion was withdrawn from York in the fourth century, they were reinforced by auxiliaries who did carry round shields'.

Similarly, excavations by archaeologist Peter Wenham and others established that remains of the Roman road known as the Via Decumana, leading from Roman York's north-eastern gate to its legionary headquarters, lay just about eighteen inches below the floor level of the Treasurer's House cellar. Not only does this road run towards the Minster, taking the route along which Joan saw the Romans moving, height-wise also it is at the level at which she and Harry [Martindale] saw their Romans.

This would seem to explain why the lower portions of the men's legs were apparently missing, and also illustrates an intriguing aspect of apparitions that seem to be psychic recordings: they move through space exactly as they would have done in their own time, regardless of any changes to the environment occurring over the intervening years. As Ian Wilson notes, apparitions of this type seem 'frozen in both time and space ... because they are able only to repeat certain movements that they performed at a crucial moment when alive'.

HARLAXTON MANOR

Harlaxton Manor in Lincolnshire, England, is a grand and striking stately home. The house itself was built early in the nineteenth century and owned by the Gregory family, who put it up for sale in 1935.

Violet Van der Elst, although born into humble circumstances, had become a successful and wealthy businesswoman (manufacturing and marketing the first brushless shaving cream). In 1938 she bought Harlaxton and renovated it, installing electricity (which took twenty miles of wiring) and adding new plumbing throughout. Violet adored the place, not least because it implied the aristocratic background she so desperately wanted. She renamed the house Grantham Castle, and used it as a base from which to organize her frequent demonstrations against capital punishment, to which she was passionately opposed. According to Peter Underwood, Earl Attlee once presented to Parliament a petition containing 100,000 signatures on Violet's behalf, and was of the opinion that she was instrumental in securing the abolition of capital punishment in Britain.

Her husband, John Van der Elst, had died in 1934, prompting the idiosyncratic Violet to become deeply involved with spiritualism. She would spend days on end in the Old Library (now known as 'Mrs Van der Elst's Room') attempting to communicate with John. Indeed, by all accounts the house was a most unnerving place to be: while Violet, dressed all in black, conducted her seances, surrounded by black decorations and furniture, vases and other household objects would move around, apparently guided by unseen hands, and strange, dark forms would be glimpsed moving through the labyrinthine corridors of the house.

When the maintenance of Harlaxton eventually became too much even for Violet's considerable resources, she was forced to put the house up for sale. (She lived to see the abolition of the death penalty, her great project, before dying in a nursing home in Kent in 1966.)

Harlaxton was then bought, in 1948, by the Jesuits who found that the supernatural influences were still very strong. Disturbed by the atmosphere, they extensively exorcized the house before selling it. After a brief ownership by Stanford University, California, Harlaxton was sold to the University of Evansville, Indiana, which maintains it to this day as its British campus.

Peter Underwood was invited to Harlaxton to give a lecture in his capacity of famous and well-respected ghost investigator. He reported:

A few years ago the curator, Francis Watkins, spoke of 'many' students and teachers over the years reportedly 'seeing ghosts in the house and several members of staff leaving unexpectedly, saying that they felt uneasy living there . . .' One visitor described the house as 'alive with the spirits of the past' and perhaps it is. A teacher who was resident at Harlaxton for two years had told of having a number of unnerving experiences including encountering the 'hazy outline of a tall man standing in the doorway of the library for some twenty minutes' while she and some of her students watched in turn.

It seems that Violet was, as she had claimed, a catalyst or focus for the supernatural, since, as Peter Underwood informs us, all the ghostly happenings at Harlaxton date from her time there. Although he saw no ghosts himself during his visit, Underwood did speak to two students who reported strange experiences in the house. One of the students told how he suffered from terrible nightmares while sleeping in a certain room, and on one occasion woke up to catch a brief glimpse of a 'sub-human' face close to the bed. On other occasions, he saw a dark-robed figure gliding through the room. The other student to whom Underwood spoke said that he had had similar experiences when he had stayed in the room.

There have also been other sightings of a black-robed woman moving through the rooms and corridors, implying, perhaps, that Violet Van der Elst found a way, after all, to remain at her beloved Harlaxton Manor.

THE HAUNTED BOMBER

In his *Nights in Haunted Houses*, Peter Underwood reports on a strange set of phenomena occurring in and around a Second World War Avro Lincoln bomber kept at the Aerospace Museum at Royal Air Force (RAF) Cosford in Shropshire, England. Intriguingly, however, this aircraft never saw active service. Looking into the background to the case, Underwood discovered that the first reported incidents occurred while the aircraft was being renovated. One man saw a figure approaching and, thinking it to be his friend who had been working in the cockpit, began to say something, when the figure vanished. From then on, various strange things were experienced by people in the hangar containing the Lincoln, including whistling sounds, unexplained temperature variations and the appearance of a figure in a blue battledress jacket.

In 1977, an ex-RAF engineer named John Small had several strange experiences while supervising repairs on the bomber. On one occasion, he saw a man wearing a pilot's helmet looking out at him from the astrodome (the observation bubble on top of the fuselage).

One of the most striking observations occurred in 1984 during the filming of the television series *Wish You Were Here*, which carried an item on holidays in the west Midlands. Chris Kelly, producer, writer and presenter, was sitting in the Lincoln's cockpit, when the cameraman on the ground outside called up to him to ask the man behind him to leave the cockpit, since he was in the shot. Kelly turned around, but saw no one; as far as he was concerned, he was alone in the aircraft. However, the cameraman maintained that there was someone in the cockpit with Kelly, someone who could be seen both with the naked eye and through the camera. Again Kelly turned around, and again he assured his colleague that there was no one else in the aircraft. Eventually, the other person in the cockpit disappeared.

In 1985, five members of a ghost research group went to the museum to investigate the phenomenon and discovered several 'cold spots' inside the Lincoln. Two members also reported feelings of light-headedness while in the cockpit. On a subsequent visit, they left a tape recorder running inside the aircraft, which recorded 'morse code blips, ghostly hangar doors opening and closing, Merlin engines running out of synchronisation' and other noises.

Although a psychic recording would seem to be the likeliest explanation for the various noises and sightings of the phantom airman, Peter Underwood came across some information that implies some self-awareness on the part of the ghostly airman:

Early on I had come across a story associated with the bomber suggesting that one pilot so loved the aeroplane that he said he would never leave it, even after death. He was killed in a flying accident soon after making that statement in the presence of several of his fellow officers.

Among the later theories to account for the appearance of the phantom airman at Cosford is the idea that it may be the ghost of an engineer who killed himself after a bomber he was responsible for crashed in the 1940s killing all the crew; some parts of the crashed bomber finding their way into the haunted hangar as the Aerospace Museum.

The idea of components from a downed aircraft causing the haunting of another is somewhat reminiscent of one of the theories put forward to account for the so-called 'Ghost of Flight 401', which we will examine later in this book.

Peter Underwood conducted his own investigation of the museum, along with other members of the London-based Ghost Club. They placed a number of thermometers through-out the Lincoln, and also placed several 'trigger' objects at various locations. The trigger objects were intended to estab-lish some kind of link with the past, and included service badges, coins from the 1940s, a pair of binoculars, a Second World War postcard and an old ashtray.

The thermometer in the aircraft's tail registered 4°F lower than elsewhere in the aircraft. During the vigil, it was discovered that several of the trigger objects, which had been placed in chalk circles, had been moved. Several members of the group also saw the figure of a man moving around the hangar. One of the investigators, Philip Moore, took several photographs of the Lincoln, and in two of them he was able to discern a figure wearing what looks like an oxygen mask, sitting in the cockpit.

In his account of the vigil, which was published in the Ghost Club *Newsletter*, Philip Moore writes:

My particular experience occurred midway through the vigil. It was reported that the atmosphere near the bomber had altered. I climbed the ladder at the rear of the plane and entered the aircraft to be immediately confronted with a sudden wave of static electricity. It felt as though a wall had been erected and the air was alive, and although I could see nothing the feeling of expectancy remained. The experience lasted for about two minutes before everything returned to normal. I cannot explain this experience, maybe it was part imagination, but the feeling was so strong and vivid that I believe the event could be classed as supernatural, certainly something that cannot be easily explained.

THE GHOSTS OF HERSTMONCEUX

Herstmonceux Castle in Sussex, England, is one of the most haunted buildings in the country. Over the years there have been numerous reports of ghostly experiences and encounters, the best known of which is with the 'White Lady', who has been frequently seen attempting to swim the castle's moat. The story behind these sightings is, as is so often the case, a tragic one. The castle was built in 1440 by Sir Roger de Fiennes, and legend has it that one of his sons invited a girl from the nearby village to his room. He promptly made rather unsubtle advances to her, which she resisted, and managed to escape from the castle. However, the moat stood in her way and, after an unsuccessful attempt to swim across it to freedom, she was recaptured by the young Fiennes and dragged back to his bed, where he murdered her. It is the ghost of this unfortunate girl which has been seen frantically trying to swim across the moat.

In 1910, the castle was owned by Colonel Claude Lowther, who discovered a young woman, apparently in a state of anguish, in the courtyard one night. When he approached to ask her if she needed help, Lowther noticed that her hands were shrivelled, perhaps as a result of being immersed in water. Before he could glean any information from her, she vanished before his eyes.

An earlier legend originated from 1708, when the castle was bought by a George Naylor. Although the motive has never been discovered, it is said that his daughter Grace was starved to death by her governess in a room in the eastern part of the castle. After her burial in the family vault at All Saints Church in Herstmonceux, her sobs could still be heard echoing through the castle corridors, and the figure of a young girl was also sometimes seen floating through the building.

Towards the end of the nineteenth century, a descendant of the Naylors, Georgiana, lived in the castle, and was reputed to have an abiding interest in the occult. Apparently, it was her curious daily habit to ride a white ass to a spring in the surrounding park, from which it would drink. Georgiana would dress in a white cloak embroidered with magical symbols and be accompanied by a white doe. When the doe was attacked and killed by a pack of hounds, Georgiana left Herstmonceux, never to return. Since her death in Lausanne in 1906, her ghost has returned to the park around Herstmonceux Castle, and now rides the white ass through the rooms and corridors of the castle itself.

One of the most haunted rooms in the castle is the so-called Drummer's Hall, which plays host to a curious figure that has been seen banging a drum with glowing drumsticks. According to local legend, which originates in the last century, a member of the Dacre family lived secretly in the castle with his beautiful bride. To deter the attentions of the other men in the village, Dacre dressed himself in a drummer's uniform, smeared himself and his drum with phosphorous and stalked the castle's battlements, banging maniacally upon the drum.

There is another legend associated with the Dacre family, in which a young Dacre lad and some friends were trespassing for fun on the land of Lord Pelham, when they were discovered by one of Pelham's gamekeepers. An argument ensued, and Dacre struck the keeper with his sword and killed him. After Dacre's death, his spectre was seen riding through the grounds of Herstmonceux Castle. Should anyone attempt to engage him in conversation, he immediately rides for the moat, plunges into it and disappears in a milky cloud.

'WICKED' WILL DARRELL

According to local legend, Littlecote Manor in Wiltshire, England, was the scene of an appalling crime, and it is not surprising that the place should have retained some imprint of the infamous events. In the sixteenth century, Littlecote was home to the Darrell family, the most notorious of whom was 'Wicked' Will Darrell. He was known to have counted his own sister among his many mistresses, and it so happened that in the 1570s, one of them – it is unclear which – became pregnant.

According to the deathbed testimony of a midwife named Mrs Barnes, she was summoned one night to deliver a child. Such was the secrecy surrounding the birth that she was blindfolded and taken to a house. When the child had been delivered, a man snatched it away from Mrs Barnes and threw it into a fire. He then held it down in the flames with his foot until it was dead.

Thinking quickly, the midwife cut a small piece from the bed curtains, and also counted the stairs down which she was led (again blindfolded) on her way out of the house. After Mrs Barnes's death it was proved that Littlecote was indeed the scene of the gruesome crime, and Darrell was committed for trial at Salisbury. However, he was acquitted and (perhaps significantly) the judge, Sir John Popham, was left Littlecote Manor when Darrell died in 1589.

The bedchamber in which the baby was murdered is said to be haunted, with phantom bloodstains appearing occasionally on the floor. The ghost of the terrified Mrs Barnes is also occasionally seen with the screaming baby in her arms.

Another local legend has it that Darrell was out riding one day, when an apparition of the baby, surrounded by flickering flames, appeared in front of him. His panic-stricken horse immediately reared up and threw him; his neck was broken in the fall.

Writing in 1971, Peter Underwood tells of other ghostly manifestations associated with Littlecote Manor:

Littlecote has belonged to the Wills tobacco family for fifty years now and although the present owner, Major George Wills (who does not live there), will tell you that he had never seen a ghost he is no sceptic. This may be due to the fact that his brother, Sir Edward Wills, saw a ghost in the passage beyond the Long Gallery. In 1927, while sleeping in their room which was the first up the few stairs from the Long Gallery, both Sir Edward and his wife were disturbed by the sounds of somebody or something coming up the creaking stairs from the Long Gallery. The third time Sir Edward heard the sounds, he quietly stepped out and saw a lady with a light in her hand which cast a shadow on the ceiling of the passage. Her hair was fair, she was not very tall and wore a pink dress or nightdress. Sir Edward followed the figure that disappeared into the room occupied by his younger brother, the present owner of Littlecote; he, however, slept through it all and knew nothing of the affair until told of it by his older brother. One curious thing about this ghost is that it appeared to open the door of the room into which it disappeared.

It is indeed curious that a ghost should open a door in order to pass through; however, it may be that some spectres are more capable of physically interacting with their environment than others, and are more inclined to behave in ways that were familiar to them when they were alive.

It is also said that the ghost of Darrell himself appears in certain places in the house, and where he walks, the wood of the floor rots away and has to be replaced.

THE GHOSTS OF RAYNHAM HALL

Situated in Norfolk, England, Raynham Hall was for many generations the home of the Townshend family, and is also home to a number of ghosts, including the famous 'Brown Lady', otherwise known as Dorothy Walpole, sister of Sir Robert Walpole. Sir Robert was the 1st Earl of Orford and, as leader of the Whig administration, is regarded as Britain's first prime minister, although this was in the seventeenth century and the office as not officially recognized until 1905.

Dorothy Walpole was married to the 2nd Viscount Townshend; the union was not a particularly happy one and the centre of Dorothy's life was occupied by her children. There is an undoubtedly apocryphal story that the Viscountess was starved to death at Raynham Hall, an unlikely fate in view of the proximity of her powerful brother. What is a little closer to the truth is that after her death, Dorothy Walpole returned to the scene of her unhappiness in life and was seen on many subsequent occasions, mostly on the hall's principal staircase.

In 1849, there was a house party at Raynham, which was then owned by Lord Charles Townshend. One of the guests, Major Loftus, was making his way upstairs to his room when he was startled to see a lady wearing a brown silk dress standing before him. In those days, ladies did not make a habit of staying up until the small hours; in addition, Major Loftus had not seen her before, but when he politely inquired as to her identity, she vanished.

Intrigued by this strange encounter, the major sat up for most of the following night, hoping to meet the mysterious lady again. She reappeared before him, but then moved away, and Loftus gave chase, finally catching up with her in a side passage. She was certainly a beautiful woman, although her appearance was somewhat spoiled by the two empty sockets where her eyes should have been.

News of this shocking event quickly made its way to the servants, who immediately gave their notice, leaving Lord Charles Townshend to fend for himself. Townshend suspected that some trickery was to blame for the appearances of the Brown Lady, and he decided to replace his staff with a large group of detectives, who stayed with him at Raynham for several months. They were, however, unable to discover the identity of the practical joker – if such a person were indeed to blame for the ghostly activities.

A later guest at the hall, a writer of adventure stories called

Captain Marryat, also encountered the Brown Lady in one of the corridors. He responded in a singular way, by firing his pistol into her face at point-blank range. Doubtless offended, the apparition instantly vanished, and the bullet struck the door behind it.

In addition to the Brown Lady, there are the ghosts of two children at Raynham Hall, one of whom haunts a room known as the Stone Parlour. She was seen on one occasion by Miss Baumer, the German governess of the Marchioness Townshend in the early years of the twentieth century. Miss Baumer had been delegated by the Marchioness to receive Lady Norah Bentinck, her two children and the Dowager Countess of Gainsborough, the Marchioness having arranged to open a bazaar in King's Lynn.

When the guests were inside, Miss Baumer mentioned to Lady Norah that she had seen three children with her, whereas she had thought Lady Norah was bringing only two. Lady Norah replied that she had indeed brought only two children, and that she had no idea what Miss Baumer was talking about. The governess said that she had distinctly seen three children climbing the steps leading to the hall's entrance, the third of whom ran into the Stone Parlour.

One afternoon in October 1935, Marchioness Townshend's friend Maude ffoulkes encountered the ghost of a spaniel, as she was on her way to the principal staircase via a small, dim vestibule. Once inside the vestibule, she heard the sound of a small animal running towards her and, thinking it to be the Marchioness's son's dog, she stooped to pat it. When she realized that there was actually no dog there, she ran back into the Marble Hall, from which she had come, to find the dog still there, asleep by the fire.

There have been other apparitions seen at Raynham, and Marchioness Townshend believed that they signalled the death of a member of the family. On one occasion, the Marchioness gave a party at the hall, during which Miss Baumer noticed a tall woman in a pink dress holding a handkerchief to her face. Miss Baumer asked the Marchioness whether any such woman had arrived at the hall, to which she replied in the negative. They both decided that the mysterious woman's appearance was an ill omen of some kind. Sure enough, shortly afterwards Marchioness Townshend's mother-in-law died from an illness from which she had been suffering for some weeks.

The Marchioness's sister-in-law, Lady Agnes Durham, later told her that when Raynham Hall had been let some time previously, the tenants reported being awakened by the sound of a large number of people walking up and down the staircase. They got up to investigate, and to their shock witnessed a procession of black shadows moving past them. A couple of days later, Lady Agnes's father, the 5th Marquis, died in Paris.

Finally, according to the Marchioness Townshend, there is a rather more charming, though no less puzzling, supernatural manifestation associated with Raynham Hall. To celebrate the anniversary of the return of the Townshend family to the hall after the period in which it was let, she made a habit of burning incense in a small oratory within the building. However, on an occasion when the family was absent from the house on the anniversary, the scent of incense still wafted through the rooms and corridors of Raynham Hall, causing much puzzlement to the housekeeper, who had not lighted a single stick.

THE RETURN OF RUPERT BROOKE

In January 1919, Dr A. I. Copeland returned to Cambridge, England, after his demobilization, and rented rooms in the Old Vicarage at Grantchester, which had been occupied in the pre-war years by the poet Rupert Brooke, who had died in the First World War. In *True Ghost Stories* Marchioness Townshend and Maude ffoulkes describe the sitting-room:

The sitting-room at the Old Vicarage gave Dr Copeland the impression of still being lived in; there was not the slightest feeling that the bright young life associated with the place had met with such sudden extinction. How well one knows the atmosphere of a man's room when he is the healthy out-of-doors type, and where the aftermath of good tobacco blends with the never-to-be-forgotten smell of leather-bound books, and you appreciate the 'homeliness' of photographs, the favourite ashtrays, and the odds and ends so characteristic of the man.

On a certain winter evening, Dr Copeland was happily reading in the sitting room, more than content to continue the occupation of the Old Vicarage so cruelly cut short when Brooke met his fate four years earlier. Copeland's bulldog, Caesar, was fast asleep on the sofa, and beyond the French windows the still, clear night was held in the thrall of a heavy frost.

Without warning, Caesar stirred and awoke from his deep slumber, rising a little and listening intently. Alerted by the dog's behaviour, Dr Copeland put aside his book and listened also. He heard the sound of footsteps approaching the windows of the sitting room. They were slow and measured, and Copeland at first assumed them to belong to his landlord, Mr Neave. Rising from his seat, Copeland went over to the French windows and opened them, with a greeting for Neave on his lips.

There was no one there, however, and Copeland stepped out through the window to see where Neave might be, but he found himself completely alone in the garden. Somewhat puzzled, he returned to the warmth of the sitting room and rang for the landlord. When Neave arrived a few minutes later, Copeland told him about the strange footsteps he had heard approaching along the side of the house.

Mr Neave replied: 'We are used to these footsteps; they've happened ever since Mr Brooke was killed – they belong to his ghost, which up to now nobody has seen. The footsteps come close to the window, but there's no one there . . . I hope, sir, you've not been upset.'

Copeland assured Mr Neave that he was not, and that, apparently, was the end of the matter. Again we are left to wonder whether psychic recordings can be made as a result of great happiness and contentment as well as great anguish. There is no doubt that Rupert Brooke loved the Old Vicarage at Grantchester, and perhaps it was for this reason that Dr Copeland heard the sounds of a pleasant midnight stroll through the frost of winter.

4

INTERACTIVE GHOSTS

THE HAUNTED POLICE STATION

The building stood on North Newstead Avenue, a convenient business location a mere ten-minute drive from downtown St Louis, Missouri. It would be ideal for the purposes of its new owners, Matt and Denise Piskulic, who were in the process of starting up a computer graphics company. At the beginning of 1992, the couple moved into the converted police station, intending to live there until their new business took off and they could afford to keep it exclusively as their offices and move elsewhere.

Built in 1904, the building had been at the centre of the Bobby Greenlease kidnapping case of the 1940s. This notorious case involved the abduction of a young boy in Kansas City. The kidnappers demanded a ransom of $600,000 from the boy's wealthy St Louisan father. Although the money was handed over (at the police station on North Newstead), the boy was killed, and half the ransom went missing, leading to accusations of police corruption. In 1945, a man suspected of theft was beaten to death in his cell, and although three police officers were indicted for manslaughter, there was insufficient evidence to secure convictions.

In the years following, the station was converted to a private residence, and many of the occupants reported strange sounds, such as heavy footsteps echoing through the building. It was during this time that 14 North Newstead acquired a sinister reputation as the site of ghostly activity.

In the 1960s, it came to the attention of Gordon Hoener, a St Louisan who had an interest in parapsychology. In the company of a reporter from the *St Louis Globe-Democrat* and two independent observers, Hoener conducted a seance in the building. Also present were the then residents, Helen and Howard Jones. The group set up a ouija board and attempted to contact whatever restless spirit walked the high-ceilinged rooms.

In his article on the case, published in the October 1995 issue of *Fate*, D. Douglas Graham quotes the *Globe-Democrat* of 4 April 1975, in which staff writer Walter E. Orthwein describes the results of the ouija board experiment:

> Moving across the letters and number on the board, the pointer spelled out answers to the group's question.
>
> 'Did a man die here?' [the] reporter asked.
>
> 'Y-E-S.'
>
> 'A policeman?'
>
> 'N-O.'
>
> 'A prisoner?'
>
> 'Y-E-S.'
>
> 'Would the presence manifest itself to the group?'
>
> 'Y-O-U 4 N-O.'
>
> This was taken to mean that the 'ghost' wanted no truck with the four outside observers, but had no objection to showing itself to the Joneses.

When the Piskulics moved in in the early 1990s, they almost immediately began to hear the sound of footsteps in the house. One night, Denise was awakened by what sounded like a baby crying; the sound seemed to come from a wall next to their bed. Since there were no adjoining buildings, a neighbour's baby was out of the question as a cause for the 'heart-wrenching' cries. As the couple were puzzling over the possible origin of the sound, they heard a shriek coming from the attic.

The following day, Denise telephoned the couple who had previously occupied the building, the Fosmires, asking them if they had experienced anything unusual during their tenure.

Corey Fosmire replied that one night, he had heard a voice calling his name impatiently. He was alone at the time. On another occasion, he and his family had spent an entire day varnishing the hardboard floor in the central studio. When he returned the following day, Fosmire discovered footprints all over the floor – footprints that abruptly stopped in the centre of the room.

According to D. Douglas Graham:

The final outrage occurred as the [Fosmire] family was sleeping one night. A loud scream erupted in the house. Corey described it as neither animal nor human. It came from everywhere and nowhere in 14 North Newstead, and it was so intense that it seemed to rock the whole building. Fosmire's wife was so terrified that she tried to crawl underneath him in bed, using his body to shield herself from whatever was making the terrible din. The screaming drove the family out into the street. They left for good shortly thereafter.

While the Piskulics lived at 14 North Newstead, they experienced a number of strange occurrences. On one occasion, Denise heard a woman calling 'hello', although she was alone in the building. The mysterious footsteps continued, appearing to be concentrated on the front staircase, which, although thickly carpeted, echoed with the sounds of someone walking on concrete.

In March 1993, Denise saw an apparition (this was the first time one of the ghostly phenomena manifested itself visually). She was working in her office, when she turned to see a man in the doorway. Instantly, the man ducked out of sight. Denise assumed that it was Lars Hamilton, who was working for the Piskulics in a sales capacity and had an office across the hall from Denise's. Seeing the man reminded her that she needed to ask Hamilton a question related to business. However, when she went across the hall to Hamilton's office, she found it deserted. Hamilton had been in the bathroom at the time Denise had seen the 'man'.

The Piskulics were not the only ones to suffer these super-natural episodes: their employees also experienced unexplained phenomena. One woman, Mary Adler, felt someone blowing in the back of her neck. Unamused, she turned to give whoever was responsible a good dressing down, only to find herself alone.

That the spirits present in the old police station were capable of interacting with the percipients was rather embarrasingly demonstrated when another employee, Chelsea Kersten, was confronted by an old man as she was using the toilet. Clearly as taken aback as she was, the phantom excused himself and left. Chelsea searched for him (more or less) immediately, but could find no one matching his description in the building.

The Piskulics decided to call in some help and contacted the St Louis Metaphyiscal Society, which sent along six psychics to look the place over. They concluded that 14 North Newstead was full of ghosts, only some of which had taken up permanent residence. The psychics were of the opinion that the building possessed some attribute that encouraged spirits who had nothing to do with its history to drop in. According to D. Douglas Graham, the old police station 'seems to function as a kind of motel on the highway to the hereafter, [encouraging] the roaming dead to just drop in from time to time'.

This varied cast of supernatural characters includes a black caretaker named Willie, a woman from the Depression era (who apparently is fascinated by such miracles of technology as television and microwave ovens), and an Officer O'Brien, who is very pleased with the Piskulics' renovation work on the building.

Graham also quotes the impressions noted by the psychics as they moved through the house during their visit:

Felt uncomfortable in lounge area. Man stood in lounge – like to look out the windows, said it gave him much peace in unpeaceful times when he worked in the building. He said he

74

spent more time in the building than he did at home. Comes back to visit. Older male with fringe of white hair around side of his head.

Older police officer on back steps by kitchen. [This is probably O'Brien.] 'I like this place. I spent my entire life in charge of so many. I am just visiting. No harm, no harm. I was a police officer. I spent my life protecting people. I want only good. I only visit, only visit.'

The Piskulics now share the premises with another company, whose employees have reported the odd behaviour of their computers, which frequently turn themselves on overnight, and telephones, which make strange screeching noises. However, it seems that the living residents of the house are content to share their premises with their supernatural guests, since the latter have no desire to frighten them or coerce them into moving away. Indeed, their frequently playful attitude probably makes the working day that much more interesting.

THE BLACK VELVET RIBBON

The most interesting ghost reports, with regard to the possibility of an afterlife, are those in which the ghost imparts some information that can be later verified, and which strongly imply that the ghost possesses some form of consciousness (as opposed to psychic recordings, which seem to be nothing more than mindless moving images). One such report, from the eighteenth century, is recounted by Lord Halifax in his *Ghost Book*. It concerns a brother and sister, Lord Tyrone and Lady Beresford.

On a certain morning, Lady Beresford surprised her husband at breakfast by wearing a black ribbon around her wrist. She was pale and obviously deeply troubled by something, which prompted her husband to ask if she were unwell. She replied: 'Let me beg you, Sir, never to ask about this ribbon again. From this day forward you will not see me without it.

If it concerned you as a husband, I would tell you at once. I have never denied you any request but about this ribbon I can say nothing and I beg you never to bring up the subject again.'

Her husband's concern was further roused by the fact that Lady Beresford was anxiously awaiting the post. When he asked her if she was expecting an important letter, she replied that she was, and that it would inform her of the death of her brother, Lord Tyrone, the previous Tuesday at four o'clock. The post duly arrived; it indeed included a letter telling of the death of Tyrone.

Lady Beresford then informed her husband that she had absolutely no doubt that she was expecting a child, and that it would be a son. This assertion likewise proved accurate: she gave birth to a boy seven months later.

When her husband died a few years later, Lady Beresford moved in with a clergyman and his wife. Before long, she entered into a romance with and married the couple's son, who was somewhat younger than she. In spite of some severe problems with the marriage, caused no doubt by the difference in their ages, she presently gave birth to another boy. A few weeks later, she celebrated her forty-seventh birthday; however, the clergyman gave her what he assumed to be some good news. He had looked up her date of birth in the parish register and discovered that, in fact, she was only forty-six. To the clergyman's surprise, Lady Beresford reacted with horror, and said: 'You have signed my death warrant!'

By this time, her son by her first marriage was twelve, and she summoned him, together with her friend Lady Cobb, to her room. There, she at last divulged to them the secret reason she had worn the black velvet ribbon around her wrist throughout the years since the morning on which she had learned of her brother's death. She told them that she and her brother had agreed that whoever should die first would appear to the other at night. This Lord Tyrone did, telling his sister that he had died the previous Tuesday at four o'clock. He also gave her information regarding the future, including the birth of her first son, her first husband's death and her second marriage. Lord Tyrone's ghost then said to her: 'You will die in the forty-eighth year of your age.' This, he added, could be avoided only if she resisted the temptation to marry again.

Lady Beresford asked the ghost for some proof of its existence, asking it to touch her wrist. When the ghost did so, the nerves and muscles in her wrist were instantly withered. The ghost told her to cover the wrist with a black ribbon, and never to let anyone see it.

When she reached the age of forty-seven, Lady Beresford assumed that the warning had not been accurate and she had avoided the death that had been foretold. However, since she was actually only forty-six, it became clear to her that it would still come to pass. On the day of her forty-seventh birthday, she died. Driven by curiosity, Lady Cobb took the black ribbon from her friend's wrist and saw that it was indeed withered.

BETHAN AND BRIAN JAMES

Just as violent and traumatic events can cause psychic recordings to be imprinted on to the atmosphere, to be replayed again and again in later years, it is possible that such events can also cause interactive ghosts to return to the places they knew in life, sometimes to impart important information, sometimes to offer final reconciliation to friends and loved ones. The following case occurred in Wales in the 1960s, and was investigated by the Revd J. Aelwyn Roberts, who describes it in his book *The Holy Ghostbuster*. It concerned a young couple, Bethan and Brian James, who lived on a smallholding on the island of Anglesey, which he had inherited from his father.

The couple had two children, who became a considerable drain on their meagre resources, and eventually Brian decided to get a job in a factory in the nearby village of Llangefni. One evening, Brian returned home at seven o'clock, looking uneasy. He had taken some cows to Builth Wells, in order to earn a little extra money, and on his way home he had been stopped by the police. In order to save money, Brian had foolishly cancelled the insurance on his van; in addition, the tax had expired, and the police, he was sure, would prosecute him. The resulting fine would almost certainly be more than the family could afford.

Bethan was absolutely furious, and shouted that Brian was a fool and that she would have been better off marrying the village idiot. Brian left the house, and a few minutes later, Bethan heard the sound of a shotgun. Rushing outside, she found her husband's body by the paddock stile.

At the coroner's inquest it was noted that Brian's death did not appear to be a suicide, since Brian had apparently died while climbing the stile, and thus it was much more likely that the gun had gone off accidentally. Accordingly, the coroner entered a verdict of accidental death. Although this soothed Bethan's conscience somewhat, she could not rid herself of the suspicion that Brian's death had indeed been suicide.

Five months later, Bethan was preparing to go to bed, when she heard a whistling sound in her bedroom, which she instantly recognized as the sound Brian used to make through his teeth whenever he had something on his mind. She also heard a tapping sound, as if someone were tapping their fingernails on the chest of drawers. This was another of Brian's habits. The sounds returned several nights a week and deeply disturbed Bethan.

Eventually, Bethan's parents suggested that she leave the house, which she did, taking the children to live in a cottage in Llangefni. All was peaceful for three months, and then the tapping sounds and the whistles started again, prompting Bethan to contact the Revd J. Aelwyn Roberts to ask for help. Roberts agreed, and asked if he might bring a friend of his to the cottage. Elwyn Roberts, he told Bethan, was a research scientist who was also a 'sensitive' (a person who can sense the presence of disembodied spirits).

The two men went to the cottage, and while they were talking with Bethan, she suddenly told them that her husband was there, which Elwyn Roberts confirmed. He was able to communicate with Brian, who said that he had committed suicide on the stile. It had been a spontaneous act which he immediately regretted; the reason for his returning was his desire to let Bethan know how sorry he was for all the grief he had caused her and their children. In fact, on the nights he visited her, he had shouted to her in an attempt to make himself heard, although of course Bethan had heard nothing but the gentle whistling and the tapping of his fingers on the chest of drawers.

However, with the aid of the sensitive Elwyn Roberts, Brian had now made his wife understand, and it seems that this was enough to release his spirit and allow it to commence whatever unfathomable journey awaited it. After that night, Bethan James and her children were left in peace.

THE GHOST OF RICHARD TARWELL

The following case from the early eighteenth century is reminiscent of Athenodorus's encounter (which we examined at the beginning of the book), in that a spirit apparently returned to Earth in order to guide someone to the site of its murder, and thus to achieve a posthumous justice. In 1730, George Harris owned a large estate in Devon, England. He was often in London, where he held a prominent position in the court of George II, and on one such occasion, he received an urgent message from his butler, Richard Morris, who asked him if he would return to the estate as quickly as he could.

When Harris arrived, Richard Morris told him that there had been a break-in at the house. Morris had heard noises coming from the butler's pantry during the night, and had entered the room thinking that some of the servants were to blame: the house had been locked and secure, making it unlikely that anyone could have gained entry from outside.

But when he threw open the door to the pantry, he was confronted by two robbers and a boy, named Richard Tarwell, who had recently been taken into employment in the kitchen. The robbers tied up Morris and made their getaway with a quantity of the house's silver, and Tarwell in tow. Morris suggested to George Harris that it had been Tarwell who had let the robbers into the well-secured house.

In spite of extensive searches, neither the robbers nor Richard Tarwell were apprehended. However, as George Harris lay in bed one night, he became aware of a young boy standing in his room. He recognized the boy as Richard Tarwell, and was somewhat surprised to see him there, not least because he had earlier gone around the house with Morris, watching as the butler secured every single door and window. He concluded that Tarwell must have been hiding in the house since the night of the robbery.

Like Athenodorus's ghost, the boy beckoned to Harris, who realized that the boy was moving absolutely silently, and that he was in fact seeing an apparition. He felt compelled to follow as the ghost made its way down the stairs and walked to one of the house's side doors, which stood open despite having been locked by Morris earlier in the evening. John and Anne Spencer make the interesting observation that 'although Tarwell may have been able to move through matter in the classic ghostly manner, he had apparently made provision for Harris's need for a more conventional exit'.

The apparition led Harris away from the house and towards a large oak tree, where it pointed to the ground and vanished. The following morning, Harris instructed two footmen to dig at the point indicated by the ghost. They discovered the body of Richard Tarwell.

At this point, it occurred to Harris that Tarwell could not have let the robbers into the house, since Morris kept the keys with him at all times. He began to suspect that it was Morris, rather than Tarwell, who had been in league with the robbers, and that the boy had stumbled upon them. When Richard Morris was confronted with his employer's suspicions, he broke down and confessed that he had indeed let the robbers into the house and that Tarwell, woken by the sounds of their activities, had walked in upon them. One of the robbers had killed the boy, then buried his body. Morris had been tied up to make it look as if he were the innocent witness to the robbery.

Morris was later hanged for murder, an outcome that presumably allowed the spirit of Richard Tarwell to rest in peace thereafter.

THE ANGRY SPIRIT

In her book *True Hauntings: Spirits With a Purpose*, ghost investigator Hazel M. Denning relates an interesting case which she personally investigated and was able to resolve. The case, from the 1970s, concerned a young woman whom she calls 'Helen', who was lying in bed one night, drifting off to sleep, when she had the sudden sensation of another presence in the room. She tried to look around to see who might be there, but to her surprise she found herself completely unable to move. She became extremely frightened when she tried to call out to her parents for help but was unable to make a sound. Presently, however, the paralysis left her and she was able to get out of bed. Helen considered going to her parents' room and telling them what had happened; but she suspected that they would dismiss her experience as a nightmare. Reluctantly, she returned to bed, and was able, eventually, to drift off to sleep.

The mysterious paralysis returned several times over the next few weeks until, during one such episode, Helen became aware of a voice which kept repeating: 'Speak to me, speak to me.' Helen opened her eyes to see a young man kneeling by her bed. She tried to scream, but once again the paralysis prevented her from doing so. She shut her eyes tightly, and when she opened them again, the young man had disappeared.

The following day, Helen told her friend 'Margaret' what had happened, and Margaret suggested that they approach Hazel Denning for help. At that time, Denning was working with a sensitive named Gertrude Hall. Denning reported: 'Following introductions the first thing I heard was Gertrude saying, "Well, I am sorry, young man, but I *am* going to do something about this." She then explained that an angry spirit was present. The moment he saw her he said, "You stay out of this. She is mine and you can't make me leave her." Gertrude Hall then proceeded to walk around Helen, sprinkling 'a combination of herbs' on the carpet, apparently in a kind of New Age exorcism ritual. The troublesome spirit was infuriated by this, complaining that he could no longer get to Helen.

Denning began to explain to the spirit how it could enlist the aid of others in its dimension to find peace. According to Denning, who received his responses through Gertrude, the conversation went as follows:

'There are people in your dimension who will help you if you will just ask. You must have relatives who have gone before you, maybe a grandmother or grandfather . . .'

He broke in indignantly. 'I never had any truck with my relatives when I was on earth. I'm not about to start over here.'

'Well, then, perhaps you had a friend who died before you did who could come to help.'

As I finished this sentence, Gertrude broke in to tell us that another spirit had come into the room. He slapped our spirit on the back and said, 'Ralph, you old son-of-a-gun, what kind of mess have you got yourself in now?'

Ralph replied, 'I just wanted to talk to this girl.'

'Don't you know you can't mess around with a young girl and not get into trouble?'

'But I only wanted to talk to her. She can hear me. Nobody else could.'

82

Denning asked 'Ralph' how he was able to paralyse Helen during his earlier visits, and he replied that he had been a boxer when alive, and thus knew the correct pressure points to press. The two spirits then began to converse with each other, and eventually Ralph's friend convinced him that there were people on the other side who would be able to explain everything to him.

Apparently, the reason he could be heard only by Helen was that she was an unwitting psychic sensitive. Ralph then left with his friend, and Helen was not troubled again.

AMERICA ON THE MOVE

One summer in 1943, a travelling salesman was on the night train from Minneapolis, Minnesota, to Butte, Montana. He was trying, without much success, to get some sleep as the train swayed constantly from side to side. In addition, he was prevented from getting any rest by a curious feeling of uneasiness, which he could not quite define, but which refused to leave him in peace. In an interview with a Chicago newspaper reporter some months later, he said: 'I couldn't put my finger on what was troubling me. There were no strange or unusual noises in the train. I could detect nothing that sounded wrong in the steady clicking of the wheels. For some reason, I decided to lift the shade of my window.'

Peering out into the night, the salesman was astonished to see a native American brave riding at breakneck speed alongside the train. The brave was bent low, wringing every last drop of speed from his jet-black mount. The salesman later described the apparition as seeming to be solid flesh, but with a strange shimmering effect around the edges, like 'a strip of really old movie film being projected on the prairie'.

On subsequent journeys, the salesman saw similar apparitions sweeping across the darkened landscape, and he was not the only witness. Railway workers throughout the

Dakotas and Wyoming often saw the phantom native Americans, who seemed to be engaged in races with the trains.

One such phantom was even the subject of a painting by the respected artist Frederic Remington, who sketched it from life (so to speak) from his train. Remington called his picture *America on the Move.* He believed that the phantoms were attempting to win their races with the 'iron horses' of the white men, because to do so would represent a victory which might force the invaders to leave the lands they had conquered.

Although it might seem at first glance that these reports are examples of psychic recordings, it is important to note the apparent intention of the phantoms to race the trains across the landscape. This implies an awareness of the part of the long-dead native American braves, and an endless desire to beat the white men to the horizon.

THE SKULL AT BURTON AGNES HALL

Among the most eerie and spine-chilling of ghostly encounters are those associated with certain skulls, which are apparently the focus for the activities of the restless spirits of their owners. One such tale, related by Charles G. Harper in his book *Haunted Houses,* concerns the skull kept at Burton Agnes Hall, situated between Bridlington and Driffeld in Yorkshire, England.

The estate on which Burton Agnes Hall stands came into the possession of the Griffith family during the reign of Edward I in the thirteenth century. By the time of Elizabeth I's reign, three centuries later, the family had been reduced to the three daughters of Sir Henry Griffith, who decided that the old, fortified hall was no longer sufficient for their needs. Since the family was still immensely wealthy, the three heiresses decided to build a completely new mansion upon the site of the old. It was Anne Griffith who took the greatest interest in the project and devoted herself completely to it.

Not long after the magnificent Burton Agnes Hall had been completed and the three sisters moved in, Anne decided to pay a visit to some friends at Harpham, one mile away. Fearful for the safety of an unprotected girl on a country road, her sisters insisted that she take with her their pet dog. Her sisters' fear were well founded, for on her way to Harpham, Anne came upon two wanderings beggars who asked her for some money. As she was taking some from her purse, they noticed a ring she was wearing and demanded that she hand it over. When she refused, saying that it was a family heirloom, the beggars attempted to snatch it from her. The dog barked, but was otherwise useless, and one of the men struck Anne on the head with a cudgel, knocking her unconscious.

By the time Anne was found lying by the roadside, the thieves had long since made their getaway. She was carried back to her beloved Burton Agnes, where she died five days later. According to Harper:

In her last conscious intervals she besought her sisters, for the love she bore their home and the affection they owed her, when she was dead to sever her head from her body and to preserve it within the walls of the mansion, there to let it remain to all future time. 'Never,' she implored, 'let it be removed; and make this, my last wish, known to any who might come into ownership. And know, and let those of future generations know, that if my desire not be fulfilled, my spirit shall, it if be permitted, render the house uninhabitable for human beings.'

A few days later, Anne was interred in the family vault. Her sisters, assuming her final entreaties to be no more than the products of a deranged and damaged brain, disregarded them and left the body intact. The quietness of the surviving sisters' mourning was soon interrupted by a loud crash in one of the upstairs rooms. On inspecting the room, they discovered that no object had fallen. A few nights later, doors throughout the house were slammed again and again, and although the occupants searched the rooms and corridors, ready to confront any intruders, nothing was found amiss. From then on, the house was plagued with strange noises, including the apparent groans of a dying person.

Perhaps unsurprisingly, the surviving sisters wondered if their broken promise to Anne might be the cause of their problems, and consulted the local vicar, who advised them to disinter the body, remove the head and take it into the house, as Anne had requested. When they opened the coffin, so the legend goes, they were appalled and astonished to discover that, while the body was perfectly preserved, the head had been severed and the flesh had decomposed completely, revealing the skull beneath. When it was removed and interred within the house, all of the supernatural manifestations ceased, and the sisters were never again troubled by Anne's spirit.

However, many years later, when Burton Agnes Hall passed into different ownership, and the legend associated with it had been dismissed as foolish superstition, a mischievous maidservant disinterred the skull and threw it into a passing farm cart. The horse immediately stopped in its tracks, and no amount of whipping could induce it to move. The maidservant, suddenly terrified and thinking better of her rash action, retrieved the skull from the cart and took it back into the house, whereupon the horse went on its way.

The next family to own the estate, the Boyntons, likewise took the legend with a large pinch of salt, and had the skull buried in the garden. They were plagued with bad luck until they saw sense and once more returned Anne's skull to its rightful place within the house.

In the 1860s, the Hall was unoccupied, and Matthew Potter, the gamekeeper on the estate, invited his cousin John Bilton to come from London for a visit. Potter warned Bilton that the house was haunted, but the latter scoffed at the notion, and declared himself content to stay the night there. Charles Harper describes what happened next.

Keeping very close together on their way to the bedroom, they went to bed in the dark, and shared the same bed, for the sake of security; but not in peace, for there came a shuffling of feet in the passage, like that of a considerable crowd.

'What's that?' asked the startled visitor.

'Jenny Yewlats,' returned the gamekeeper, with a yawn, giving the local Yorkshire name for owls.

'But owls don't wear hob-nailed boots and bang doors,' returned the visitor, ducking his head under the clothes as the noises increased.

'Bats, then,' said the gamekeeper.

'Bats be blowed,' remarked his friend, with more force than politeness.

'Aw, then, 'tis Owd Nance [the local nickname for Anne Griffith],' said the gamekeeper unconcernedly, and went to sleep; but the stranger to these things thought it was more like Old Nick, and lay long awake, listening to the unearthly tumult. He did not sleep another night at the Hall.

THE HAUNTED TOWER OF LONDON

It can surely come as little surprise that the Tower of London is reputed to be haunted by many restless spirits, in view of the large number of people forced to depart their lives there over the long and bloody centuries of its history. While the most famous apparition is that of Anne Boleyn, second wife of Henry VIII, who apparently carries her head underneath her arm in the traditional and clichéd ghostly fashion, a far more interesting sighting was made by Edmund Lenthal Swifte, who in the early years of the nineteenth century was the Keeper of the Crown Jewels, and who wrote of his experience in *Notes & Queries* in 1860.

In 1814 I was appointed Keeper of the Crown Jewels in the Tower, where I resided with my family until my retirement in 1852. One Saturday night in October 1817, about the 'witching hour,' I was at supper with my wife, her sister, and our little boy, in the sitting-room of the Jewel House, which – then comparatively modernised – is said to have been the 'doleful prison' of Anne Boleyn, and of the ten bishops whom Oliver Cromwell piously accommodated therein ... The room was – as it still is – irregularly shaped, having three doors and two windows, which last are cut nearly nine feet deep into the outer wall; between these there is a chimney-piece projecting far into the room, and surmounted with a large oil picture. On the night in question, the doors were all closed, heavy and dark cloth curtains were let down over the windows, and the only light in the room was that of two candles on the table. I sat at the foot of the table, my son on my right hand, his mother fronting the chimney-piece, and her sister on the opposite side. I had offered a glass of wine and water to my wife, when, on putting it to her lips, she paused, and exclaimed, 'Good God! what is that?' I looked up and saw a cylindrical figure, like a glass tube, seemingly about the thickness of my arm, and hovering between the ceiling and the table; its contents appeared to be a dense fluid, white and pale azure, like the gathering of a summer cloud, and incessantly mingling within the cylinder. This lasted about two minutes, when it began slowly to move before my sister-in-law; then, following the oblong shape of the table, *before* my son and myself; passing *behind* my wife, it paused for a moment over her right shoulder (observe, there was no mirror opposite to her in which she could there behold it). Instantly she crouched down, and with both hands covering her shoulder, she shrieked out, 'O Christ! it has seized me!' Even now, while writing, I feel the fresh horror of that moment. I caught up my chair, struck at the wainscot behind her, rushed upstairs to the children's room, and told the terrified nurse what I had seen. Meanwhile, the other domestics had hurried into the parlour, where their mistress recounted to them the scene, even as I was detailing it above stairs.

Interestingly, although Edward Lenthal Swifte and his wife experienced this apparition, neither his sister-in-law nor his son saw anything unusual (apart from the couple's odd behaviour). This would seem to weigh against the idea, mooted at the time, that someone in another building in the Tower might have been projecting light from a mirror into the room, in which case the other two people present would have seen the light; Swifte also maintained that all the curtains were tightly drawn. In addition, of course, beams of reflected light cannot physically grab people.

Swifte also tells of a report made by one of the night sentries at the Jewel House:

> [The sentry,] a man who was in perfect health and spirits, and was singing and whistling up to the moment of the occurrence, was alarmed by a figure like a huge bear issuing from under the Jewel Room door. He thrust at it with his bayonet, which stuck in the door, even as my chair had dinted the wainscot; he dropped in a fit, and was carried senseless to the guard-room.
>
> When on the morrow I saw the unfortunate soldier in the main guard-room, his fellow-sentinel was also there, and testified to having seen him at his post just before the alarm, awake and alert, and had even spoken to him. I saw the unfortunate man again on the following day, but changed beyond my recognition; in another day or two, the brave and steady soldier, who would have mounted a breach, or led a forlorn hope with unshaken nerves, *died* – at the presence of a shadow.

Charles Harper admits that it was unclear whether the soldier had seen a genuine apparition, or was perhaps the victim of a practical joke, but what is certain is that there were a number of bears kept in the Royal Menagerie in the Tower. It is possible that one might have briefly escaped, although there are no records of such an occurrence.

THE HAUNTED INN

The Oliver House in Bisbee, Arizona, was built in 1909 by Edith Ann Oliver, the wife of the mining tycoon Henry Oliver, as a boarding house for executives from the Arizona and Calumet Mining Company. In its early days, the house was the site of three murders and one suicide. An employee named Nat Anderson was killed by an unknown assailant on 22 February 1920, and at an undetermined date a man is said to have discovered his wife in bed with another man; he shot them both and then turned the gun on himself.

In 1986, Dennis Schranz bought the Oliver House with the intention of turning it into a bed and breakfast, in spite of the fact that the previous owner, in a fit of conscience, had informed him that it was haunted by five ghosts, one of which was 'violent', and that he probably shouldn't buy the place. Schranz did not believe in ghosts, so considered the house's reputation to be of little relevance, and it was without any apprehension that he moved in with plans to begin renovations.

The ghosts lost no time in making their presence known: on his first evening in the house, Schranz heard water running through pipes that had been ripped out years before, followed by the sound of footsteps coming down the hall towards the door to his room. Although a sceptic, Schranz was prepared to believe that intruders might have broken into the house. He had locked the door to his room, and so felt reasonably secure, at least in the very short term. However, to his astonishment, the footsteps continued through the locked door and approached his bed. No harm came to him that night, and Schranz continued with his plans to turn the house into a bed and breakfast.

There were many other strange manifestations at the newly named Bisbee Bed & Breakfast. A manager named Terri King encountered a strange presence in several of the rooms. On one occasion, she was changing sheets in the Captain's Room, when she heard a voice shout: 'Get out!' Rather courageously, she replied in an equally hostile manner: 'What do you mean "Get out"? Who else is going to clean up this room? You get out!' This seemed to have the desired effect and Terri never heard the voice again. This is interesting, since it echoes the testimony of numerous other ghost percipients, who have said that telling a ghost to 'get lost' results in the presence leaving.

In October 1992, parapsychologist William G. Everist organized an investigation of the Bisbee Bed & Breakfast. The team consisted of nineteen of Everist's students (who were also psychic sensitives), two local residents and two professional psychics. Everist's strategy was to go through the house with the professional psychics and record their impressions. Following this, the rest of the team were each assigned a room in which to spend the night, and were provided with a journal and a list of adjectives to describe the nature of whatever they might perceive.

The following morning, the team regrouped to discuss what (if anything) had transpired. Reporting on the investigations in the September 1996 issue of *Fate*, Everist relates what he was told after breakfast:

The man who had been assigned to the room at the top of the stairs on the second floor, near the alleged location of Nat Anderson's shooting, reported hearing metallic sounds in the night, like jewelry or coins rattling.

'At about 3.30 a.m.,' he stated, 'I awoke to hear a voice. It was my roommate having a dream. As I went back to sleep, I heard two female voices in the distance. A short while later, I heard another female voice whispering near me, but when I opened my eyes, no one else was in the room.

'Shortly thereafter, I had an unusual dream. I dreamt that someone from our group had laid down on the bed to my right. I told them that they did not belong there and I woke to find no one there. I went back to sleep and began to dream again. This time I was walking the darkened halls of the Oliver

House, first upstairs then downstairs. Then I sat with someone in the parlour where we had dinner earlier last night. After that I went back up to my room. As I went back to sleep in my dream, the same person again laid down on my right side. I told them they did not belong there and they left.'

The man woke when he heard the metal rattling sound next to his right ear. It was about 5.30 a.m., and he noticed the sound of poker chips from the right corner of the room and the sound of coins being poured into a sack.

The sensitive described his impressions of the presence that had been with him. It had, apparently, been a man in his late forties, with a craggy face and dark hair, who seemed to be extremely frustrated. The whisperer had been a slender woman in a red dress.

The two female investigators who had slept in the room next door reported similar experiences of dreams in which they were walking through the house. One of them said: '"I dreamt I woke up from the dream and saw the clothes rack on the other side of the room in front of me. To the left of the clothes rack, I felt a presence. The presence was just watching us sleep. I didn't know what to do, so I began crying. I was terrified, but this was in my dream and then Janice woke me up. But it felt real to me."'

Another woman, who was sharing a room with three other investigators, felt the powerful presence of a man whom she suspected of having done 'something terrible to someone' while alive. It seemed to her that he was 'somehow being punished'.

In his interpretation of the data supplied by the sensitives, Everist notes that many of them reported out-of-body experiences (in which a person's consciousness somehow becomes separated from his or her physical body, and is able to move about freely), disguised as dreams of walking through Oliver House. He also notes the reports of awakening during the dream (which he considers to be another kind of out-of-body experience) and becoming aware of a discarnate presence near by. Everist goes on to ask the intriguing question: could these experiences signify contact by a ghost *within* a dream state? Of course, the sceptical answer would be a resounding 'No!' – probably accompanied by a deep guffaw. After all, these are *dreams* we are talking about, and many weird and wonderful things can happen in the dreaming state. However, the fact remains that the sensitives in the Oliver House apparently experienced *shared* dreams, which is slightly different from a single person dreaming in isolation.

Indeed, Everist is well aware of the sceptical argument:

> In reviewing the Bisbee dream haunting experiences, one might logically ask, 'Could these experiences be nothing more than dream incubation?' That is, were the dreamers experiencing something similar to collective programming or self-fulfilling prophecy since each of them were [sic] at the Oliver House for the specific purpose of having some sort of paranormal experience?

Once again, however, there is a problem with this interpretation. While they may have been expecting some kind of paranormal experience, no one expected precisely the sort of experience that was reported by the sensitives. At the time of publication of his article, Everist was planning to conduct further research, not only into the apparent haunting at the Oliver House, but also into the dream haunting experience in general.

A LEGLESS SPECTRE IN BOSNIA

The war which erupted in the first half of the 1990s with the collapse of the former Yugoslavia left a hideous scar on the face of Europe which will perhaps take decades to heal. Indeed, the conflagration was partly the result of suppressed hostilities and tensions going back centuries. The aftermath for the living has been tragic enough, but if recent reports are to be believed, the catastrophe in the Balkans, in common with the wars of years past, has generated its own unhappy company of restless souls.

On 25 May 1995, a mortar attack killed seventy-one people in Kapija Square in Tuzla's old town. Today, the square is shunned after midnight, not for fear of more attacks, but for fear of the ghost of a girl killed in the attack, who still searches for her severed legs. The ghost was first encountered in December 1995 by a military police officer named Mustafa Piric, who stopped a girl with long, blond hair after curfew and asked for her identification papers. She had her back to him, and when she turned around, Piric saw that she had no face. As the police officer stood rooted to the spot in utter shock, he heard a girl's voice cry: 'Give me back my legs!'

Alma Ahmedbegovic, a twenty-year-old radio reporter who had helped to pull the dying from the rubble of the square after the mortar attack, said: 'A lot of people here believe in ghosts and spirits. They believe this girl's spirit can't rest because she was buried without her legs.'

According to Maida Hamzic, a nineteen-year-old nurse who suffered minor injuries in the attack, the ghost was later seen by three police officers while on patrol in the square. She maintained that 'the fact that they all saw the same thing means the story is true. I believe the stories about people hearing strange sounds and moans coming from there late at night. In fact, many people lost limbs, or were decapitated, when the mortar struck, and were buried in a mass funeral, which was held in the middle of the night for fear of another attack.'

In addition to the apparition haunting Kapija Square, there are tales of people awakening from nightmares to see their dead friends and relatives standing in front of them. While these tales may refer to hypnopompic visions, in which dream imagery is briefly carried over into the transitional state between sleeping and waking, the Kapija Square apparition might be the product of superstition, or it might just be one of the victims of the Bosnian war being unable to find the peace that has, at least tentatively, returned to that tragic region.

MONTROSE AERODROME

In 1987 a woman driving near Montrose aerodrome in Scotland watched as a Hawker Hurricane fighter flew past, so low that she was able to see every detail of the khaki-painted aircraft. Surprised by what she had seen, she reported the sighting to the Montrose Aerodrome Museum Society. Research later revealed that a Hurricane had been among several aircraft which crashed near Montrose during the Second World War, when the aerodrome had been operated by the RAF.

Strange phenomena at Montrose and the surrounding area began before the 1980s; in 1943, a member of the NAAFI heard the sound of an aircraft returning to the base, and prepared some tea for the crew. When no one entered the canteen, she went outside to check where they were. In fact, no aircraft had landed. The NAAFI canteen was the sight of another supernatural event, when a flying officer entered the canteen and approached the assistant. When she greeted him, he vanished in front of her.

These were not the only ghosts to be seen at Montrose. In 1942 an airman was involved in a fatal crash soon after take-off, and his spectre also was seen on numerous occasions around the base. In fact, so common was his appearance that new arrivals to Montrose were warned about the ghost. As is often the case, one particular airman scoffed at the tales of the phantom pilot, but soon changed his tune when he encountered a figure in flying suit, helmet and goggles, his apparel failing to hide his deathly pale skin.

The manifestations took the form of strange sounds in addition to visual apparitions. On one occasion, an RAF policeman named Norrie Webster heard footsteps, which had no apparent cause. Intrigued, he began to follow them, whereupon they apparently turned and began to approach him.

In a conversation with Ian G. McIntosh of the Aerospace Museum Society, Peter Underwood was told that the hauntings continue at Montrose aerodrome, which is still used by light aircraft. In 1990 a woman walking her dog on the airfield heard a disembodied voice near by say 'I'm here' four times; and he reports:

> Twice, once at the end of 1990 and once early in 1991, an unidentified figure has frightened people off the airfield at dusk. Three girls saw 'something' beside one of the old hangars and left, fast; and in 1994 footsteps, door opening and door handle rattling were experienced and a shadowy figure was seen by the Museum Society principal's son. If special areas attract ghosts and ghostly activity Montrose Aerodrome seems to be a special place with a powerful attraction.

AN ANGEL OF MERCY

St Thomas's Hospital, founded in the thirteenth century, stands on the Albert Embankment in Lambeth, London. The ghost known as the 'Grey Lady', who walks the wards and corridors of the ancient building offering solace to the sick and dying, takes her nickname from the old-fashioned grey uniform she wears. She is consistently described as being middle-aged and very nice. The part of the hospital in which she has been seen most often is Block 8, a wing that at one time was dedicated to the treatment of malignant diseases.

When Peter Underwood heard of the haunting, he lost no time in visiting St Thomas's and interviewing those who had encountered the Grey Lady, in addition to examining the records of earlier ghostly manifestations. A member of the staff named Charles Bide told him that in 1943, he was working in Block 8 the night after a bomb had struck the building, causing extensive damage. As he was clearing up the debris, he noticed that a mirror was surprisingly undamaged, and so he lifted it up to re-hang it. As he did so, he saw the reflection of a woman in the glass. She was about thirty-five and wore an old-fashioned grey nurse's uniform.

Bide's initial assumption was that the nurse must have been taking a short rest there; however, he began to feel intensely cold – an unnatural cold that made him afraid, even though he felt no malice from the nurse. He quickly left Block 8, and later regretted that he had done so, since he had also had the feeling that the nurse wanted to tell him something important. According to his wife, Bide never forgot the expression of anguish on the nurse's face, a memory that 'troubled him for the rest of his life'.

The look of anguish on the nurse's face was also a key feature of a later encounter in the hospital, in which a former superintendent named Edwin Frewer was walking along a corridor with his superior, Mr French, when they saw a nurse, dressed once again in the old-fashioned grey uniform, approaching them from the direction of Block 8. They too suddenly felt an intense coldness. The nurse then disappeared, and although both men checked, they could find no means by which she could have left that particular section of corridor. Edwin Frewer said: 'The memory of her face, with its look of anguish, remains with me after all these years.'

The most interesting element in this case is the interaction reported between the Grey Lady and certain patients who were terminally ill. A night nurse told how she was going from bed to bed, filling the patients' water jugs, when she reached the bed of an old man who was dying of cancer. The old man thanked her and said that he had already been given a glass of water. Since she was the only night nurse on duty, she asked him who had given him the water. The old man smiled and pointed to the foot of his bed; there was no one standing there. The old man died two days later.

Two months later, another nurse was washing another cancer patient, when he asked her about the 'other nurse', and if they always worked together. She asked him who he was talking about, and, like the previous patient, he pointed to someone the nurse could not see. The old man mentioned that the other nurse had been most kind and helpful, and had been to see him several times. He too died not long afterwards.

Just over a year later, another cancer patient asked who the nurse was who was warming her hands over a nearby radiator. The nurse who was at his bedside asked him to describe the person he was seeing, since she could see no one there. He replied that she was wearing a grey uniform. Like the other patients, he died two days later.

Over the next year or so, two additional terminal patients, both women, told their nurses of visits by a very kind, grey-uniformed nurse, who offered them considerable comfort. The two women also died shortly after seeing the ghostly nurse.

The fact that the figure was invariably described as being dressed in grey is extremely interesting in view of the fact that the present sisters' uniform of Oxford blue with white apron and collar came into use in the early 1920s. Previously a grey dress had been worn. In addition to these experiences, which were all written down and signed by the nurses concerned, a number of other reliable accounts of the Grey Lady appearing to patients who died soon afterwards were obtained by word of mouth but dates, times and other details are no longer available.

Underwood goes on to describe one other well-attested case, in which a state registered nurse was called during her night duty to supervise the administration of a powerful drug to a dying patient. She then asked the patient if she could do anything to make her more comfortable, to which the patient replied that the other nurse had already seen to her needs. There was, of course, no other nurse on duty that night.

While accepting that a sceptic would point to the use of pain-killing drugs as evidence of hallucinations on the part of the patients concerned, Underwood counters with an interesting argument:

> All the patients in the six accounts described would have had analgesic drugs at the ward sister's discretion; these drugs have opium derivatives or synthetic analogues of morphia, and the hallucinogenic properties of these drugs have not been fully explored, yet the fact that six quite separate reports are so similar would seem to outweigh objections on this score. It is extremely interesting to notice that more than a dozen dying patients in one unit of a massive hospital had almost identical 'hallucinations'. These 'hallucinations' had all the impressions of reality to the person concerned who was able to reconcile the apparition with specific articles and particular parts of the ward, and was able to describe, soberly and sensibly, the experience to nurses and others.

There are a number of possible identities for the Grey Lady, such as a sister who fell down an empty lift shaft at the turn of the century. Another story has it that an administrator committed suicide in the part of the hospital where the manifestations occur; while a third tells of a nurse who killed herself after inadvertently causing the death of a patient.

In a conversation with Peter Underwood, the chaplain at St Thomas's, the Revd Kingsley R. Fleming, said that he was convinced of the veracity of the encounters, adding that hospitals, due to the nature of their function, possess a 'terrific supercharge of emotion'. This must certainly be true of the noble people who work in hospitals all over the world, and it may be that such charges of emotion can provide the energy source necessary for some workers, such as the Grey Lady of St Thomas's, to continue with their care of the sick and dying even after they themselves have left this life behind.

THE GHOST OF ANNE BOLEYN

The case of the ghost of Anne Boleyn, second wife of Henry VIII, is especially interesting, since she is said to haunt at least three separate locations – not only the Tower of London but also Blickling Hall and Hampton Court – which may be said to imply some form of consciousness on behalf of the ghost, or at least some desire to shift between these locations.

The reports of her appearances over the years include imagery that is part and parcel of the traditional idea of ghostly behaviour. At Blickling Hall, Anne's family home in Norfolk, there are numerous tales of her headless ghost, together with those of a headless horseman driving his headless steeds. Her ghost has also been seen wandering through the rooms and corridors of Blickling Hall itself, in spite of the fact that the present building was built 100 years after her execution. It seems, therefore, that she is attracted to the *site*, rather than any particular building.

One night in 1985, Steve Ingram, the administrator of Blickling Hall (in which he kept a flat with his wife), was awakened at 1.30 a.m. by what sounded like the footsteps of a woman shuffling along the corridor just outside the bedroom door. As Ingram listened intently, he became aware of subtle changes in the quality of the sounds as if someone were stepping from rushing matting to carpet. Lying there in the darkness, he realized that the footsteps were actually moving from the matting in the corridor to the carpet in the bedroom itself. Since he was not prone to unnecessary jitters, Ingram assumed that his wife must have gone to the bathroom and was now returning to bed.

Ingram then turned on the bedside light and saw that his wife was actually fast asleep in bed next to him, and that the room was empty apart from them. It was only on the following day that Ingram realized that he had in fact heard the disembodied footsteps on the anniversary of Anne Boleyn's death.

An earlier encounter with Anne's ghost occurred after Blickling Hall had been taken over by the National Trust in 1946. One of the administrators, named Sidney Hancock, watched the figure of a woman walk down towards the lake from the kitchen window. Since no one was supposed to be in the grounds of the hall at that time, Hancock followed her to the lakeside and asked her if she was looking for someone. According to Hancock, the lady, dressed in a long grey gown, replied: 'That for which I seek has long since gone.' She then vanished from the lakeside. Although on the former occasions she wore the same blue dress she wore for a certain portrait hanging there, on this occasion she appeared minus her head.

At the Tower of London, which was the site of Anne Boleyn's execution, a well-documented sighting occurred in 1864. A captain of the guards found one of his men unconscious, and when he was revived, he told of how he had challenged a woman he saw approaching him from the room in which Anne Boleyn had spent her last night on earth. He had told the woman to stop, but she had kept coming at him, so he stabbed at her with his bayonet. The weapon went straight through the figure, and the guard had realized he was in the company of a ghost, whereupon he dropped in a faint.

The captain considered it more likely that his man had simply fallen asleep while on duty than that he had seen a ghost, and so he instituted court-martial proceedings against him. However, several other soldiers came forward claiming that they had seen both the ghost approaching the guard and him fainting. The charges against the soldier were therefore dropped, although one is obliged to wonder whether this was merely camaraderie, rather than genuinely corroborative testimony.

THE EVIL AT ETON VICARAGE

The strange and terrifying events that occurred in and around the vicarage at Eton, Berkshire, England, were first reported in two national newspapers. The *Daily Mirror* report ran as follows:

A congregation has been forced to abandon its church – because they say it is haunted by evil spirits. The parishioners are so scared that they are moving out at the end of the year. They believe that their 130-year-old parish church beside the Thames at Eton ... was built on a spot where devil worship and pagan rites, including human sacrifice, were performed centuries ago.

Vicar's wife Mrs Annie Johnson, said: 'I have never felt happy here, nor has my husband.' Several years ago church authorities called in an exorcist to banish the ghosts. He failed. Mrs Johnson added: 'He heard young girls screaming and shrieking. He told us the forces were very powerful.' Since then strange things have continued to happen. Fires have been lit in the altar. Pews and mats have been moved.

The vicar, the Revd Christopher Johnson, believes that the church was recently used for pagan rituals. His wife explained: 'He found a window smashed, his vestments stolen and candles had been placed round the church and lit as if for some awful purpose.'

Two days later, the *Daily Express* ran the following report:

The parishioners walked slowly, their faces pinched by the bitter cold of the morning. Just eleven answering the summons of a single ring from the bell of a church some say has been taken over by the devil.

The vicar's wife, speaking softly, not too keen to speak at all, said: 'The devil has won this time, but it's not over yet.' Sunday service at St John the Evangelist at Eton, Berkshire, came and went yesterday with an alleged shadow of evil cast across the joy of Christmas. St John's will close down in the New Year because not enough people pray there any more and because there is not enough cash to keep it going. And, say the vicar

102

and his wife, because of the atmosphere created by the presence of dark forces.

The Rev. Christopher Johnson, vicar of . . . St John's nestling on the edge of the playing fields of Eton College said: 'There is much I would like to say about the evil here, but I have been forbidden to do so.' He added: 'The Archdeacon has told me not to comment.'

His wife Anne was, however, free to speak of the evil some say have given the devil a victory. She said: 'There is evil here. It has driven people from the church. It is real and it is frightening.' The Johnsons have been at St John's for thirteen years. Nine years ago an exorcism was performed. Mrs Johnson reckoned the prince of evil took a few knocks, but then returned. She added: 'We have not imagined any of this. The then bishop called for the exorcism, not us. It was a subtle force, certainly evil. The exorcist found that the church had probably been built on a pagan burial ground. Windows have been broken, vestments taken, candles unaccountably lit. I agree, it sounds like vandalism, but it is more than that. I have felt physical pain. I have been frightened. It may sound irrational but there are forces here to be reckoned with. After the exorcism, the forces seemed less powerful, but they are still here. The congregation used to be large. This was a fine family church. Once we had a thousand people here. The devil has won this time. But it's not the end of the story. We will not give up. The evil that is here will be driven out.'

But parishioner Mrs Elizabeth Hazell, a grandmother whose husband is a house master at Eton, said: 'Ghosts? I have never seen any and I've been coming here for thirty years. It's all cock and bull. There are no evil spirits.'

On reading of the events at Eton Vicarage, Peter Underwood decided to ask permission from the Revd Johnson to conduct an investigation with a team of researchers from the Ghost Club. In the course of these investigations, Underwood was told of the strange sounds afflicting the vicarage, which included the rattling of the large, Victorian letterbox on the front door. The rattlings would occur frequently, but as soon as the Revd Johnson or his wife went to see if any mail had arrived, the letterbox would be found to be empty. These unexplained rattlings had been heard through the years by the vicarage's numerous incumbents.

The Revd Johnson, however, discovered a possible origin for these sounds. It seems that more than 100 years ago, the first incumbent of the vicarage maintained an extremely strict control over his family, as the Victorians were wont to do. He did not allow any of his five daughters to receive visits from the local men. However, the potential suitors conceived the idea of slipping notes through the letterbox, which was so noisy that the father, whose office was in the room nearest to the front door, was invariably alerted, and he snatched the notes away before any of his daughters had a chance to read them.

According to one exorcist who had examined the house, three of the girls' bedrooms retained some impression of their erstwhile occupants. On several occasions, ghostly forms were seen in those rooms. The exorcist claimed, however, to have released the spirits.

In addition the Johnsons reported to Underwood that there had been some cases of spontaneous possession. On one occasion, Mrs Johnson awoke one night to hear her husband speaking in a 'strange tongue'. He subsequently began to behave in uncharacteristic ways, leading his wife to suspect that he had been somehow taken over by some evil entity.

During their investigation, Peter Underwood and the other members of the Ghost Club attempted to communicate with whatever entities were present in the vicarage. They tried holding a seance and then using a ouija board, but were initially unsuccessful. After a short rest, they tried again with the ouija board, and this time both the glass and the table began to move, at first fitfully and then faster and faster.

One of the sitters, Frances Jones, suggested using the

standard seance code, with a movement of the table to the right meaning 'yes', and to the left meaning 'no'. It soon became apparent that whatever entity was present had been responsible for the death of a child in the house. It claimed that the child's body had been buried in the garden, although no evidence was ever found of this. The entity requested the sitters to pray for it, which they did; the table then stopped moving.

Frances Jones later told Underwood that she had no doubt that Eton Vicarage was haunted by several female ghosts, together with a 'domineering male ghost'. She added that she had encountered the male ghost on the stairs, and had succeeded in persuading him to leave the house in peace. Indeed, according to Underwood, the Johnsons suffered no further disturbances after the Ghost Club investigators had left.

THE GREAT-GRANDFATHER

When the Marchioness Townshend was searching for material for the book she published with Maude ffoulkes, *True Ghost Stories*, she asked an acquaintance, Dr Francis Edwards, if he knew of any interesting supernatural reports. Dr Edwards replied that an old gentleman he had known told him of a most unusual experience that had happened to him some time previously. He even furnished Edwards with a manuscript, 200 pages in length, which he had written not long after the events, and which described in exhaustive detail the circumstances of his experience. Dr Edwards passed on the salient points of the manuscript to the Marchioness Townshend, who included it in *True Ghost Stories*. The drastically abridged account, which I shall quote in full, read as follows:

I was born when my father was over sixty years of age, so he was a very old man when I left home [for Australia during the

Gold Rush of 1850], and I had not been long in Australia before he died, leaving me, amongst other property, our house at Bath.

I had no inclination to return, and, as I intended to lead my life on broader and more unconventional lines, I instructed our lawyer to see that the house was kept in good order, and a responsible caretaker installed. I had inherited many family possessions which it would have been foolish to allow to fall into disrepair, and I did not wish to disperse them.

I married in Australia, and brought up a family. One of my sons died a few years after his marriage, and his wife, who only survived him a year, left me guardian of their orphan daughter, then just seven years old.

Mary was a happy little creature, a perfectly normal child (I mention this as necessary to remember in the face of what happened afterwards) . . . We became very fond of each other, so much so, that I decided to give her an English upbringing. There was the house at Bath ready to step into; my affairs in Australia were so well ordered that our departure need not be delayed, my other children had made their own lives, and were not dependent on me. I had no ties. [His wife, presumably, had died.]

When Mary and I arrived at Bath, I found that my instructions had been well carried out during these long years of absence, and the house and its contents were as well preserved as in my father's lifetime. Mary was too young to appreciate family portraits and period furniture, but she loved the old-fashioned garden, and as she wasn't lonely without playmates of her own age, I did not send her to school, but planned to educate her at home. For the moment it was one long holiday for us both.

Autumn came, and when the days began to draw in Mary and I used to sit in the library, the child playing with her dolls, whilst I read. The library was a warm, comfortable room, and we spent many quiet hours there.

One evening, just before 'lighting-up' time, Mary, who was nestling by my side before the fire, suddenly exclaimed:

'Look, Grandpapa, *whoever* is the old gentleman sitting in the big chair with "ears"? He *does* look funny, he's dressed so oddly.' And she began to laugh.

'There's nobody there, you silly child,' I told her.

'Oh, but there *is*, Grandpapa,' she said. 'Why, he's just nodded his head. I *believe* he knows me. I didn't see him come into the room, did you?'

'Run away, and see if there are any letters,' I said. I did not want to humour the child in strange fancies, so I lit the gas, and when she came back:

'Well, Mary, where is the funny old man?' I asked.

Mary looked round the room. 'Oh . . . he's gone – but he *was* here five minutes ago. Perhaps he'll come again. I *do* hope he will; I *like* him, Grandpapa.'

After this the visitor often returned, and Mary described his appearance and dress so minutely that I was convinced, against my will, that the appearance (unseen by me) was none other than my old father, wearing the clothes fashionable in the first years of the nineteenth century, which he had refused to discard for anything more up-to-date.

It was useless to allow Mary to think that her friend was a ghost, so I let things take their course, hoping they would right themselves, although I could not imagine why my father had come back to haunt his former library, or why he wanted to get in touch with Mary.

A few weeks elapsed, and, incredible though it may seem, Mary and her great-grandfather carried on long conversations, the substance of which she gave me verbally, since, needless to say, I was never audibly, or visibly, aware of my father's presence.

I have endeavoured to set down some of these conversations exactly as Mary repeated them to me, and when I told her to ask my father about certain family matters, known only to himself and me, the answers no longer allowed me to doubt the existence of a state of things beyond my comprehension. My last lingering doubts were eventually dispelled by the child herself.

One day I said: 'Ask Great-grandpapa what becomes of the little babies who die before they have time to open their eyes.'

Mary looked at the invisible occupant of the chair with 'ears'; spoke to him, waited a few minutes, then: 'Great-grandpapa says that *still-born children* go on living in heaven,' whispered Mary; 'but what does *still-born* mean, Grandpapa?'

'It's another word for death,' I told her. After this I never doubted that these ghostly conversations were real, as the child had never heard the word '*still-born*' until my father used it. Proof conclusive, wasn't it?

Winter passed and spring returned. Mary's first English spring, and one morning when the crocuses in the garden flamed in the sunlight, Mary said:

'Great-grandpapa told me yesterday that he isn't coming here any more, because he says I'm soon going to live with him. Where does Great-grandpapa live? I hope it's not far away. Why *must* I go and live with him? I'm quite happy here – but' – brightening – 'I expect I'll be able to come and see you every day.'

My heart stood still ... I understood my father's meaning only too well, but I dared not tell the child that his 'house' was a grave in the churchard of Bath Abbey, although the spirit which loved his little descendant was free of mortal environment. But Mary, all unknowingly, had received her summons to another world. Her great-grandfather never came again, and within a month she was dead.

These, Dr Edwards, are the outlines of the story – you will read the facts for yourself – but, after this, you will understand *why* I believe in ghosts.

If we accept this as being a more or less accurate account of what happened, and there is little reason not to, we must assume that, for some unknown and perhaps unknowable reason, the ghost of Mary's great-grandfather was despatched to earth to prepare her for her destiny, and to help her accept it without fear.

RADIANT BOYS

The appearance of young boys who glow or are surrounded by flames is a tradition which extends throughout most of Europe, and it is generally accepted that whoever sees one of these mysterious child apparitions is doomed. In the nineteenth century, the English politician Viscount Castlereagh encountered such a 'Radiant Boy', with dreadful consequences. There are a number of versions of his experience, but the best known is as follows.

The young Castlereagh was out hunting one day in Ireland, when he was caught in a violent storm, and sought shelter in a large house near by. He was admitted by the butler, who said that although he was most welcome to spend the night, there were already a large number of guests at the house, and there was only one room available for him. Castlereagh accepted the room, and after dinner that night was shown up to it. He discovered that the room was completely empty, except for a makeshift bed that had been placed in front of the hearth, in which there burned a splendid fire.

Bidding the butler goodnight, the Viscount lay down and was soon fast asleep. Several hours later, though, he awoke suddenly to see the room flooded with light, although the fire had since become dead ashes. Looking around the room, his gaze alighted upon a handsome young boy, who was surrounded by light and was looking directly at him. After some moments, the apparition faded away and the room grew dark.

Castlereagh was a stern man, whose sense of humour was practically non-existent. Suspecting that some kind of practical joke had been played upon him, he spent the rest of the night in a foul mood, and the next morning he stormed down to his host, declaring that he would be leaving the house immediately. When asked by his host what had angered him so, Castlereagh told him what had happened the previous night and how he was certain some impertinent trickery had been afoot. His host agreed with him, and asked his other guests if they knew anything about it; they all denied any knowledge.

The host then called in the butler and questioned him. The butler informed his master, with great contrition, that he had put Castlereagh in 'the boy's room'. Upon hearing this, the host flew into a rage, saying that he had told the butler time and again never to allow anyone to sleep in that room. He then explained to Castlereagh the reason for his anger. The glowing boy was the spirit of an ancestor who had been murdered by his own mother during an attack of madness. He added that the spirit occasionally returned to the scene of his death, and that whoever chanced to see him would first become extremely prosperous, and then, at the height of his success, would be violently killed.

Castlereagh was not particularly upset by this rather outlandish tale: for one thing, as the second son of the Marquis of Londonderry, he stood to inherit little. In addition, his military career meant that violent death was an ever present possibility that he was prepared to accept.

As might be expected, things did not quite turn out the way Castlereagh thought they would. Not only did his older brother die in a boating accident several years later, making him his father's heir, but he himself left the military and went into politics, rising quickly to become both immensely powerful and hugely wealthy.

However, his innate ill-humour eventually turned into deep-seated paranoia and, ultimately, serious mental illness. He was confined to his country house by his worried family, who took care to remove all sharp objects from his vicinity, fearing that he would do himself harm. Unfortunately, these fears proved well founded, for in August 1822, Castlereagh came upon a penknife that had been missed by the family and cut his own throat.

THE GHOST OF THE PURPLE MASQUE

The Purple Masque is the name given to the campus theatre at Kansas State University in Manhattan, Kansas. The theatre occupies what was once a cafeteria in the 1950s on the main floor of East Stadium, and near by there was also once a dormitory for athletes. According to local legend, a football player named Nick was badly injured during a game, and was brought into the cafeteria, where he died before a doctor could treat him.

In 1964, a drama professor named Carl Hinrichs was contributing to a production of *My Fair Lady* at the Purple Masque. He was in the process of painting some scenery and was working well into the early hours to finish the job on time. At 2.00 a.m. he went to the scene shop to refill his bucket with paint from a large drum, and then returned to the stage. Suddenly, there was a loud noise which seemed to come from the scene shop. When Hinrichs went to investigate, he found the large paint drum upturned in the middle of the floor. It seems that the ghost of Nick, the dead football player, was to blame.

Nick appears to be a rather mischievous spirit who enjoys helping as much as hindering with productions at the Purple Masque. For instance, on one occasion, a student named Kay Coles was helping with the preparations for a production, and was supervising a crew which unloaded a large number of chairs for the audience. The chairs were left in the theatre, to be set up later, while the men went outside for a break. When they returned a few minutes later, all the chairs had been set out, and a programme had been neatly placed on each one.

According to Beth Scott and Michael Norman in their book *Haunted Heartland*, Kay Coles had another experience with Nick in 1971. She had been working with another student on the sound system in the theatre. When they had finished work, they switched off the system and left, locking the place behind them.

'Suddenly, music started playing,' said Coles. Her companion unlocked the theater and found the tape running. He turned off the machine and again locked the theater.

The music started again. 'It . . . came on four more times,' Coles explained. 'We looked for someone playing a joke, but there wasn't a soul around.'. . .

Another inexplicable Purple Masque incident involved two technicans working together on a set that included a bed and a couch. In the early morning hours they decided to take naps. One took the bed, the other the couch.

They hadn't slept long before the fellow on the couch struggled awake. He seemed to be choking to death. Squinting through one eye, he saw the fire extinguisher discharging in midair. But no one held it! The apparatus, like a torpedo, zeroed in on him, the nozzle spraying a malevolent chemical into his face. The student leaped from the couch and ran.

Apart from contributing to or hindering various productions, Nick is also fond of stomping loudly through the theatre, and was heard by many people on many occasions. On an evening in autumn, three students were working on a production, when they heard what sounded like a 'two-hundred-pound person' walking around on the floor above. None of the students felt particularly inclined to go upstairs to check on who might be making such noises.

At that point, the theatre's heating system started up, with its familiar clanking of pipes. Some time later, the students learned that the boilers had been switched off on that day, and had not been fired up until three weeks later.

In addition to Nick, there also seems to be another, far more malevolent presence in the Purple Masque theatre. One female visitor, who did not know of the theatre's reputation, commented that she felt someone unseen was there. She could not even remain in one particular room, saying that there was something extremely dangerous there.

When enquiries were made into the history of the university, it was discovered that there had indeed been a football player named Nick at Kansas State. However, his supposed death in the cafeteria remains unestablished as a historical fact.

FROM BEYOND A FROZEN GRAVE

In the winter of 1873, the state of Minnesota fell victim to a dreadful blizzard which swept across the prairies, killing and freezing everything in its path. One of the unfortunate people who set themselves against the forces of nature in a pitiful effort to stay alive was Mary Weston of Nobles County. Her husband, John, had ventured out into the hellish whiteness to search for more firewood, without which they and their three-year-old daughter, Margaret, would surely freeze to death.

Although the family's log cabin had been well built, the walls could not completely prevent the bitter winds forcing their way through here and there, and Mary Weston's heart grew heavier and heavier as she used up the last of their firewood in the stove. John had now been gone for nearly three days, and Mary knew that he must return very soon with more fuel if they were to survive the still-raging blizzard.

Eventually, though, the winds began to die down, and when she finally moved to a window and looked out, Mary saw that the vast, white world beyond had become perfectly still, and utterly silent. The silence was then broken by the sounds of footfalls through the deep snow, and Mary cried to her daughter in relief that John had at last returned.

At that moment, there was a knock on the door; but as Mary hurried across the room towards it, she heard a neighbour's voice shouting: 'Mrs Weston, John is frozen to death!'

Her heart plunging instantly from joy to anguished disbelief, Mary opened the door to be confronted by . . . nothing. Nothing but the vast, pristine whiteness greeted her. There was no neighbour, not even any footprints in the limitless carpet of snow. Not knowing what else to do, Mary sat in a chair, exhausted by her ordeal and its uncertain conclusion. Eventually, some friends arrived at the cabin with some food and firewood. Later, Mary would learn that the neighbour whose voice she had heard was still in his own cabin at the time.

Six days later, with still no sign of John, Mary was paid a visit by another neighbour, Elmer Cosper. In a halting voice, he told her that he had seen John that very morning. He was in his barn, when he looked up to see John standing in the doorway. John stepped into the barn and bid his neighbour good morning. Elmer told him how surprised he was to see him: he had assumed that John had been frozen to death. John replied that that was indeed the case: he was dead, and his body lay a mile and a half to the north-west, near the village of Hersey.

'After your husband spoke to me, ma'am,' said Elmer, 'I seen the wind shake his coat about his knees. Then ... well ... just like a mark wiped from a slate. I searched all around, but there weren't no footprints. No sign of anyone.'

The people in the area, hearing of Elmer's encounter, searched the land around Hersey, but John Weston's body was never found. Mary lived the rest of her life in their cabin, always hoping that one day her husband would return through the snow of the harsh, Minnesota winter.

OHIO'S HAUNTED INN

The Buxton Inn in Granville, Ohio, was built in 1812 by Orrin Granger, who had originally intended it as a post office and stage coach stop. In the 1920s, the inn was taken over by Mary Stevens Sweet, who quickly began to sense strange presences throughout the building. In addition, various guests reported to her that they awoke to be confronted by a transparent figure leaning against the bedposts.

One night, Mary Sweet's son, Fred, went down to the

pantry to get himself a snack, when he encountered a ghost. Fred had had his heart set on a piece of apple pie, but unfortunately, the ghost was just finishing the last piece! Seeing that the young man was rather put out by this, the ghost introduced himself as Orrin Granger, and, by way of recompense for his consumption of the last piece of pie, entertained Fred with tales of the Buxton Inn's early history as a stage coach stop. He added that he was very pleased with the way Fred's mother was running the place and told the young man that there was no need for him to remain. With that, he waved goodbye and vanished.

Decades later, in 1972, the inn was purchased by Orville and Audrey Orr, having heard tales not only of Orrin Granger's ghost but also of the spectre of a lady in blue, who haunted the inn. During the restoration of the inn, Orr told the workmen of the lady in blue and how she had, over the years, appeared to guests. The workmen took these stories with a large pinch of salt, saying that they would need proof before they believed any such nonsense.

Evidently, the ghost heard this, for she soon appeared to the workmen, walking across the rear balcony of the building and vanishing as she descended the stairs. She then appeared before them every evening at six o'clock precisely, which prompted the workmen to pack up and leave a little earlier from then on.

It is generally accepted that the ghost is that of Ethel Bounell, who ran the inn from 1934 until her death in 1960. Little more was known for certain, until the inn was inspected by a medium from Cincinnati, named Mayree Braun. Knowing nothing of the history of the Buxton Inn or Ethel Bounell, Braun claimed to see a woman in a blue dress accompanying her and Audrey Orr through the rooms and corridors of the building. In *Haunted Heartland*, Beth Scott and Michael Norman describe how 'The psychic said the ghostly lady was beautifully dressed, had once been on the stage and obviously liked hats. Mrs Braun also remarked that the spirit was pleased with the restoration work the new owners were doing, especially the work done in the ballroom. The medium had unknowingly described [Ethel] Bounell.'

As it happened, Orville Orr also claimed psychic abilities and reported strange incidents in the building, including disembodied footsteps and slamming doors. He witnessed a shadowy figure, evidently a man, whom he suggested was Major Buxton, owner of the inn from 1865 to 1905. According to Orr: 'When we first purchased the building, employees would even set a place for the Major at the table. One waitress claims to have seen the Major sitting in a rocking chair before the fireplace.'

Since the ghosts of Orrin Granger, Ethel Bounell and Major Buxton have been so frequently encountered at the inn, it seems that the place holds a particular place in their affections, not unlike the haunted police station in St Louis, which we examined at the beginning of this chapter, compelling them to return from beyond the grave to watch over it.

5

POLTERGEISTS

As mentioned earlier, the word 'poltergeist' means 'noisy spirit'. Poltergeist hauntings vary greatly in intensity and duration, and range from a single unexplained and unrepeated sound, to years of terrifying events that seem to have no basis in rationality and can drive percipients to the point of utter despair. Most poltergeist visitations are somewhere in between these two extremes, lasting about six to eight weeks and causing disorder and frustration, but presenting no real danger to their victims. There is much debate among ghost researchers as to what poltergeists actually are: whether they should even be treated as similar phenomena to ghost visitations, or whether their explanation lies firmly in the realm of psychology. In the majority of cases, the focus for the poltergeist activity seems to be a young person, usually an adolescent and usually a female, a fact that has led to the conclusion that such manifestations must be the result of the tension and emotional turmoil commonly experienced at that time of life, which have, through some as yet unknown process, become externalized to the extent that they have a physical effect upon the environment.

Perhaps the most famous poltergeist case of all centred on Borley Rectory in Essex, England, and was extensively investigated by Harry Price, whom we met earlier. The rectory was built by the Revd Henry D. E. Bull in 1863. Early claims that it was built on the site of a thirteenth-century Benedictine monastery were discovered to be untrue in 1938 by the Essex Archaeological Society. According to local legend, a monk from the monastery had eloped with a nun from a convent at Bures, eight miles away. The couple were caught, however, and the monk was beheaded, while the nun was walled up alive in the convent. Their ghosts are said still to haunt the area.

Borley Rectory was taken over after Revd Henry Bull's death by his son, Harry. According to Harry's daughter, he saw many ghosts there, including a phantom horse and carriage, in which the unfortunate couple who had tried to elope had fled. Harry Bull also had a rather chilling encounter in the garden, when his retriever suddenly howled with terror and he saw a pair of legs standing under a fruit tree. Thinking it was an intruder on his property, Bull followed the legs as they moved towards a postern gate, whereupon he realized that no other part of the intruder's body was visible. The legs disappeared through the closed postern.

The next occupants of Borley Rectory, who moved there in 1928, one year after the death of Harry Bull, also had their share of strange experiences. One evening, not long after they had moved in, the Revd Guy Smith and his wife heard the doorbell ringing stridently. When he answered the door, there was no one there. When it happened again, he hurried to the door and got there before the peals had stopped, but there was still no one at the door. Shortly afterwards, all the keys in the house dropped from their keyholes, and later vanished altogether.

The couple then began to hear soft footfalls in the house, and the lights began to switch themselves on and off. Small pebbles were thrown by unseen hands, and a disembodied voice in the chapel whispered the arcane entreaty: 'Don't, Carlos, don't.'

Revd Smith's parishioners were well aware of these strange goings on and were reluctant to visit him at the rectory, which concerned him deeply and prompted him to contact the *Daily Mirror*, asking if there were a psychical investigator who might offer some help. The *Daily Mirror* contacted Harry

Price, who conducted an investigation that would last several years.

In October 1930, after Smith and his wife had given up on the place and moved to Norfolk, Borley Rectory was taken over by Revd L. A. Foyster and his young wife, Marianne. Foyster had come to England from Amherst, Nova Scotia, the scene of another well-known poltergeist haunting in 1878 (which will be discussed later), and much was made of this fact in subsequent evaluations of the Borley case by the Society for Psychical Research. However, Colin Wilson thinks it unlikely that Foyster would have faked any of the spectacular phenomena his incumbency saw. These phenomena included mysterious footsteps and ringing bells; bricks were thrown, and one night a jug of water was poured over Foyster and Marianne as they lay in bed. Several apparitions were seen, including the legendary nun, and Henry Bull, who had built the rectory.

In his book *Poltergeist: a Study in Destructive Haunting*, Colin Wilson writes:

There is much independent confirmation of all these events. A Justice of the Peace named Guy L'Estrange visited Borley at the invitation of the Foysters, and wrote a lengthy account of it. As soon as he arrived, he saw a dim figure near the porch, which vanished as soon as he approached. Mrs Foyster had a bruise on her forehead – something 'like a man's fist' had struck her the previous evening. The Foysters were telling L'Estrange about mysterious fires that kept breaking out in locked rooms when there was a loud crash in the hall; they found it littered with broken crockery. Then bottles began flying about. L'Estrange notes that they seemed to appear suddenly in mid-air. The bottles were coming from a locked storage shed outside. All the bells began to ring, making a deafening clamour – but the bell wires had been cut. L'Estrange shouted: 'If some invisible person is present, please stop ringing for a moment.' Instantly, the bells stopped – stopped dead, as if each clapper had been grabbed by an unseen hand. Later, sitting alone in front of the fire, L'Estrange heard footsteps behind him; he turned, but the room was empty. The footsteps had come from a part of the wall where there had once been a door. In bed, L'Estrange felt the room become icy cold, and saw a kind of shape materialising from a patch of luminosity; he walked toward it, and had a feeling of something trying to push him back. He spoke to it, and it slowly vanished. He was luckier than another visitor who thought that the ghostly figure was someone playing a joke, and tried to grab it; he was given a hard blow in the eye.

During the Foysters' incumbency, strange messages were written in pencil on the walls, all of which appeared to be addressed to Foyster's wife, Marianne. Many were totally illegible, being written in a chaotic scrawl, but some could be read, and said things like 'Marianne light mass prayers' and 'Marianne please help get'.

In 1937, Harry Price decided to rent the rectory (the Foysters had moved away two years earlier) and took up residence with a team of investigators. In March 1938 they held a seance with an ouija board, which spelled out the message that the rectory would be destroyed by fire, an event which came to pass in February 1939. The ghostly phenomena, however, continued around the ruins; these included patches of light and the sounds of footsteps.

Harry Price decided to excavate the cellars of the rectory, where he found some fragments of a human skull, with an abscess on the jawbone. Some researchers have suggested that the skull belonged to the ghostly nun, who always appeared to be quite miserable.

In the years following Price's death, his reputation was seriously damaged, not least by the SPR, which conducted a detailed review of his Borley investigation, and concluded that the haunting there was 'a house of cards built by the late Harry Price out of little more than a pack of lies'. While it is true that Price was a shameless self-publicist, he was also an extremely diligent and level-headed investigator of the para-normal. Indeed, as Colin Wilson reminds us, Price spent many years searching for a vocation into which to channel his considerable intelligence and energies; and it seems unlikely that, having found that vocation, he would risk being forced to abandon it, as would surely have been the case should he be revealed as a hoaxer.

As a postscript, it is worth noting that in the 1960s, a local psychical investigator named Geoffrey Croom-Hollingsworth decided to carry out his own investigations on the site of the rectory, along with his assistant Roy Potter. In Brian Innes's book, *The Catalogue of Ghost Sightings*, Croom-Hollingsworth describes what happened one night while they were at the site:

> Suddenly I saw her quite clearly, in a grey habit and cowl as she moved across the garden and through a hedge. I thought, 'is somebody pulling my leg?' Roy was out in the roadway . . . and I shouted to him. The figure had disappeared into a modern garage, and I thought that was that, but as Roy joined me we both saw her come out of the other side. She approached to about 12 feet from us, and we both saw her face, that of an elderly woman in her sixties, perhaps. We followed her as she seemed to glide over a dry ditch as if it wasn't there, before she disappeared into a pile of building bricks . . . Roy and I saw the nun quite clearly for a period of about 12 minutes.
>
> I don't give a damn if Price invented things or not. The basic question is – is the place haunted? And you can take it from me it is. I have invented nothing.

'BUTTON CAP'

In his book *Haunted Houses*, Charles Harper writes of the haunting of Barnack Rectory in Northamptonshire, England, in the early nineteenth century. The rectory, built in the fourteenth century, contained a 'haunted room', which was said to be troubled by a ghost known as 'Button Cap'. The Revd Charles Kingsley was placed in the room as a boy, and subsequently wrote of the strange noises with which it was filled. Of Button Cap, Kingsley has this to say:

> He lived in the Great North Room at Barnack. I knew him well. He used to walk across the room in flopping slippers, and turn over the leaves of books to find the missing deed, whereof he had defrauded [an orphan and widow]. He was an old Rector of Barnack. Everybody heard him who chose. Nobody ever saw him; but, in spite of that, he wore a flowered dressing-gown, and a cap with a button on it ... Sometimes he turned cross, and played *poltergeist*, as the Germans say, rolling the barrels in the cellar about with surprising noise, which was undignified. So he was always ashamed of himself, and put them all back in their place before morning. I suppose he is gone now. Ghosts hate mortally a certificated National school-master, and (being a vain and peevish generation) as soon as people give up believing in them, go away in a huff – or perhaps someone has been laying phosphoric paste about, and he ate thereof and ran down to his pond, and drank till he burst. He was rats!

While he has his tongue in his cheek to a certain extent, Kingsley raises an interesting point in speculating that the ghost left when people stopped believing in him. However, since this is connected to the various theories of the origin and nature of ghosts and spirits, we shall put it aside until the final section of this book, in which we shall examine them more fully.

THE BARBADOS COFFINS

In the early nineteenth century, there was a series of outrage-ous and unexplained events inside the Chase family vault in Bridgetown, Barbados: events which remain a mystery to this day. Although the vault has come to be known as the Chase vault, it is unclear who actually built it, and the Chases were not the only people to be buried there.

In 1808, the coffin of Mary Ann Chase, the two-year-old daughter of Thomas Chase, a wealthy and much-hated land-owner, was interred in the vault, followed in 1812 by that of her sister Dorcas who, according to local rumour, had starved herself to death in a suicidal depression brought on by the cruelty of her father. Some weeks later, Thomas Chase himself died (of remorse, according to some) and the vault was duly opened to receive his coffin.

When the vault was opened by the funeral party, it was discovered that none of the coffins were in their original places: all had been cast about the chamber, leaving a scene of sacrilegious chaos. The funeral party were horrified and deeply angered, assuming that tomb robbers had broken in. They quickly realized, however, that the concrete seal around the single vault entrance, which was replaced after each interment, had not been broken. This made it unlikely that common tomb robbers were the culprits. The coffins were returned to their original places, and Thomas Chase's extremely heavy lead coffin was placed in its assigned position.

Four years later, on 25 September 1816, the coffin of eleven-year-old Charles Brewster Ames was taken to the vault. When the funeral party chipped away at the concrete seal and opened the vault, they saw that the coffins had again been strewn about, including that of Thomas Chase, which had taken eight men to shift into position.

Less than two months later, the remains of Charles Brewster Ames's father, Samuel, were taken to the Chase vault for interment. This time, the procession included numerous people who were curious about the strange goings-on in the vault and wanted to see if they had been repeated this time. Once again, the contents of the vault had been tossed around, in spite of the concrete seal – which had been carefully examined prior to opening – remaining completely intact.

The moving coffins in the Chase vault had, by this time,

gained notoriety throughout the island. Three years later, on 17 July 1819, another funeral was held; again, the concrete seal was chipped from around the heavy marble slab covering the entrance to the vault, and again the coffins inside were scattered all over the chamber. This time, the only coffin to escape the attentions of the mysterious tomb-defiler was a fragile wooden one containing the first person to have been buried in the Chase vault, Mrs Thomasina Goddard, who had been interred in July 1807. In spite of comprehensive investigations ordered by the governor of the island, Lord Combermere, no clue as to the identity of the culprit was found.

The coffins were arranged as they had been before, with the larger one on the ground, the smaller children's coffins resting on top and the wooden coffin leaning against a wall. Lord Combermere ordered sand to be sprinkled on the floor of the vault, in the hope that if anyone broke in, they would leave their footprints. When the vault was closed and sealed, Combermere and two other men pressed their private seals into the wet cement. This time, if anyone broke into the vault, they would also destroy these seals.

On 18 April 1820, Lord Combermere's curiosity got the better of him and he decided to open the vault to see if there had been any more disturbances. Taking along some interested friends, he went to the vault and examined the entrance; the seals were still in place. However, when the vault was opened, the coffins were again scattered about – except for the wooden coffin of Thomasina Goddard. The sand that had been sprinkled on the floor showed no sign of any footprints.

At this point the governor decided that these disturbances could not go on, and ordered that the coffins be taken away and buried elsewhere. They were never again disturbed and the Chase vault was never used again.

The events in the Chase vault remain a mystery, in spite of the various theories put forward to explain them. These include earth tremors and flooding; but a tremor powerful enough to scatter the coffins, which included Thomas Chase's lead casket, would have been recorded, and there were certainly no signs of flooding. It seems feasible that the disturbances were caused by poltergeist activity, probably connected to the unfortunate Dorcas (the disturbances began only after her interment). There are many reports of suicides being unable to pass on to the afterlife, their despairing and restless spirits being trapped on Earth indefinitely. In the event, the removal of the coffins to other burial locations seems finally to have laid her spirit to rest.

THE CASE THAT INSPIRED *THE EXORCIST*

When William Peter Blatty's best-selling novel *The Exorcist* was made into a film by the respected director William Friedkin, it caused a storm of controversy, not least because of its astonishing and horrific visual effects. Both the novel and film are regarded as among the finest in the 'horror' genre, and have lost none of their ability to shock and move. One of their selling points was that the tale of Regan and her possession by the demon god Pazuzu was actually based on a genuine occurrence, although Blatty changed the story quite radically, so that little of the original remains in *The Exorcist*. In fact, the source case was more one of poltergeist activity than true possession.

As with Blatty's story, the events occurred in a suburb of Washington DC. The year (not as in Blatty's story) was 1949, and the vicim was a fourteen-year-old boy named Robert Mannheim. The Mannheim family first noticed that something was not quite right when they began to hear odd noises coming from the walls of their home. Suspecting mice, they called in an exterminator, who was unable to find any such pests. Presently, the disturbances became more extreme and occurred only, it seemed, when Robert was near by. House-hold objects would fly around, including a picture which floated off the wall and then moved back to its position. Robert Mannheim was the most afflicted by these disturbances, which included the rattling and vibrating of his bed.

Not knowing what else to do, the family turned to the Church for help, and in February 1949, the Revd M. Winston spent a whole night watching over Robert. Although initially highly sceptical, when Revd Winston subsequently attended a meeting of the Society of Parapsychology in Washington, at which he described the details of the case, he told the meeting how strange scraping noises had issued from the walls of the room in which he and Robert passed the night. He asked Robert to sit in an armchair, but as soon as the boy did so, it began to move around the floor, before tilting sharply and throwing him off.

Winston thought it would be better to keep Robert away from furniture, so he asked him to sleep with some blankets and a pillow on the floor. The result was the same, with Robert sliding about the room, as if pushed by unseen hands.

Robert was taken to two hospitals in Washington, Georgetown and St Louis University, both of which were run by Jesuits. He was examined both physically and mentally, and it was concluded that there was nothing wrong with him.

Once again, his family were at a total loss as to what to do about the disturbances, which showed no signs of stopping. Once again, they turned to organized religion and enlisted the aid of a Roman Catholic priest to perform an exorcism upon whatever evil was afflicting the unfortunate boy. The priest prepared for the ritual by fasting on bread and water for two and a half months. The exorcism itself had to be repeated no less than thirty times, during which Robert went into convulsions and screamed obscenities, sometimes in Latin, a language of which he had no knowledge.

In May 1949, the priest performed the exorcism ritual for the thirtieth time and received no reaction from Robert, leading him to conclude that, at last, he had succeeded and the evil influences had departed the hapless child.

From then on, the Mannheim family were left in peace. Anyone who has read or seen *The Exorcist* will note that the phenomena were not quite as extreme in the Mannheim case: there was no vomiting of green bile and Robert's head did not turn 180 degrees. Indeed, it seems that the case was an 'average' one of poltergeist activity that stopped after a couple of months or so, as most poltergeist activity is wont to do (and thus the exorcism may or may not have had anything to do with its cessation).

As far as Robert's curious ability to blaspheme in Latin goes, this may actually have been an instance of what is known as cryptamnesia, in which information is received by the unconscious mind to reappear much later. Since the Mannheims were a religious family, it seems likely that Robert may, at some point in his young life, have been exposed to the Latin language, which he unwittingly absorbed and spontaneously recalled during the exorcism.

THE BLACK MONK OF PONTEFRACT

This case, which occurred in the town of Pontefract in Yorkshire, England, has come to be regarded as something of a classic in the annals of the supernatural. In August 1966, the Pritchard family were living at 30 East Drive, Pontefract. Jean and Joe Pritchard decided to take a holiday in Devon during the Bank Holiday, and took their twelve-year-old daughter Diane with them, while Phillip, aged fifteen, decided to stay behind with Mrs Pritchard's mother, Mrs Sarah Scholes, who was looking after the house.

On Thursday, the weather was fine, and Phillip was sitting in the garden reading a book while Mrs Scholes sat in the lounge, knitting a cardigan. Just before midday, there was a strong gust of wind that rattled all the windows. Phillip came in to make himself a drink and his grandmother asked him if the weather was becoming more unsettled. He replied that it was still quite calm.

When he returned from the kitchen, Phillip was astonished to see a cloud of white powder falling gently through the air around his grandmother, who was still knitting happily, unaware of what was happening. Phillip alerted her to the strange powder and they both looked up to the ceiling, assuming that something had made the paint flake off. It was then that they noticed that the cloud of dust occupied only the lower half of the room: above their heads the air was completely clear.

Mrs Scholes was surprised but not afraid, assuming that there had to be some rational explanation for the curious fall of dust. She went across the road to her other daughter, Marie Kelly, and asked her to come and take a look at the Pritchards' lounge. Marie remarked, on seeing her mother, that she looked 'like a snowman'. In the Pritchards' house, the powder was still falling, and they decided that the best thing to do would be to clear up the stuff.

When she went to the kitchen, Marie discovered a large pool of water on the floor. As she tried to mop it up, she saw other pools forming; but when she pulled up the edge of the linoleum to see if the water was coming from underneath, she discovered that the floor was completely dry.

Enid Pritchard, who was married to Joe Pritchard's brother, had heard the puzzled voices from next door and came around to see what was going on. She found the stop-cock under the sink and turned it off, but the water continued to collect on the linoleum floor. Not knowing what else to do, they called the water board and explained the problem.

While Mrs Scholes and Phillip began to clean up the white powder, which had by now stopped falling, the man from the water board inspected the kitchen floor, searching for a possible burst pipe. He then moved outside and probed the drains with a rod, searching for any blockage. However, he found nothing wrong, and went back to report his puzzlement. After he had left, the pools of water stopped appearing as mysteriously as they had started.

At about seven o'clock that evening, the strangeness started again, when Phillip discovered sugar and tea leaves scattered all over the kitchen work surface. The button on the tea dispenser attached to the wall was continually being pressed by some unseen force, which did not stop until the dispenser was empty. The crockery cupboard then began to vibrate. Phillip opened the door and the vibrations instantly stopped. The chill in the air, which Mrs Scholes had experienced earlier, now returned.

She and Phillip then decided to ask Marie Kelly to come and have another look at the strange occurrences. Marie stayed with them until 9.30 p.m., during which time she also saw the crockery cupboard shake and rattle. After she had left, Phillip decided to go to bed and his grandmother retired a little later. When she went into Phillip's room to kiss him goodnight, they both saw the wardrobe in the corner of the room begin to sway. They both decided that they would not be staying in the house that night and went to Marie Kelly's where they were put up in spare beds.

Marie's husband Vic had become intrigued by what was happening across the road and called the police in to investigate. When three officers arrived, they, along with Vic and Marie, went into the Pritchards' house and searched it from top to bottom, but could find nothing untoward.

At this point, they had the idea of asking a friend of theirs, Mr O'Donald, who was interested in ghosts, to come and investigate. Mr O'Donald lived just up the street and, since the lights in his house were still on, they knocked on his door and asked for his help. Immediately interested, O'Donald sat with them in the Pritchards' house, explaining the habits of poltergeists, including their fondness for destroying photographs. When nothing more occurred, he left. Vic and Marie were about to leave the house also when they heard a loud crash and discovered two small oil paintings lying on the floor of the lounge. Another picture – a photograph of Jean and Joe Pritchard on their wedding day – had been slashed as if with a knife.

When Jean and Joe Pritchard returned home the following Saturday, Mrs Scholes and Phillip told them everything that had happened. When Joe asked them what kind of knocks they had heard, there were three louds bangs in reply.

The poltergeist did not return to the Pritchards' house for

two years. When it did so, it resumed its antics, playing a number of apparently pointless tricks on the family. There were more unexplained noises and several household implements were thrown around. Colin Wilson describes the typical poltergeist as a 'mad practical joker' whose 'mentality seems to be that of an idiot child'. Like a precocious (but not necessarily idiotic) child, it seems that poltergeists demand attention, although they never seem to put that attention to any use when they receive it, since on the rare occasions when they communicate with their victims they seldom have anything useful – or even coherent – to say.

At one point in the Pontefract case, Phillip suggested that they might have the poltergeist exorcized, not knowing that exorcism never works in such cases, the poltergeists apparently treating the ritual with contempt. However, they contacted a local vicar, the Revd Davy, who agreed to pay them a visit. The Revd Davy arrived at seven o'clock one Thursday evening and explained the exorcism service to the family. The poltergeist (whom the family called 'Mr Nobody') was silent throughout, until the Revd Davy finally made to leave. Jean Pritchard apologized for the lack of any demonstration on the part of Mr Nobody. In *Poltergeist* Colin Wilson describes what happened:

And as she spoke, the house resounded to loud thumps that came from overhead. And a small brass candlestick jumped off the mantlepiece on to the floor.

'There,' said Jean Pritchard.

Mr Davy looked thoughtfully at the candlestick. 'I think I know what your problem is. Subsidence.'

'But subsidence,' said Marie [the Kellys had been invited over], 'can only make things fall. And . . .'

The other candlestick rose up from the shelf, floated across in front of the vicar's nose, then dropped to the floor.

'Do you think *that's* subsidence?'

There was a tremendous crash from the next room, one of

those spectacular sounds like a piece of heavy furniture falling through the ceiling. They all rushed into the lounge.

Scattered all over the carpet was every cup, saucer and plate from the china cupboard. Yet not a single one was broken, or even cracked.

The Revd Davy became convinced that there was 'something evil' in the house and advised the Pritchards to move; they declined, being unwilling to surrender their home to a 'ghost'. From then on, the manifestations became more extreme, with items of heavy furniture being moved around (including a grandmother clock which was thrown down the stairs). It also began to manifest itself visibly, in the form of a large shadow that was accompanied by an icy chill in the air.

The Revd Davy seems to have been disinclined to perform the exorcism, so a few months later, Vic Kelly, who was a Catholic, suggested that he obtain some holy water and sprinkle it throughout the house. This only served to inspire anti-Christian activities on the part of Mr Nobody, who responded on Easter Sunday by painting inverted crucifixes in gold on all the doors.

According to Colin Wilson:

The phenomena reached a kind of climax one evening when Diane had gone to the kitchen to make coffee. The lights went out, and while Jean Pritchard was groping for the torch, she heard Diane scream. It was dusk, and there was, in fact, enough light to be able to see their way around the house. They found that Diane was being dragged up the stairs, and it was light enough to see that her cardigan was stretched out in front of her, as if 'Fred' [Diane's nickname for the poltergeist] was tugging at it; his other hand was apparently on her throat. Phillip and Jean Pritchard rushed up the stairs and began trying to pull Diane down again; she was yelling with terror – this was the first time it had 'laid hands on her', so to speak. Phillip and Jean Pritchard went tumbling backwards down the stairs with Diane. Phillip had the impression that it was his thought of trying to touch the presence that caused it to let go. He made the interesting comment: 'It always seemed to be ahead of you.' Diane had to be given a large brandy. In the light, they saw that her throat was covered with red fingermarks.

Not long after this attack, the poltergeist manifestations ended and the Pritchards were finally left in peace to set about repairing the damage to their house, not to mention their nerves.

The name by which the case has come to be known – the Black Monk of Pontefract – came about as a result of a theory that the poltergeist was actually the ghost of a Cluniac monk who had committed rape and murder in the sixteenth century, and had been hanged for his crimes. However, subsequent research revealed that no such events had occurred in Pontefract. On reflection, it seems that the Pritchards' name for the poltergeist – Mr Nobody – is more accurate. It is worth considering that there was a certain amount of tension between the sport-loving Joe Pritchard and his bibliophile son Phillip, and that the latter had just passed the age of puberty when the manifestations began. It seems at least feasible that Phillip thus provided a 'focus' for some external agency that was attracted to the house by the presence of this tension, which provided the psychic energy necessary for its needs. Alternatively, the manifestations could have been the externalized result of the psychic tensions prevalent in the house at the time.

Colin Wilson quotes the researcher Guy Lyon Playfair:

'It's a kind of . . . football of energy. It somehow gets exuded from disturbed teenagers at puberty. Along come two or three spirits or elementals, look through this window, and see the football lying around. And they do what any group of school-boys would do – they go and kick it around, smashing windows and generally creating havoc. Then, as often as not, they get tired and leave it. In fact, the football usually explodes. Oddly enough, it turns into water . . .'

THE CENTRAHOMA POLTERGEIST

As with many poltergeist visitations, the first unusual events to be noticed in the tiny hamlet of Centrahoma, Oklahoma, were merely puzzling rather than obviously supernatural. The evening of 15 June 1990 was oppressively hot, and Bill and Maxine McWethey were sitting in their front yard with their eighteen-year-old daughter Twyla and her baby Desirée. Suddenly, a stone clunked against the side of the house, followed by another and then a third, flying out of the darkness.

Thinking that some local children were playing a prank, Bill McWethey stood up and shouted at them to stop. The stones kept coming, however, and would not stop for the next twenty-four hours. They ranged in size from about half an inch in diameter to the size of a golf ball. There was no police station in the village (the population of Centrahoma is a mere 150), and so the McWetheys were obliged to enlist the support of their neighbours and carry out a makeshift investigation themselves; but they could find no stone-throwing culprits.

The attacks began again the following evening, and occurred sporadically throughout June and July, prompting the McWetheys to wonder whether some supernatural agency might be responsible. By July, news of the stone-throwing phenomenon had spread through the village, and one night a group of about fifty people gathered at the McWethey house, in an attempt to apprehend whoever was responsible. Someone had the idea of marking some of the stones with nail polish and throwing them back into the surrounding darkness. The marked stones were promptly thrown back by the unseen miscreant. The people then threw the marked stones into a nearby pond; they were thrown back wet.

In August the McWetheys contacted the Coal County

133

Sheriff's office, and a deputy was dispatched to check out the area. As soon as he arrived, he was pelted with stones, and left after a quick and fruitless search for the stone-thrower. The culprit then began to throw other small objects, such as coins and nails, at the family and even began to tap away on an old typewriter in the toolshed.

That winter, the stone-thrower (obviously disturbed by the cold) moved indoors and began to throw whatever it could lay its 'hands' on; it also stripped the beds of their sheets and draped them over chairs. The McWetheys contacted the local newspaper, the *Coalgate Record Register*, which sent along two reporters. As soon as they arrived, Maxime McWethey ushered them into the kitchen, where they and the family were subjected to forty-five minutes of stone-throwing. One of the reporters, Helen Langdon, was deeply disturbed by the manifestations and asked aloud if they could be 'of God'. Instantly, the stones were directed at her. They all retreated to the lounge, but the poltergeist followed them and placed a number of stones underneath Twyla, who had been sitting on the couch. Twyla claimed that stones were also placed under her when she was in bed.

Kym B. Chaffin, whose article on the case appeared in *Fortean Times* Number 79, suggests that Twyla was the focus for the manifestations.

> There was no doubt that Twyla was the focus of the phenomenon. In his massive *Encyclopedia of Psychic Science*, psychoanalyst Nandor Fodor states that poltergeists are 'noisy spirits, causing periodic disturbances of a malicious character in certain places in the presence of a certain, mostly unsuspecting sensitive person'. Twyla was clearly the 'sensitive person'. It is also observed that the focal person is usually an adolescent. Twyla, though a single mother, was then 18.

Chaffin investigated the case personally, arriving at the McWethey house with a writer named Peggy Fielding on Saturday 16 July 1991. When they arrived, they found a number of people who had spent the previous night in the house in the hope that the poltergeist might manifest itself. They had not been disappointed: it had pulled their hair, scratched them and pushed them around. They told Chaffin and Fielding that it had gone into town with Twyla and would be back in a few minutes.

One of the people present, an amateur psychic investigator named Shirley Padley, claimed to have tape-recorded the sounds made by the poltergeist. The sounds were high-pitched and 'metallic', and seemed to be saying: 'This is Michael.'

Chaffin became aware of an oppressive, 'electromagnetic' quality to the atmosphere. At that point, there was a high-pitched mewling sound that began to move around the house. Apparently, 'Michael' would pick whoever was most frightened and concentrate his attacks on them. He had told Twyla that he was an alien from Saturn, and had taken her to a nearby field containing a flattened patch, as if 'something had landed there'. Maxine McWethey qualified this by adding: 'Course, he lies a lot.'

The psychic investigator Shirley Padley claimed: 'He followed me home one time. On the way home my daughter said she felt something in the car with us and when we got there we could hear him wandering around the house and the phone kept ringing over and over but no one was there.'

Michael also drew strange symbols on mirrors with lipstick. The family showed copies of some of them to Chaffin, who recognized one as the astrological symbol for Saturn. Chaffin concluded:

> I was ready to leave. Driving away, I reflected that the McWetheys were very good people. I could see why a ghost would pick them. It told them, they said, that it learned to talk by watching television with them. As for the theory that the poltergeist is a projection of someone living in the house, there is no doubt that it is tied to Twyla. Some time ago an off-duty police officer from a nearby town came out here to investigate the ghost, fell in love with Twyla and married her. Now the

ghost usually went with them. But, Mrs McWethey told me, it sometimes stayed with her for days without Twyla present. My belief is that something about Twyla allows it to manifest, but that it is very much a separate being.

This case is especially interesting for two reasons: first, because (most unusually) the 'voice' of the poltergeist was captured on tape; and second, because the family had no obvious problems or tensions that might have given rise to a traditional poltergeist visit – although it is true that Twyla was a teenager at the time of the phenomena. Cases of this kind would seem to weigh in favour of the idea (by no means universally accepted by researchers) that poltergeists might actually be disembodied spirits, as opposed to the externalized tensions and frustrations of adolescents.

THE HEOL FANOG HOUSE HAUNTING

When self-employed artist Bill Rich moved into the fourteenth-century Heol Fanog House in St David's Without, near the Brecon Beacons in Wales, with his wife Liz and their three children, he had no idea that he and his family would be sharing their home with a phenomenon that produced smells of sulphur and church incense, footsteps and other unexplained sounds, a phantom figure, and enormous electricity bills.

Bill Rich explained: 'Since we moved in the electricity bills have been remarkable. We had one for £750 the first quarter we were here. Whatever it is also uses the electricity when all the appliances are off and even when we are away. We estimate that altogether we have had to pay for about £3,000 worth of electricity that we haven't used.'

Bill and Liz also experienced feelings of intense fatigue for no apparent reason. They enlisted the aid of several exorcists, including representatives from the Spiritualist Church in Cardiff, who claimed to have expelled four ghosts. When the

Revd David Holmwood inspected the house, he claimed to have met a man who died at the end of the last century and had been 'stuck in a thorn bush ever since'. The Revd Holmwood blessed the house, and the noises seemed to abate, although the family was still plagued with ghostly figures and Bill was forced to tape down the light switches to prevent them from being turned on during the night.

In March 1994, the famous medium Eddie Burks visited Heol Fanog House and claimed to have encountered the most intense concentration of evil he had ever experienced. It was, he said, feeding off the house's electricity supply, not to mention the psychic energy of the family.

Burks went into a trance state, in which he was able to draw the malign energy from the house and into himself. He appeared to have been successful, for the Rich family's daily electricity costs fell from £5 to £2 and the ghostly figures ceased to appear. The family applied to SWALEC, the local electricity board, for a rebate of £3,000. Apparently, they were unsuccessful.

This is one of those occasional cases in which the entity seems to be connected with electricity in some way (if the reader will excuse the pun). The terrifying 'Something' that inhabited 50 Berkeley Square produced an 'electric horror', which could be felt through the walls of the house (see p. 241). The Heol Fanog House poltergeist seemed to have slightly unusual energy requirements, in that it was apparently obliged to access the house's electricity supply in order to manifest itself.

THE ROCHDALE POLTERGEIST

The following case comes from the files of the Northern Anomalies Research Organization (NARO), two of whose members, Alicia Leigh and Stephen Mera, read a newspaper article describing the tribulations of a family in Rochdale in the north of England. The Gardener family was, it seemed, suffering from unexplained drips of water coming from the ceiling of their prefab bungalow. The local council had been called in and had been unable to get to the bottom of the mysterious dampness. Ironically, these mysterious falls of water occurred at the height of the incredibly hot and prolonged summer of 1995, in which hosepipe bans were in place all over the country.

The manner in which the water dripped from the ceiling was extremely strange. According to the Gardeners: 'It would start dripping in one place then shoot from corner to corner. The edges were jagged like broken glass, and it would finish at a point.' The council inspected the loft for leaking pipes and came to the conclusion that either the Gardeners had a serious problem with condensation or they were liars. Indeed, two council officials accused the family of turning a hosepipe on the ceiling in order to be rehoused, and threatened to have them evicted.

The dripping water was not the only mysterious phenomenon to plague the family: doorhandles were turned by unseen hands, the doors opened and closed when there was no one near by and the smell of cigarettes began to pervade the house. Intriguingly, the cigarette smell included liquorice. Jim Gardener smoked a pipe, but his wife Vera's previous husband, Geoffrey, had rolled his own cigarettes in liquorice papers; he had had a heart attack and died in the hall. Presently, the sounds of a man coughing began to be heard in the house.

The case was investigated, while the phenomena were occurring, by Alicia Leigh, Stephen Mera and the well-known writer and chairman of NARO, Peter Hough. At one point during the investigation, Vera's grown-up daughter, Jeanette, came out of the bathroom with her hair wet (she had not used the bath or basin). In the hallway they discovered a damp patch on the ceiling, close to a trap-door leading to the loft. Taking a torch, Peter Hough climbed into the loft and inspected it, but could find no sign of any dampness there whatsoever. This sparked off a major fall of water all over the house, while Alicia Leigh suddenly complained of nausea and a pressure in her chest.

In the *Fortean Times* Number 89 Hough explains:

> We searched the house. In the back bedroom water was falling from the ceiling and had formed on the walls and door frame. We resumed questioning the Gardeners, but Stephen who was standing in the doorway between the living room and the hall, suddenly called us.
>
> Water had suddenly flashed across the ceiling in the hallway, just as Jim Gardener had described it occurring previously. Stephen told us what he had seen. 'It was as if the ceiling was the floor and someone had thrown a cup full of water across it' The phenomenon had defied gravity!

Searching for the focus of the activity which, as we have seen, is common in such cases, the investigation team wondered if Vera's daughter, 33-year-old Jeanette, might qualify. The phenomena began only after she had moved in ten months previously. She had also been deeply involved with a serious family crisis that had driven her irrevocably apart from her father, Geoffrey.

At this point, the team took stock of what they had seen and came to the conclusion that the phenomena were amenable to one of only two explanations. One, obviously, was that the family were hoaxing all the strange episodes, an explanation that was considered unlikely, in view of the nature of the phenomena and the profound distress of the family, as observed by the team and testified by the neighbours they interviewed. The other explanation was that the phenomena were genuine manifestations of a poltergeist presence.

The team arranged for additional investigators to join them for an evening without the Gardeners, who had agreed to spend the night elsewhere. Preparations were made, including making a video record of the positions of all the moveable objects in the house.

Peter Hough writes:

Just after 10 o'clock we all heard Alicia cry out. When we rushed in, she was seated in an armchair near the kitchen doorway, pointing towards a bronze statuette on the carpet. 'I was looking into the kitchen,' she gasped. 'As I turned my head to make a comment to Steve, I saw the statuette standing on the floor near the television set. I swear it wasn't there moments before!'

'Great!' I remarked. 'It must be on film.'

Stephen shook his head and looked embarrassed.

'I was fiddling with the camera and unfortunately it was pointing towards the hallway at the time.'

As Hough notes, evidential near-misses such as this are all too well known to paranormal investigators: the mysterious entities that apparently cause such phenomena are noted throughout the literature on ghosts and poltergeists for their mischievous sense of humour. Although a sceptic would point to this as evidence that nothing unusual whatsoever is actually happening in these cases, it is not at all unusual for an 'entity' to wait until an investigator is changing the battery in his camera, or performing some other task which briefly interferes with his equipment's ability to register or record, to cause some astonishing manifestation, such as the materialization of the statuette witnessed by Alicia Leigh.

About one and a half hours later, at 11.30 p.m., the investigators began to hear strange, disembodied voices drifting through the house. One percipient, Carole, compared them to the voices on a police radio, and could not work out what they were saying.

In the early hours of the morning, a wheezing was heard in one of the bedrooms, and as he sat on the bed, Stephen Mera received a 'flick' which made him jump and left a temporary red mark just above his waistline. The investigators were inclined to link this laboured breathing with Geoffrey Gardener, who had suffered from severe asthma. In addition, the radio-like voice Carole had heard seemed to be linked with Geoffrey's occupation as a taxi driver.

Peter Hough concludes that when Jeanette moved into the house ten months previously, the wrath of her deceased and unreconciled father was raised. Water, Hough reminds us, is a purifying symbol, and the statuette which materialized was of Themis, the goddess of law and justice. It seems that the poltergeist might have been trying to tell the family to leave the past behind them, or might just have been 'hell-bent on making life a misery ... According to Vera, he was not the nicest of men.'

THE ENFIELD POLTERGEIST

The Enfield Poltergeist case, which occurred in the late 1970s, was investigated by two highly regarded researchers, Maurice Grosse and Guy Lyon Playfair. The manifestations began on 31 August 1977 in the Enfield, north London, home of Mrs Harper. That evening, she was putting her daughter Janet and one of her sons to bed, when a chest of drawers began to slide across the floor, followed by four loud raps that came from one of the walls.

Suddenly afraid, Mrs Harper hurried next door to ask her neighbours, Vic and Peggy Nottingham, for help. Vic and his son searched the house, but could find nothing untoward. Unsatisfied, Mrs Harper then called the police, and WPC Carolyn Heeps was sent to investigate. According to her written statement, she and the other witnesses watched as a chair slid across the floor, apparently of its own volition.

The following day, several household objects began to move around, and when Mrs Harper touched them, she found them to be hot. She contacted the *Daily Mirror*, which sent photographer Graham Morris to the house on 4 September. As he was taking a photograph of the family, a toy brick struck him on the head. When Morris reported the incident to senior reporter George Fallows, the latter decided to inform the Society for Psychical Research of the case.

At that time, Maurice Grosse was still mourning the death

of his daughter in a traffic accident, an event which kindled in him a profound interest in parapsychology. He had recently joined the SPR and requested that he be put in charge of the Enfield investigation. Grosse went to the Harpers' house on 8 September and witnessed several apparently poltergeist-related phenomena, such as a child's marble being thrown at him, and the opening and closing of a door when no one was near by.

When Guy Lyon Playfair joined the investigation, it was decided to try to communicate with whatever was causing the knockings on the walls of the house. As with many other cases, such as the Hydesville rappings examined earlier, they discovered that they could communicate using a simple, one-knock-for-'no'-two-knocks-for-'yes' code. When Grosse asked how long the 'spirit' had been in the house, it replied with fifty-three knocks, which of course could have meant hours, days, weeks or years.

Although these raps were recorded successfully on tape, when Playfair attempted to record other mysterious sounds he found that the tapes were invariably damaged or wiped clean when he later tried to play them back. Attempts were made to capture something photographically, with the electronics company Pye leaving an infra-red television camera in the children's bedroom. This machine likewise malfunctioned unaccountably.

Several apparitions were seen around the house, including a grey-haired woman, a child and an old man. As with the case of the Black Monk of Pontefract, pools of water began to form at various locations, without apparent cause. Also Janet Harper was attacked on several occasions by something that was apparently attempting to choke her; and both she and her brother Jimmy began to speak in strange, guttural voices which, it was claimed, it would have been impossible for them to achieve normally. As with the Borley Rectory haunting, writing began to appear spontaneously on the walls, with the letters occasionally being formed from adhesive tape. Several times Janet was carried up off her bed, these instances of apparent levitation being captured on high-speed film.

The investigative team was joined by physicist David Robertson of Birkbeck College, London, who handed Janet a large, red cushion and asked her to make it disappear. At this moment, a passing tradesman, who claimed to have had no knowledge of the events in the house, saw a red cushion on the roof of the house. He also claimed to have seen, through the upstairs window, Janet floating horizontally across the room. Mrs Hazel Short, a school-crossing lady, also claimed to have seen Janet floating horizontally in the air.

In October 1978, the Enfield disturbances gradually lessened in intensity and then faded away altogether, in common with all other such cases. However, four years later an experiment was conducted by Professor J. B. Hasted, head of the physics department at Birkbeck College. In this experiment, Janet Harper was placed on a platform that was connected to a chart recorder. Intriguingly, while Janet sat perfectly still on the platform, the chart showed that, over a period of thirty seconds, she became lighter by 2 lb.

As with virtually all such cases, there is a depressing side to the Enfield investigation: other members of the SPR criticized the investigation conducted by Grosse and Playfair. For instance, Anita Gregory, a member of the society's council, visited the house and concluded that the manifestations were nothing more extraordinary than pranks played by the children. She concluded that, while there may have been some genuine phenomena in the early stages of the case, the attention aroused by those phenomena probably persuaded the children to make them a little more dramatic.

THE AMHERST INCIDENT

In the town of Amherst, Nova Scotia, in 1878, there occurred one of the rare cases in which a poltergeist causes serious harm to its human victims. The scene of the manifestations was a two-storey cottage in which lived Daniel Teed with his wife, Olive, their two young sons and two of Olive's younger sisters, Jeannie and Esther Cox.

The disturbances began with odd noises coming from the girls' bedroom. A couple of days later, Esther woke up screaming that she was dying, and indeed it was discovered that her face and arms were severely swollen, which caused her considerable pain. As the family tried to calm her, the house was assaulted by a series of thunderous knocks. The family searched the house, looking for the cause, but were unable to find anything that might have caused them.

After a few hours Esther's swelling went down (apparently, she visibly 'deflated' while the rest of the family watched in astonishment) and all was quiet for the next four days. There then began a series of what we have come to recognize as typical poltergeist manifestations, such as covers being torn from beds and small objects being tossed around. It is clear that Esther Cox was the focus of the activities – a message was scratched on the wall, reading: 'Esther Cox You Are Mine To Kill.'

News of the strange goings-on quickly spread and large crowds congregated around the Teeds' house, hoping to catch a glimpse of the unusual. Predictably, there were also many sceptics who insisted that Esther herself was the cause of the disturbances, in an attempt to gain attention. However, Esther fell seriously ill, apparently suffering from diphtheria. During the time she was confined to her bed, the poltergeist attacks stopped. Daniel Teed decided that during her convalescence it would be better if Esther stayed at the house of another sister in New Brunswick; and while she was away, the Teed house was spared the attentions of the poltergeist.

When she returned, the disruptive activities resumed, and this time they included the spontaneous appearance of lighted matches (the poltergeist, whose name apparently was 'Bob', had informed Esther of its intention to burn down the house), which started numerous small fires. Daniel Teed was unsure what to think about these phenomena, but was inclined to side with the sceptics who claimed that Esther was somehow faking them. He ordered her out of the house and she was forced to find employment in a local restaurant owned by a man named John White. However, when chairs and tables in the restaurant began to be strewn around, apparently by the poltergeist, White dismissed her and she was taken in by another man, Captain James Beck, who intended to conduct a scientific examination of the poltergeist phenomena.

The poltergeist had other ideas and refused to manifest itself, so Beck's plans came to nothing. Thinking that the entity had at last gone on its way (or alternatively, that Esther had grown out of her attention-seeking phase), Daniel Teed decided to take her back, whereupon the disturbances began all over again.

At this point a travelling showman named Walter Hubbell arrived in Amherst, and had the idea of putting Esther on the stage and making some money out of her. Daniel Teed agreed to split the profits with him. But this plan, too, came to nothing: as soon as Esther got up on stage, the poltergeist would desert her, leaving the angry audiences to demand their money back.

Teed banished Esther from his house for good, and she spent the rest of her life wandering from job to job. She also spent time in prison for arson, having been blamed for the burning down of one employer's barn, an event she blamed on the poltergeist.

Interestingly, the poltergeist manifestations began shortly after Esther went for a carriage ride with a local youth named Bob MacNeal, who was something of a ruffian and apparently tried to rape her but was disturbed by the sound of another buggy approaching. Understandably enough, this traumatic event upset Esther considerably and she cried herself to sleep for the following few nights.

It is, therefore, surely significant that the poltergeist's name was Bob and that Esther was the focus for the activity. She perfectly fits the criteria for the psychological origin of poltergeist manifestations (i.e. a young and deeply disturbed woman), and it is this explanation (along with the sceptical one of outright fraud) which has most consistently been offered to account for the events at Amherst. Colin Wilson adds another theory in *Poltergeist*:

> [The] abrupt termination of the 'haunting' seems to favour the view that Esther's own unconscious mind was responsible ... Esther was sexually frustrated, and if Bob MacNeal had adopted a more gentlemanly way of seducing her, there would have been no [phenomena]. Esther was a classic case of 'the divided self': a part of her longing to give herself to her lover, while the inhibitions induced by her background and training made this impossible. So when she rejected his advances, and he vanished into the night, her unconscious mind said, in effect: 'Now see what you've done, stupid!' and set out to punish her.

THE BELL WITCH

Although the name suggests otherwise, the Bell Witch was a poltergeist, and an extremely troublesome one at that. It also had the rare attribute of speech. The manifestations took place on the farm of John Bell in Robertson County, Tennessee, in 1817. Bell was moderately prosperous, and lived a quiet life with his wife, four sons and daughter; the family were well liked in their community. Typically, the disturbances began with strange noises, such as knocks and scratchings, but there were other manifestations that set the case apart from others of its kind. At about the time the noises started, John Bell saw a curious animal that looked something like a dog, but which wasn't a dog. He grabbed his gun and fired at it, but apparently missed. He also saw something that looked like a turkey, but wasn't. Again, he fired at it, and again he missed.

The poltergeist's activities then grew more violent: whenever a family member tried to prevent it from snatching their bedclothes away, it slapped them hard on the face. Once again, the focus for the haunting seemed to be a young female: Bell's daughter Elizabeth, then twelve years old. The family tried to keep their problems secret, but Bell himself began occasionally to act rather strangely, as when he went to a friend's house for dinner. He spoke and ate very little, which caused his friends some concern. Later, he explained his curious behaviour: 'All of a sudden my tongue became strangely afflicted. Something that felt like a fungus growth came on both sides, pressing against my jaws, filling my mouth so that I could not talk.'

The Bells turned to a local lay preacher for help. James Johnson visited the house and became convinced that there was indeed an evil presence there. He returned with a committee of local residents, who inspected the house, searching for some evidence of fakery, but could find nothing to suggest that the Bell family were not telling the truth. Since their Protestant background precluded the idea of ghosts, the residents concluded that the Bells' unwelcome visitor was a witch, hence the name by which the case has come to be known.

Although the poltergeist initially communicated with a rapping code, it quickly acquired the power of speech, which progressed from a squeak, to a whisper, to a loud shrieking. When those present asked the entity who or what it was, it gave several contradictory replies, one of which was: 'I am a spirit from everywhere, Heaven, Hell, and the Earth. I'm in the air, in houses, any place at any time. I've been created millions of years. That is all I will tell you.' Another reply was: 'I am the spirit of a person who was buried in the woods near by and the grave has been disturbed and my bones scattered, and one of my teeth was lost under the house. I've been looking for that tooth.'

The poltergeist allowed the Bell family to waste some considerable time digging in their yard, trying to find the tooth, before telling them that it had been joking. This predilection for pointless lying is common to many alleged communications from beyond the grave; it is an often quoted maxim that nothing received via seance or ouija board should ever be taken at face value.

The poltergeist lied to them on another occasion, and once again they fell for it. It told them: 'I am the spirit of an early immigrant who brought a large sum of money and buried my treasure for safekeeping until needed. In the meantime I died without divulging the secret and I have returned in the spirit for the purpose of making known the hiding place. I want Betsy [Elizabeth] Bell to have the money.' The Bells duly began to dig, but were rewarded with nothing but the scathing laughter of the poltergeist.

Interestingly, the community's suspicion that the poltergeist was a witch was confirmed by another communication, in which the entity stated: 'I am nothing more nor less than old Kate Batts, witch.' Kate Batts was a local woman with a dreadful temper, who seems to have harboured a considerable dislike for John Bell. Her reputation was somewhat ambiguous: while some thought it likely she was a witch, it was nevertheless well known that she had a fondness for quoting Scripture. An additional problem was that Kate Batts happened to be alive at the time. However, few took seriously the idea that she could be responsible for the disturbances.

What is certain is that the poltergeist (for some reason that was never made clear) despised John Bell, while expressing an extreme fondness for his wife, Lucy. Indeed, the entity stated its aim as nothing less than the destruction of 'Old Jack Bell'. The 'witch' also involved itself with the Bells' daughter, Elizabeth. At one point, a local man named Joshua Gardner announced his intention to marry Elizabeth (although she was too young to marry). This infuriated the entity, which pleaded with Elizabeth never to marry him and even resorted to physical intimidation, such as punches and slaps. In the event, the marriage to Joshua Gardner never happened.

The disturbances continued for the next three years (rather longer than the average poltergeist visitation, which usually lasts around six months). Eventually, they took their toll on John Bell, whose health was seriously affected. In spite of the

148

attempt by a doctor to treat him, Bell fell into a coma on 19
December 1820. The poltergeist responded to this with the
words: 'It's useless for you to try and revive Old Jack – I have
got him this time. He will never get up from that bed again.'
Then, as Daniel Cohen in *The Encyclopedia of Ghosts*, explains,

> One of his sons rushed to the cabinet where the medicines were
> kept, but instead of the usual bottles he found 'a smoky looking
> vial, which was about one-third full of a dark colored liquid.'
> The doctor was sent for, but the witch announced that it was
> too late ... When asked about the bottle with the strange-
> looking liquid, the witch said, 'I put it there and gave Old Jack
> a big dose out of it last night while he was fast asleep, which
> fixed him.'
>
> The liquid in the bottle was tested on a cat, and the cat died
> instantly. John Bell lingered a bit longer. He died the following
> day. The witch was exultant. Even during the funeral the air
> was filled with loud and derisive shouts and songs.

In the months following the death of John Bell, the manifestations gradually lessened in intensity, until the poltergeist
declared that it was leaving the family, but would return in
seven years. Seven years later, it did return, but by that time
Elizabeth had married and moved away, as had John Bell Jr.
Lucy Bell remained in the house with her other three sons.
There were strange noises, and bedclothes were ripped from
the beds, but there were no voices, and this time the poltergeist
manifestations were short-lived.

The psychologist and psychical researcher Nandor Fodor
re-examined the Bell Witch case in 1951, and commented on
the similarity between Elizabeth's fainting fits and trance
mediumship. Admitting that he was purely speculating, Fodor
went on to suggest that John Bell might conceivably have
molested Elizabeth when she was very young, and that his
own illness might have been the result of a profound guilt
complex. This, in turn, might have been enough to trigger a
split in Elizabeth's personality, with part of her subconscious

being somehow responsible for the poltergeist manifestations. Whatever the true nature of those manifestations, the case of the Bell Witch remains unexplained and its status as a genuine instance of poltergeist activity remains intact.

THE STRANGE CASE OF GEF, THE TALKING MONGOOSE

Throughout his life, Harry Price investigated many strange phenomena, but none were as strange as the case of Gef, the talking mongoose. In 1932, Price heard about a family called Irving, who lived at Cashen's Gap on the western side of the Isle of Man, in the Irish Sea. The Irving family, so the story went, had made the acquaintance of a mongoose that could not only speak several languages, but could also read minds. Price was intrigued, but was too busy at the time to make the trip to the island himself. However, his friend Captain M. H. Macdonald offered to look into the Irvings' claims on his behalf.

On his arrival, Macdonald learned that the family had first noticed the presence in their home of something untoward when they were disturbed by strange barking and spitting noises coming from the walls of their farmhouse. Whatever was making the noises proved too cunning for Mr Irving, who tried laying down poison and even went looking for it with a gun.

Eventually Irving tried communicating with it by making animal noises and was surprised to hear the animal imitating them. Voirrey, his thirteen-year-old daughter, began to sing it nursery rhymes, which it also repeated. When the creature finally revealed itself to the family, they saw that it was a small mongoose, which claimed to have come from India. Although Mr Irving rarely saw the creature – which the family called Gef – it frequently appeared to Mrs Irving and Voirrey.

Gef did not take kindly to the arrival in February of Captain Macdonald, and refused to appear to him. When he left the farm to go to his hotel, they all heard a high-pitched voice cry: 'Go away! Who is that man?' The following day, Macdonald returned to the farm and heard Gef apparently talking to Mrs Irving and Voirrey in an upstairs room. When he called out to invite the mongoose down to meet him, it declined in no uncertain terms, screeching: 'No, I don't like you!' Macdonald tried to creep upstairs to surprise it, but unfortunately a creaking stair betrayed him. Gef screamed: 'He's coming!' and left the house, not to return for the remainder of Macdonald's visit.

Irving told Macdonald of Gef's other talents, which included proficiency in Russian, Spanish and Welsh, a fine singing voice and the ability to strangle rabbits. Gef was also able to tell them what was happening miles away without leaving the farm; his information would later be discovered to be accurate. When asked about his origins, the mongoose replied that he was 'an earth-bound spirit'.

On one occasion, Gef plucked some hairs from his tail and left them on the mantelpiece for Irving. One has to wonder why the mongoose would do such a thing, and in view of the fact that the hairs were promptly forwarded to Harry Price – obviously as 'proof' of Gef's existence – this event sounds rather contrived. When Price had them analysed, they were discovered to be dog hairs (the family owned a collie dog). When Price finally went to the Irving farm, Gef was neither seen nor heard, and returned only after he left.

The case of Gef has remained the most bizarre in the annals of psychic research, and some commentators have suggested that its very strangeness militates against its being a hoax. Assuming, for the moment, that it *wasn't* a hoax, that Irving did not pluck some hairs from his dog and send them to Price, that some member of the Irving family wasn't a fine ventriloquist . . . what might Gef have been?

There are aspects to the appearance and behaviour of Gef that would seem to place him in the category of elemental, or nature spirit. In his book *The Black Arts*, Richard Cavendish has this to say on the subject of elementals:

In the fifth century Proclus divided spirits into five groups, four of them connected with the elements of fire, air, water and earth, and a fifth group which live underground. Psellus, in the eleventh century, added a sixth category – *lucifugum*, 'fly-the-light'. In sixteenth- and seventeenth-century authors the fire-spirits are usually described as living in the upper heavens and having no contact with men. The spirits of air are ferocious and violent. They hate human beings, cause storms, and can make themselves visible bodies of air. Water-spirits, which are cruel, passionate and deceitful, generally appear in female shape. They wreck ships and drown swimmers. Spirits of earth live in the woods. Some are friendly to men, but some set traps for them and lead travellers astray. The spirits who live underground are exceptionally malicious. They attack miners and treasure-hunters, cause earthquakes and eruptions, and lure people below ground to their deaths. The fly-the-lights, which naturally never appear in the daytime, are entirely beyond human understanding or control – mysterious, restless, icily malignant. They pursue and kill those incautious enough to travel by night.

These spirits are the medieval and modern survivals of the widespread primitive belief that all Nature is alive as man is, that the spirits live in every stream and mountain, in clouds and breezes, in trees and fields and hedgerows, in boulder, crags and caves. They are unpredictable and mischievous as Nature is, sometimes kindly but more often cruel.

That these spirits of nature should influence the affairs of humanity – not to mention interact in various ways with those travelling through or living in isolated regions – was accepted unequivocally by our ancestors, however much we might look down our noses at them for doing so. As Cavendish suggests, the capriciousness and cruelty of nature inspired ancient peoples to impose anthropic attributes upon it. Perhaps the Irving family, living in an isolated part of the country in the first half of this century, were continuing that tradition. It should be remembered that Mr Irving very seldom saw Gef (indeed, he may not have seen the talking mongoose at all); Voirrey was an adolescent, and might be expected to have suffered some of the emotional traumas and insecurities to which most adolescents succumb, including a desire for attention. That her mother shared her experiences with Gef might be put down to a case of hysterical contagion, in which the perception of strange events – born of a deeply ingrained superstition – can be shared by others.

THE EPWORTH GHOST

The disturbances that occurred in 1716–17 at the parsonage at Epworth, England, which was the birthplace of John Wesley, the founder of Methodism, have been extensively investigated in the many years since. Although John Wesley himself was not a direct witness to the phenomena, many members of his family did experience the events, and he wrote a lengthy account of what occurred for *The Arminian Magazine* in 1784. Such accounts, written at the time of ghostly manifestations by those at the centre of them, are few and far between, and for that reason, I shall quote at length from the Revd Wesley's record.

On December 2nd, 1716, while Robert Brown, my father's servant, was sitting with one of the maids, a little before ten at night, in the dining-room, which opened into the garden, they both heard someone knocking at the door. Robert rose and opened it, but could see nobody. Quickly it knocked again, and groaned. 'It's Mr Turpine,' said Robert; 'he used to groan so.' He opened the door again, twice or thrice, the knocking being twice or thrice repeated; but still seeing nothing, and being a little startled, they rose up and went to bed. When Robert came to the top of the garret stairs, he saw a handmill, which was at a little distance, whirled about very swiftly. When he related this, he said, 'Naught vexed me but that it was empty. I thought if it had been but full of malt he might have ground his hand out, for me.' When he was in bed he heard, as it were, the gobbling of a turkey-cock close to the bedside, and soon after the sound of one tumbling over his shoes and boots; but there was none there; he had left them below.

The next day he and the maid related these things to the other maid, who laughed heartily, and said, 'What a couple of fools you are! I defy anything to fright me!'

After churning in the evening, she put the butter in the tray, and had no sooner carried it into the dairy than she heard a knocking on the shelf where several puncheons of milk stood; first above the shelf, then below. She took the candle and searched both above and below, but, being able to find nothing, threw down the butter tray, and all, and ran away as if for life.

The next morning, my sister Molly, then about twenty years of age, sitting in the dining-room, reading, heard as if it were the door that led into the hall open, and a person walking in who seemed to have on a silk nightgown rustling and trailing along. It seemed to walk round her, and then to the door, then round again; but she could see nothing. She thought, 'It signifies nothing to run away, for, whatever it is, it can run faster than I.' So she rose, put her book under her arm, and walked slowly away. After supper, she was sitting with my sister Sukey (about a year older) in one of the chambers, and telling her what happened. Sukey made light of it, telling her, 'I wonder you are so easily frightened. I would fain see that would frighten me.'

Presently a knocking began under the table. She took the candle and looked, but could find nothing. Then the iron casement began to clatter. Next, the catch of the door moved up and down without ceasing. She started up, leaped into the bed without undressing, pulled the bedclothes over her head, and never ventured to look up until next morning.

A night or two after, my sister Hetty (a year younger than my sister Molly) was waiting as usual between nine and ten to take away my father's candle, when she heard someone coming down the garret stairs, walking slowly by her, then going slowly down the best stairs, then up the back stairs, and up the garret stairs; and at every step it seemed the house shook from top to bottom. Just then my father knocked, she went in, took his candle, and got to bed as fast as possible. In the morning she told it to my eldest sister, who told her, 'You know I believe none of these things; pray let me take away the candle to-night, and I will find out the trick.' She accordingly took my sister Hetty's place, and had no sooner taken away the candle than she heard a noise below. She hastened downstairs, to the hall, where the noise was, but it was then in the kitchen. She ran into the kitchen, where it was drumming on the inside of the screen. When she went round, it was drumming on the outside, and so always on the side opposite to her. Then she heard a knocking at the back kitchen door. She ran to it, unlocked it softly, and when the knocking was repeated, suddenly opened it; but nothing was to be seen. As soon as she had shut it, the knocking began again. She opened it again, but could see nothing. When she went to shut the door, it was violently knocked against her; but she set her knee and her shoulder to the door, forced it to, and turned the key. Then the knocking began again; but she let it go and went up to bed. However, from that time she was thoroughly convinced that there was no imposture in the affair.

The next morning, my sister telling my mother what had happened, she said, 'If I hear anything myself, I shall know how to judge.' Soon after, she begged her mother to come into the nursery. She did, and heard, in the corner of the room, as it were the violent rocking of a cradle; but no cradle had been there for some years. She was convinced it was preternatural, and earnestly prayed it might not disturb her in her own chamber at the hours of retirement: and it never did. She now thought it proper to tell my father. But he was extremely angry, and said, 'Sukey, I am ashamed of you. These boys and girls frighten one another; but you are a woman of sense, and should know better. Let me hear of it no more.'

As six in the evening he had family prayers, as usual. When he began a prayer for the King, a knocking began all round the room, and a thundering knock attended the 'Amen'. The same was heard, from this time, every morning and evening while the prayer for the King was repeated.

The Wesley family procured a dog in an attempt to frighten away whatever was causing the disturbances; but the dog itself was frightened away. However, the Wesley children, although somewhat unnerved, were nevertheless deeply intrigued by the manifestations and even gave the ghost a nickname, 'Old Jeffrey', after a man who had died in the house.

The following year, the disturbances began to fade away and eventually left the parsonage altogether. In keeping with numerous other cases the manifestations seemed to be focused on a young woman: nineteen-year-old Hetty. Mrs Wesley reported: 'All the family . . . were asleep when your father and I went downstairs, nor did they wake in the nursery when we held the candle close to them, only we observed that Hetty trembled exceedingly in her sleep, as she always did before the noise awakened her. *It commonly was nearer her than the rest* [emphasis added].'

Intriguingly, while there are numerous letters and other writings from the family on record, there are none from Hetty herself. This is unusual, in the light of the established fact that Hetty did indeed write of the mystery. In 1791, Joseph Priestly published the letters under the title *Original Letters by the Rev. John Wesley and his Friends*, in which there are references to Hetty's writing a letter on the subject of 'Old Jeffrey'. However, the collection does not include it, and it has been speculated that John Wesley suppressed the letter, possibly because it contained information that would have been damaging to the family. It was suggested to John and Anne Spencer, in an interview conducted at Epworth, that this information may have referred to Hetty's falling pregnant, a good enough reason at the time for Wesley's suppressing the letter.

For his part, John Wesley apparently remained utterly convinced of the reality of the poltergeist manisfestations, for, as Peter Underwood has noted, he allowed his account of the events at Epworth to be reprinted in *The Arminian Magazine* more than 60 years after it had originally appeared in that publication. According to Underwood: 'This certainly suggests that he was as convinced of the authenticity of the disturbances when he was over eighty as he had been when he was twenty.'

In addition, if Hetty had actually become pregnant, as was suggested to the Spencers, and which would have been seen as something of a catastrophe in the early eighteenth century, this might well have resulted in a profound disturbance in the young woman's psyche. This could then have been the trigger which caused the disturbances to manifest.

6

CRISIS APPARITIONS

We have already examined some cases in which ghosts (for want of a more accurate term) have been reported to appear at the site of some violent or traumatic event in the past. However, there are many cases on record of apparitions being encountered at, more or less, the precise time when such events took place, the percipients usually being friends or relatives of the deceased. These events are known as crisis apparitions.

One such case occurred towards the end of the First World War, and concerned the apparition of an eighteen-year-old trainee aircraft pilot named David McConnell. On the morning of 7 December 1918, Lieutenant McConnell was ordered to fly a Camel aircraft from his home base at Scampton, Lincoln-shire, England, to the airfield at Tadcaster, sixty miles away. McConnell informed his room-mate, Lieutenant Larkin, of his assignment at 11.30 a.m. and said he expected to be back some time in the afternoon.

On the way to Tadcaster, McConnell ran into a heavy fog. He made an impromptu landing and telephoned Scampton for instructions. He was told to proceed at his own discretion; so he took off again and continued towards Tadcaster. As he approached the airfield, still swathed in fog, he became disoriented, and struck the ground at full throttle. The impact killed him instantly. When his body was recovered from the wreckage of his plane, it was noted that his smashed watched read 3.35 p.m.

At that moment, Larkin was sitting in their room, reading

and smoking, when he heard footsteps approaching. Assuming it was his friend, Larkin looked up as McConnell opened the door and offered his habitual greeting: 'Hello, boy!' Still dressed in his flying suit and wearing a naval cap (he had previously served in the naval air service), McConnell was standing no more than eight feet away from his friend, who said: 'Back again already?' McConnell replied that he had had a good trip and had arrived at Tadcaster 'all right'. After a few more pleasantries, McConnell said: 'Well, cheerio!' and left, closing the door behind him.

At approximately 3.45 p.m., Lieutenant Garner Smith walked into the room, and commented that he hoped McConnell wouldn't be back too late, since the three of them had plans to go out for the evening. Larkin replied that McConnell was already back and that he had seen him a few minutes earlier.

Larkin heard about McConnell's death later that evening and, quite understandably, assumed that McConnell had gone on another flying assignment, which had resulted in his death. It wasn't until the following day that it became clear to Larkin that his friend had died on the Scampton–Tadcaster flight – moreover, that he had died at precisely the time Larkin had looked up to see McConnell standing in the doorway to their room.

When McConnell's parents arrived at the airfield to claim his body, they heard of the incident in the two airmen's room and wrote to Larkin, who replied with a detailed account of his encounter. News of the case spread to the wider community and came to the attention of the SPR, which conducted an investigation and concluded that McConnell's visit to his friend constituted the best case on its files.

As with many elements of the paranormal, in a curious way the less spectacular an experience is, the more believable and impressive it is. We may observe this in relation to UFO sightings, especially in the case of alleged photographs of unidentified flying objects: it is a generally accepted rule of thumb that crystal-clear, close-up images of UFOs are most likely to have been faked. And with the McConnell case, we can see that the very fact of its apparent mundaneness weighs heavily in favour of its being a genuine ghostly encounter. Larkin was reliable and level-headed, and in addition wrote down his recollections only a fortnight after the event. Many cases are recalled in written form years or even decades after the encounter, and thus (due to the vagaries of memory, which has the proven ability to embellish details over long periods of time) are of less value as testimony of actual events. It would, of course, have been better had Larkin written his account as soon as he learned of the true nature of his meeting with McConnell; but, as Daniel Cohen informs us, Larkin 'did not know at the time that his experience would become a psychical research classic'. In addition, he was not particularly interested in this subject and, in common with many percipients, doubtless found it hard to believe that he had actually seen McConnell's ghost.

According to Cohen:

> Another thing that makes this case most impressive is that there was a confirming witness – not to the reality of the apparition itself, but to Larkin's belief that he had seen his roommate when in fact the man was dead or about to die sixty miles away. There is no way Larkin could have known of McConnell's death when he talked to Garner Smith. All the times are well established. The time of McConnell's death was established dramatically by his smashed wristwatch.

Cohen also points out that the SPR considered a hoax unthinkable, since it would have involved the deception of McConnell's parents by two of his comrades. Likewise, mistaken identity seems improbable, in view of McConnell's habit of wearing his navy cap around the airfield and the fact that the apparition also wore it.

PROMISES FULFILLED

In his 1985 book, *The Paranormal*, Brian Inglis describes cases in which a crisis apparition has visited a percipient after promising to do so in the event of death. For instance, the Whig politican Henry Brougham was at an inn in Scandinavia on 18 December 1799 when he encountered an apparition of a long-lost friend, 'G'. The two had been extremely close throughout school and university, and had had many discussions on the concept of life after death. They had even written an agreement in their own blood, that whoever should die first would appear to the other. As the years wore on, they had gradually drifted apart; G had moved to India, and their correspondence was sporadic.

On the day of his encounter, Brougham was relaxing in a hot bath at the inn, when he suddenly became aware of G sitting on the chair on which he had left his clothes. Brougham later said: 'How I got out of the bath I know not, but on recovering my senses, I found myself sprawling on the floor.' When he looked at the chair again, G was nowhere to be seen.

Although he told himself that this had been no more than a peculiar dream, he could not help but recall the oath he and his friend had taken, and wondered whether G had died, and had tried to let Brougham know that there was indeed an afterlife.

Upon his return to Edinburgh, Brougham found a letter from India waiting for him, informing him that G had died – not on 18 December, but on the following day.

Another such case occurred in 1863, when Baroness de Boislève gave a dinner party, which was attended by General Fleury, Master of the Horse to Napoleon III. The Baroness was anxious to hear news of the French expeditionary force in Mexico, since her son Honoré was in service there. General Fleury assured her that all was well, and that he had no particular news to give. At nine o'clock, the Baroness went to the drawing room to supervise the serving of coffee, when she was horrified to see her son, hideously pallid, and with one of his eyes missing. Not surprisingly, she screamed and fainted; when her guests rushed to her assistance and she had recovered, she told them of the awful thing she had seen.

A week later, Baroness de Boislève received the awful news that Honoré had been shot through the left eye, and had died instantly, at the very hour at which she had seen the apparition in her drawing room.

Writing in *The Paranormal*, Inglis reminds us that it is by no means unusual for such crisis apparitions to be seen by more than one person.

In 1785 two young officers, Sir John Sherbrook and George Wynyard (who was later to become a general), were sitting in Wynyard's room in barracks in Nova Scotia when a man whom Wynyard recognized as his brother John walked slowly through the room and into the bedroom. When they followed him, he was nowhere to be seen. Fearing the worst they made a note of the date, intending to keep the episode to themselves; but it quickly spread. When the next mail arrived from England, it disclosed that John Wynyard had died on the same day, and at the same time, as he had been 'seen' in the barrack room. Sherbrook had never seen John Wynyard in his lifetime; but in Piccadilly some time later he saw somebody so like the apparition that he could not resist the opportunity to introduce himself, and it turned out to be another Wynyard brother.

THE RETURN OF LIEUTENANT SUTTON

The following case is, once again, reminiscent of Athenodorus's encounter in antiquity, in that it describes how a murder victim returned from beyond the grave to achieve some form of justice. In Anthenodorus's case, the ghost of the old man required a proper burial; in the case of Lieutenant Sutton, the justice sought was the apprehension of the murderer.

On 12 October 1907, James Sutton, a lieutenant at the naval academy at Annapolis, Maryland, attended a dance. As might be expected, a lot of alcohol was consumed, and on the way back to the academy, a fight broke out. Sutton was thrown to the ground, which infuriated him to the extent that he threatened to kill his companions. When he got back to his quarters, he took two pistols and went looking for the other cadets. However, he was spotted with the weapons and approached. Such was Sutton's fury that he began to fire his weapons. One lieutenant was able to disarm him, but then took his own pistol, deliberately put it to Sutton's head, and fired.

Lieutenant Sutton's family lived on the other side of the country, in Portland, Oregon. Before she received news of her son's death (the official story being that he had committed suicide), Mrs Sutton had the inescapable feeling that something awful had happened. At that moment, she had a vision of her son standing before her. The apparition said: 'Momma, I never killed myself. My hands are as free from blood as when I was five years old.'

The apparition continued to appear for several months and recounted a number of details, both of the fight and of Sutton's injuries, which his mother could not possibly have known at the time. Eventually, the family contacted the American Society for Psychical Research, which subsequently verified the various details imparted by the apparition; and in 1909 the body of Lieutenant Sutton was exhumed from Arlington National Cemetery. According to Daniel Cohen in his *Encyclopedia of Ghosts*, 'An examination revealed that many of the wounds that had been spoken of by the apparition but not mentioned in the navy's doctor's report did indeed exist.'

The ASPR then uncovered a number of serious inconsistencies in the official version of events, including the testimonies of the witnesses and the fact that Sutton had harboured no suicidal tendencies, and certainly would not have killed himself because of a drunken fight. The revelations uncovered by the ASPR investigation seem to have satisfied the apparition of Lieutenant Sutton, for the visitations subsequently ceased.

163

7

FACES AND VOICES

GHOST PHOTOGRAPHS

As might be expected, many attempts have been made over the years to capture some evidence of the existence of ghosts and spirits; and, also unsurprisingly, photographic evidence has been at the forefront of that decades-long quest. As anyone familiar with the history of the paranormal will know, when it comes to photographic evidence, the adage 'a picture is worth a thousand words' may be true, but not one of those words ever seems to be 'genuine'.

A famous ghost photograph is that of the Tulip Staircase in the seventeenth-century Queen's House at Greenwich, London. In 1966, a retired clergyman, the Revd R. W. Hardy of White Rock, British Columbia, was touring England with his wife. Their itinerary included the Queen's House, part of the National Maritime Museum, not least because it contained the Tulip Staircase, the first cantilevered staircase in England.

The Revd Hardy took a picture of the staircase without incident, and the couple returned home to Canada satisfied. Back home, they had the pictures from their holiday developed, and were showing them to some friends, when they got to the picture of the Tulip Staircase, whereupon they were astonished to see an unmistakable hooded figure swooping up the stairs. The figure was bent low and had its left hand on the banister. On closer inspection, it became apparent that there was another figure further up the staircase, also with its left hand on the banister. The Hardys were absolutely certain that there was no one on the stairs at the time the photograph was taken.

According to research conducted soon after, in 1967, by Peter Underwood and Dorothy E. Warren, there was a 'large medieval house at Greenwich', which may have partly occupied the site of the Queen's House. It has thus been suggested that the figures in the photograph of the Tulip Staircase are the shades of long-dead prelates who occupied the thirteenth-century house.

At first sight, the Tulip Staircase photograph looks very impressive indeed – impressive enough to send a chill down the spine. And yet there are several problems with it, which have been pointed out by the author Ian Wilson. For one thing, the figures are clearly clutching the present stair-rail, which did not exist in the thirteenth century. In 1995, Wilson visited the archives of the National Maritime Museum and was given permission to examine a professional-quality black-and-white print of Revd Hardy's photograph, taken by Brian Tremain, the museum's photographer. He was also able to examine several letters from the Revd Hardy, in which he explained the circumstances under which he took the photograph.

Wilson points to the importance of the exposure time used by Hardy. He used a low-speed 64 ASA film, without a flash, and thus the camera's shutter was kept open for a relatively long time in order to make use of the limited light. In *In Search of Ghosts*, Wilson points out:

> Such a long exposure time gives rise to two problems. First, unless the camera is mounted on a tripod, or in some other way held very steady, the slightest movement will create a blur to the eventual photograph. Second, if someone moves across the camera's field of view while the shutter is open, he or she is likely to appear ghost-like two or three times, as if in a slow-motion replay of their movements.

Although Hardy succeeded in solving the first problem by holding the camera against the edge of a doorway, thus achieving an extremely sharp image of the staircase, he had to guess at the correct exposure time and was subsequently (and understandably) unable to remember exactly how long the exposure took. Wilson makes the crucial point that during this time (which was, according to Brian Tremain, probably about one second) it would have been possible for someone (living) to slip up the stairs. 'One telling feature is the two left hands, each with a ring on their third finger, that are visible at two different levels on the stair-rail.' Moreover, no one wore rings on the third finger of the left hand in the thirteenth century: both clergy and those who were married wore their rings on their right hands.

As far as the 'shroud' is concerned, which gives the main figure its monk-like appearance, it can be seen in Brian Tremain's duplicate of the photograph that the hood is actually a repeated image of the figure's shoulder, implying that someone is in the act of walking (rather than gliding) up the stairs. In Tremain's view (with which Wilson agrees), the ghostly figure is actually that of a staff member in a white lab coat, who slipped up the stairs unnoticed by Hardy as he took his photograph.

The Revd Hardy and his wife were not convinced by this explanation, however, perhaps with good reason. After all, the staircase was the subject of the photograph, and they might have been expected to notice anyone ascending at the time the picture was taken. On the other hand, they were an elderly couple, and it is perhaps not stretching the bounds of credulity to suggest that they might well have failed to notice someone slipping quietly and quickly past.

The arguments could be tossed back and forth almost indefinitely, but it has to be admitted that the solution to the mystery suggested by Tremain and Wilson is rather convincing.

Another very famous photograph is that purporting to show the 'Brown Lady' of Raynham Hall, Norfolk, England. The image was captured by one Captain Provand and his assistant Indre Shira. Provand, a former court photographer, had been commissioned by *Country Life* magazine to photograph Raynham Hall on 19 September 1936 and Shira's account of what happened later appeared in *Country Life*. It is clear that, unusually in photographic cases, the ghost was seen at the time it was photographed.

After spending the morning and first part of the afternoon photographing the interior and exterior of the house, Captain Provand and Indre Shira set up their equipment at the bottom of the main oak staircase. Provand took one photograph while Shira flashed the light. Suddenly, Shira became aware of 'an ethereal, veiled form coming slowly down the stairs'.

Shira called out: 'Quick! Quick! There's something! Are you ready?'

'Yes,' replied Provand, and removed the cap from the camera lens, while Shira pressed the trigger on the flashlight pistol.

After the photograph had been taken and the camera's shutter was again closed, Provand came out from under the focusing cloth and asked Shira what all the exitement was about.

His assistant pointed to the staircase and explained that there had been a semi-transparent figure there, through which the steps could be seen. Provand merely laughed and put it down to imagination (the apparition had since vanished). Provand and Shira took a few more photographs and then returned to town, spending the entire journey discussing the possibility of securing a genuine photograph of a ghost. Provand assured his assistant that it was quite impossible.

However, according to Shira:

When the negatives of Raynham Hall were developed, I stood beside Captain Provand in the dark-room. One after the other they were placed in the developer. Suddenly Captain Provand exclaimed: 'Good Lord! There's something on the staircase negative, after all!' I took one glance, called to him, 'Hold it!' and dashed downstairs to the chemist Mr Benjamin Jones, manager of Blake, Sandford and Blake, whose premises are immediately underneath our studio. I invited Mr Jones to come upstairs to our dark-room. He came, and saw the negative just as it had been taken from the developer and placed in the adjoining hypo bath ... Mr Jones, Captain Provand and I vouch for the fact that the negative has not been retouched in any way. It has been examined critically by a number of experts. No one can account for the ghostly figure but it is there clear enough.

At first sight, this case appears to be impressive, especially since Shira claimed to have seen the ghost shortly before Provand photographed it. And yet, in his examination of it, Ian Wilson points out some problems. For one thing, the 'ethereal' and 'transparent' apparition conforms more to the stereotypical image of ghosts than to the vast majority of sightings, in which percipients report entirely solid 'people', who are revealed to be ghosts only when they vanish, or are later discovered to have died, as in the case of Lieutenant McConnell. In fact, ghost photographs in general show transparent, ethereal or wraith-like images, which do not conform to those apparitions described by eyewitnesses. As Wilson states: 'We may have to face the possibility that if ghosts truly exist, they may do so at some spectrum which does not normally register on photographic film. No one, for instance, expects to be able to photograph television waves – these need a television receiver, just as a ghost may need a human one.'

Wilson also points to the nature of the image as no more than a 'foggy swirl' and suggests that it may just be possible that Shira might have introduced a small glass filter containing a dab of grease in front of the camera lens, without Captain Provand noticing. Indeed, it is an unfortunate but inescapable fact that fakery must be considered to be at least among the most likely explanations for photographs of this kind.

168

TED SERIOS AND 'THOUGHTOGRAPHY'

The problem of the authenticity of ghost photographs strikes at the heart of the phenomenon in general. That is, what *are* ghosts and how (assuming they exist) are they able to manifest to the extent that they are observable by living humans? And why, if they do indeed manifest themselves, are they observable by humans and yet do not register on photographic film? Ian Wilson makes a very good point when he suggests that ghosts might require the presence of a living person to appear. In effect, this is an inversion of the old solipsistic question: does a tree fall in a forest if no one is in the forest to see that it has fallen? It may well be that ghosts do not walk the corridors of 'haunted' houses unless someone is there to watch them walk . . .

And yet, in examining the phenomenon from this point of view, we come up against an additional problem: the phenomenon of 'thoughtography'. In 1963, Dr Jule Eisenbud, a psychiatrist at the University of Colorado Medical School, published an article in which he claimed that it was impossible to design a repeatable experiment to test the reality of paranormal phenomena. This, of course, has always been the keystone of the sceptical argument against the paranormal in general and parapsychology in particular. Any phenomenon that is not repeatable in strict laboratory conditions, it is argued, does not exist. Indeed, to accept otherwise would undermine the foundations of the scientific method which has proved so spectacularly successful.

After his article had appeared, Eisenbud received a letter claiming that he was wrong. The letter was accompanied by a magazine clipping about a man named Ted Serios. Apparently, Serios was able to create psychic images by holding a Polaroid camera and staring into the lens. Through the power of his mind alone, he could produce photographs of various objects, people and places.

Intrigued by these claims, Eisenbud arranged to meet Serios

(who worked as a bellhop and was, it seems, an alcoholic) and asked him to demonstrate his remarkable ability. Serios took a camera supplied by Eisenbud and placed a paper tube over the lens. He then gazed down it. After several failed attempts, he produced two blurred photographs of a water tower and a hotel. Dr Eisenbud was astonished at the results and immediately contacted several of his scientist colleagues to inform them of the experiment's success. Unfortunately, they were only mildly interested and declined his invitation to witness an experiment for themselves. Eisenbud was extremely disappointed at this attitude, although he should not have been surprised by it. He was, after all, experiencing what investigative journalist John G. Fuller calls the 'can't-happen-here syndrome': the refusal by orthodox science to open itself to the possibility that the paranormal might contain genuine and verifiable elements.

Undaunted by this lack of interest on the part of his peers, Eisenbud continued to experiment with Serio's apparent psychic abilities, in spite of his initial suspicion that the paper tube – which Serios called his 'gismo' – might have been used somehow to fake the photographs. Serios, however, assured him that the gismo was used only to help him to concentrate on the camera lens; and when he examined the gismo, Eisenbud discovered that it was indeed merely an empty tube of paper.

As is usually the case, news of Serios's peculiar talent spread quickly and came to the attention of two reporters named Charles Reynolds and David Eisendrath, who were convinced that Ted Serios was a hoaxer. In *World Famous Strange but True* Colin Wilson describes their attempt to expose him:

> [Reynolds and Eisendrath] constructed a small device that could be hidden inside the gismo, with a lens at one end and piece of unexposed film at the other. When this was pointed at the camera, the result was a picture not unlike those that Serios had produced. The account of their invention was

printed in *Popular Photography* in 1967, and it gave all the skeptics fresh ammunition. Since then, their article has been cited by people who believe that Serios is a fake, as evidence that he performed his thought photography by sleight of hand. In March, 1974 *Time* magazine ran an article on the occult revival, and included a brief account of Serios and the *Popular Photography* article. *Time* concluded: 'Many of Serio's followers were shattered. Again, the millennium was deferred.'

Eisenbud responded that Serios could well have faked the photographs in the way described by Reynolds and Eisendrath – if he had been allowed to. In the event, however, the controls on the experiments precluded this. It must be said that it is still unclear whether Serios was a faker or not; but if it is indeed possible to imprint images on photographic film through the power of the mind alone, then whatever mysterious force is brought into play may have its corollary in the force which can imprint 'ghost' images on to certain locations. This could not only conceivably account for the so-called 'psychic recordings' which we examined earlier, but might also provide a candidate for the energy required for genuine discarnate spirits to manifest themselves in our familiar, living world.

PHONE CALLS FROM THE DEAD

The history of ghostly encounters is replete with strange stories, but surely none can be as bizarre and spine-chilling as the phenomenon of apparent telephone calls from the dead. Although it sounds utterly outrageous, there are number of reports on record from people who claim to have been in contact with the spirits of family or friends via the telephone. Can there possibly be any truth to these astonishing reports?

A typical phone call from the dead (if there can be such a thing) proceeds as follows. The percipient hears the phone ringing as usual, although some have reported that it sounds curiously flat, or otherwise not quite right. When the phone is answered, the connection is usually quite bad, with the voice on the other end of the line fading in and out. However, the voice is recognizable as someone close to the percipient who has recently died. The call usually ends with either the caller breaking the connection or the line going dead.

Of course, if the recipient of the call knows the person on the other end of the line is dead, he or she may be so shocked that they say nothing and the caller breaks the connection. On the other hand, if the recipient does not realize the true nature of the call, a lengthy conversation may ensue; indeed, phone conversations with the dead have lasted up to half an hour, with the recipient finding out only later that the conversation was with someone no longer living.

Some phone calls are placed at or very soon after the time of death, and thus these calls seem to be related in some way to the crisis apparition discussed earlier; other calls have been placed anything up to two years after the caller's death. The purpose of these mysterious phone calls seems to be similar to the purpose of more traditional ghost encounters: some are no more than a farewell message, while others warn of impending danger or impart information that is required by the percipient. The American author Rosemary Ellen Guiley cites the case of the actress Ida Lupino, who received a phone call from her father six months after his death. He allegedly told her the location of some legal documents which were needed to settle his estate properly.

Even more curiously, this communication can sometimes be two-way, with people telephoning someone whom they thought to be alive, carrying on a normal conversation and then later discovering that the person was in fact dead at the time the call was placed.

There are several theories that have been put forward to explain phone calls from the dead, which seem to be related to so-called 'Electronic Voice Phenomena' (EVP), which we shall examine shortly. The most obvious of these theories is that the dead really are attempting to communicate with the living via manipulation of the telephone network. Perhaps they consider this a more reliable method of contacting the living than the more traditional mediums, possibly because the telephone network was, after all, designed with the exclusive purpose of two-way communication. Another theory, which is a good deal more complex than that mentioned above, is that the recipient of the posthumous phone call somehow unwittingly utilizes subconscious telepathy to receive information that a friend or loved one has died, and then creates a hallucination, whereby that information is imparted to the conscious mind, via the phone call.

In their book *Ghostwatching*, John Spencer and Tony Wells quote a case from the files of the late paranormal researcher D. Scott Rogo, whose source was the September issue of *Fate*. The event was originally reported by Don Owens of Toledo, Ohio, USA.

Don had a very close friend, Leigh Epps, a bachelor who had no luck with women. Consequently he valued his few close friends, who included Don and his wife, whom he called 'Sis'. After Leigh moved to another area they drifted apart, and their meetings became rare. At 10.30 p.m. on 26 October 1968 whilst Don was out, his wife received a phone call from Leigh:

'Sis, tell Don I'm feeling real bad. Never felt this way before. Tell him to get in touch with me the minute he comes in. It's important, Sis.'

Don tried to phone Leigh back many times but with no success. He discovered later that at exactly the time of the phone call, Leigh had died at the Mercy Hospital, only six blocks away.

Although phone calls from the dead are generally regarded as just that – posthumous communications – there is one very intriguing case that seems to imply that communication by this method is also possible *before birth*. In order to describe this case, I must enter briefly the neighbouring realm of ufology and alien encounters – another example of the subtle connections that tie the various elements of the paranormal together.

There is surely no one with the slighest interest in these subjects who has not heard of Budd Hopkins and his work with those who suspect that they have been abducted by extraterrestrial creatures. The case of Debbie Tomey (referred to as 'Kathy Davis' in Hopkins's book *Intruders*), perhaps more than any other, brought the alien abduction phenomenon to the world's attention when it was first published in 1987.

One aspect of this case which has rarely, if ever, been referred to in the subsequent literature on Hopkins and his work involves a series of bizarre phone calls Debbie Tomey received during her ongoing abduction experiences. In 1980, Debbie was pregnant with her second son, Tommy, when she began to receive strange phone calls, which Hopkins describes in *Intruders: the Incredible Visitations at Copley Woods*:

> Above a background noise that roared like a factory in full swing she heard a voice moaning and muttering but using no syllables she could understand. She assumed at first that it was a friend playing a practical joke on her, so she broke in and asked humorously what was going on. The voice continued without even a pause to acknowledge the question. She asked again, and after several requests and no apparent response of any sort she hung up. This occurred on a Wednesday afternoon. The following Wednesday, at about the same time – 3.00 p.m. – she received another nearly identical call. And the next Wednesday and the one after that. No words were ever audible, and there were no apparent sexual overtones. The gender of the voice itself was indecipherable.

Debbie decided to change her phone number to an unpublished listing, but this did not deter the mysterious caller; in fact, the next time it called, the voice sounded angry, and the implication was that any attempt to avoid the phone calls was futile. On one occasion, Debbie's friend Dorothy answered the phone and she too heard the bizarre, guttural mutterings.

In the early phase of their association, Budd Hopkins asked Debbie a number of questions concerning the health of her and her family. ' "Tommy, my youngest, has a speech problem. He's three years old but he doesn't talk yet. He just makes this sort of moaning sound. I've had him thoroughly tested. They've done brain stem and brain wave analysis, and so on, and he's normal. He's very bright. He just doesn't talk yet." '

What is truly astonishing is that, later, an emotional Debbie stated that the sounds made by her son Tommy were very similar to those made by the unknown caller who had tormented her during her pregnancy. Even though the question is unanswerable, we are forced to ask: could this possibly be an instance of prenatal communication via the telephone network? It seems ludicrous, and utterly beyond the bounds of rationality; the least we can say is that in exploring cases of this kind, we find ourselves plunging into the deep unknown, and it is a territory with no maps.

ELECTRONIC VOICE PHENOMENA

As mentioned, the phenomenon of phone calls from the dead is related to Electronic Voice Phenomena (EVP), first discovered in 1959 by the Swedish singer and film producer Friedrich Jürgensen, who was fond of making tape recordings of birdsong. When he played back one of his tapes, Jürgensen could distinctly hear a voice speaking in Norwegian. His first, and natural, assumption was that the tape recorder was acting as a radio receiver and he thought no more about the curious – but apparently explainable – phenomenon. However, a few weeks later, he was playing back another birdsong recording, when he heard a woman's voice saying in German: 'Friedel, my little Friedel, can you hear me?' He immediately recognized the voice as belonging to his mother, who had died several years earlier.

Jürgensen began to experiment with other ways to receive these apparent voices of the dead and came up with the idea of de-tuning an ordinary radio receiver so that it was receiving nothing but 'white noise'. He wrote up the results of these experiments in 1964 in a book entitled *Rösterma Från Rymden* (*Voices From the Universe*), which came to the attention of Dr Konstantin Raudive, a Latvian psychologist, who visited Jürgensen the following year. Raudive (after whom the phenomena would later be named 'Raudive voices') conducted his own experiments and, after months of silence, at last picked up a message in Latvian. Raudive would go on to receive more than 70,000 such messages over the next three years. In 1968, he published his findings in a book entitled *Unhörberes wird Hörbar* (*The Inaudible Made Audible*), which was translated into English in 1971 as *Breakthrough*.

In 1972, sound and radio engineers across Europe declared their interest in EVP; the chief engineer at Pye offered the opinion that the phenomena were worthy of serious investigation. R. K. Sheargold, then chairman of the Society for Psychical Research's Survival Joint Research Committee (SJRC), investigated the phenomena and succeeded in capturing voices, which prompted him to write to Colin Smythe Ltd., the publishers of *Breakthrough*, confirming that he was in a position to assure his colleagues in the SJRC that the phenomena were indeed genuine.

Between 1970 and 1972, the Society for Psychical Research commissioned D. J. Ellis to investigate EVP. However, his conclusions were less than enthusiastic: in his opinion, the phenomena were natural rather than supernatural and were more than likely random noises which were being interpreted as voices. Indeed, it must be said that EVP are never particularly clear and that those listening to them almost invariably hear different 'words' being 'spoken'. However, and this echoes Charles Fort's dictum that for every expert there is an equal and opposite expert, there are a number of other researchers who claim that groups of researchers have gone through the messages syllable by syllable (in isolation from each other), and have actually discovered extremely close correspondences in their interpretations.

John Spencer and Tony Wells point out the two main problems with Electronic Voice Phenomena. The first is that electronic equipment of any kind can pick up radio signals and that no amount of screening can prevent this possibility from undermining – potentially at least – all such recordings. The second difficulty, as mentioned above, is that the messages are almost drowned out by the surrounding static, making it extremely difficult to interpret them accurately. Sceptics suggest that what is being picked up in these cases is no more than the occasional electronic glitch. Advocates of EVP counter by stating that the messages received often are relevant to the listener, which rules out both random radio reception and electronic glitches.

Perhaps the most interesting aspect of EVP is that experiments can be done by anyone; no equipment more sophisticated than a radio receiver is required, and the phenomena offer a potentially fascinating – if ultimately rather boring – way for the average person to do a little psychic research for themselves.

'SPIRICOM'

Sceptics are forever complaining about the lack of conclusive evidence for the paranormal, evidence that can be repeated under laboratory conditions by scientists on opposite sides of the world. It is ironic that for nearly two decades there has been just such a body of evidence in the form of a refinement of the Electronic Voice Phenomena examined above. In August 1981, the American investigative journalist John G. Fuller received a curious letter from a man named George Meek, who was head of a foundation called Metascience, based in Franklin, North Carolina. A highly successful engineer and holder of many patents, Meek claimed to have headed a research effort to establish two-way communication with discarnate personalities of humans who had died. The name of this research effort was 'Spiricom'. Against his better judgement,

Fuller became more and more interested in this apparently outrageous claim, and eventually wrote a book about it, *The Ghost of 29 Megacycles*, which was published in 1985.

Meek's research proceeded along a strange path that included elements of spiritualism and hard scientific engineering. In the early days, he became acquainted with a man named Bill O'Neil who, while lacking a conventional education, possessed an innate genius for electronics, in addition to which he was an extremely sensitive psychic and healer. In basic terms, the two men combined their efforts to enlist the aid of deceased scientists in the design and construction of electronic equipment that would enable a two-way communication system to be established.

O'Neil lived with his wife Mary Alice on an isolated farm in western Pennsylvania, where he conducted his experiments both psychic and scientific. As a result of these, he made psychic contact with a discarnate person calling himself 'Doc Nick', a deceased radio ham who appeared one day in O'Neil's cluttered laboratory:

> Now he could clearly see the full, rounded form of the head and face of a man, along with his right shoulder and right arm. O'Neil was gripped in fear. All he could say was, 'My God, who are you?'
>
> He was more than surprised when the figure answered, in fully audible speech.
>
> 'They call me Doc Nick,' he said. 'I was a ham radio operator, too. What are your call letters?'
>
> Dumbfounded as he was, O'Neil gave them. 'They're N3AZQ,' he said, hardly realizing he had spoken. 'But who are you?'
>
> 'Used to be a doctor,' the figure said. His voice remained fully clear and audible to Bill, although his body only partially materialized. 'And I just want to let you know that you can become a really rare and unusual healer.'
>
> 'I want to be that,' Bill replied. 'But who are you? Where did you come from?'

'We can be getting into that later,' the figure said. 'Meanwhile, I'm going to guide you along on a regular basis. Detailed suggestions. On a regular basis.'

O'Neil began to receive help from another discarnate personality, calling himself 'Dr Mueller', an altogether more irascible character, who seemed unaware of the existence of Doc Nick. Intriguingly, during one of his appearances in the laboratory, Dr Mueller provided O'Neill with a great deal of information about his former life on earth:

Name: Dr George J. Mueller. Former Social Security number: 142–20–4640. Ancestry: English, Irish, German. BS in Electrical Engineering, University of Wisconsin. Top fifth of his class in 1928. MS in Physics, Cornell, 1930. PhD in experimental physics at Cornell, 1933. Additional training, New York University and UCLA. Meritorious Civilian Award from the Secretary of the Army. Physics Instructor and Research Fellow while at Cornell.

O'Neil passed this information on to George Meek who, after some months of research, was able to verify every item on Dr Mueller's 'curriculum post-mortem'.

With the help of O'Neil, Doc Nick and Dr Mueller, Meek and his Metascience foundation were ultimately able to construct a sophisticated radio transceiver, which was apparently capable of opening a channel of communication between this world and the afterlife, and of recording the results.

On 6 April 1982, George Meek held a press conference at the National Press Club in Washington DC. In spite of his preference for total anonymity, Bill O'Neil also attended, as did John Fuller and about thirty reporters and journalists, including representatives from the Associated Press, United Press International, Reuters, *Business Week, Harper's*, National Public Radio and the Chicago *Sun-Times*.

After playing some sample tapes of the recorded conversations between the living and the 'dead', Meek announced that he would not be patenting the Spiricom machine and that plans would be made available at a nominal fee to cover printing costs. The aim of the press conference, said Meek, was to bring to the attention of scientists around the world the potential that Metascience and Bill O'Neil had discovered for a colossal widening of humanity's awareness of the Universe, and of its own destiny.

Although George Meek is now in his eighties and in poor health, his work has been continued by researchers all over the world, most notably the American Association Electronic Voice Phenomena, Inc., which holds conferences in various countries. The association's motto is to 'Provide Objective Evidence That We Survive Death in an Individual Conscious State'.

There are now many hundreds of researchers and others interested in the ongoing quest to establish and maintain contact with the spirit world through electronic means. While most communications are composed of brief moans and hard-to-distinguish phrases, some attempts have been met with extraordinary success, and much information has been received regarding the nature of the afterlife. One of the most impressive EVP communications allegedly came from a Mr George Ohlson, who said that he would not want to return to Earth for anything.

Mr Ohlson described a kind of receiving station, in which souls find themselves immediately after death. Here the new arrivals are counselled by more experienced souls, who know how to deal with the feelings of fear and despair that are frequently felt. One reason for these feelings is that, although the spirits of the dead can easily return to Earth, the vast majority of living people are unable to register their presence, and this makes the spirits feel unwanted. Once in the afterlife, they are nurtured and cared for by the other souls, until they realize the potential of their new situation.

According to Mr Ohlson, there are vast cities in the other world, community centres and 'great halls of learning, and of music'. 'There's always something new, something more interesting, some new experience, some new place to go, new people to visit, fresh arrivals coming over from earth.' The other world itself is just as 'real' as the Earth, although it is composed not of ordinary matter, but of a substance existing on a higher 'vibration'.

Whether or not one believes that these conditions really do exist in the afterlife, or even that an afterlife exists, EVP experiments are an extremely important field in the study of the paranormal, because, unlike the vast majority of alleged encounters with the spirits of the dead, they provide physical evidence which can be studied and verified by other researchers. As such, they would seem to offer, potentially at least, the most profitable line of enquiry into the mystery of life after death.

8

GHOSTS OF THE LIVING

When most people hear the word 'ghosts', they assume that reference is being made to the spirits of the dead, which have returned to Earth for some reason. However, as we have seen, what are sometimes taken to be ghosts may in fact be psychic recordings of events that occurred years or even centuries before. The repetitious nature of their movements, coupled with the fact that they seem utterly unaware of the presence of the percipient, strongly suggest that there is no 'consciousness' inherent in the phenomenon, as opposed to those encounters in which the ghost is capable of interacting with the percipient (whether through direct communication, or simply by acknowledging the percipient's presence). There is another class of apparition which complicates matters further. In some supernatural encounters, the 'ghost' is of a person who is still alive, and yet who appears in a location in which he cannot possibly be.

DOPPELGÄNGERS

Some apparitions of living people are known as '*doppelgängers*', and are defined by the great authority on occultism, Lewis Spence, as the etheric counterpart of the physical body, which has the ability temporarily to move through space.

There are a number of encounters between famous figures and *doppelgängers* on record. For instance, the poet W. B. Yeats described in his autobiography one such experience, in which he was thinking of a fellow student for whom he had an important message.

In a couple of days I got a letter from a place some hundreds of miles away where the student was. On the afternoon when I had been thinking so intently I had suddenly appeared there amid a crowd of people in a hotel and seeming as solid as if in the flesh. My fellow student had seen me, but no one else, and had asked me to come again when the people had gone. I had vanished, but had come again in the middle of the night and given him the message. I myself had no knowledge of either apparition.

Although Yeats had no knowledge of his disembodied journey to his friend, from the latter's point of view, the apparition of Yeats looked and behaved exactly as if Yeats had actually been with him. Thus the description of these apparitions as 'doubles' is an extremely apt one. It seems that the double is an entirely independent entity, with its own will, totally unconnected with the original person.

Another famous figure, Goethe, experienced the bi-location of his friend Friederich, while he was walking home after a heavy rain. Friederich was walking in front of Goethe and was wearing Goethe's dressing-gown. When the poet arrived home, he found his friend sitting by the fire and wearing his dressing-gown. Friederich told him that he had been caught in the heavy downpour while on his way to see his friend and had been given the dressing-gown to wear by Goethe's housekeeper, while his sodden overcoat dried out.

Goethe also had a curious encounter with himself, which might more accurately be described as a timeslip. He had just visited his lover, Frederica, and was riding along, when he saw himself approaching, dressed in a grey suit with gold embroidery. Eight years later, he was riding along the same road in the opposite direction, when he remembered the curious encounter and realized that he was wearing the very same suit in which he had seen himself eight years earlier. It would seem that, somehow, Goethe caught a glimpse of his own future on that lonely highway.

183

OUT-OF-BODY EXPERIENCES

A phenomenon which seems to be intimately related to the 'phantasms of the living' is that of out-of-body experiences (OBEs). To many researchers, this is the best evidence so far discovered in favour of the idea that some component of our being has the ability to exist outside the physical body, with its attendant implication that when our physical bodies die, our minds continue on into an afterlife.

In addition, it may be that research into OBEs will ultimately provide us with a working hypothesis as to how the mechanism of separation between mind and body actually works. The potential of OBE research to increase our understanding of this mechanism is great, since it seems that some people are capable of inducing an OBE at will, thus placing it in the category of the repeatable scientific experiment.

Sceptics claim that OBEs are no more than elaborate hallucinations, brought on by various factors, such as hypnagogic and hypnopompic states (the hypnagogic state is the boundary between waking and sleeping, while the hypnopompic state is the boundary between sleeping and waking). These states are still ill understood, and it is certainly true that many bizarre visions and experiences can beset the mind at these times. However, there are many cases on record in which the person undergoing the OBE is able to gather information which could not have been known at the time and which subsequently is proved to be accurate.

We can turn to Colin Wilson's and John Grant's *Directory of Possibilities* for an example of this. The case is cited of a woman who was in the habit of controlling her OBEs and taking extended trips out of her body. On one such trip, she discovered a particularly attractive house, to which she returned again and again over the course of a year. Presently, she and her husband decided to move house, and she thought wistfully of the 'dream-house' and how perfect it would be for them. However, she had no idea where it was. She and her husband went house-hunting in London and found the 'dream-house'. It was exactly as she remembered it from her out-of-body expeditions, down to the furniture and decorations.

The house was for sale, and the asking price was remarkably low, since it had acquired a reputation for being haunted. When they called at the house to make enquiries about buying it, the owner stared at the woman, dumbfounded, and cried: 'You are the ghost!'

Although most OBEs are known as 'autoscopy' (seeing oneself from a distance), and do not result in protracted periods away from the body, some, like the one described above, include lengthy periods of exploration, which can include apparent entry on to a different plane of existence. This is known as 'astral projection'.

Perhaps the most famous practitioner of astral projection is the American Robert A. Monroe, who managed to perfect the technique and wrote of his experiences in a book entitled *Journeys Out of the Body*. One of the most intriguing aspects of Monroe's many astral experiences involves the interaction which frequently occurred between himself and the friends he 'visited' in the early phase of his experiments.

Monroe made copious notes on his experiences, many of which are reproduced in *Journeys Out of the Body*. On one occasion, he decided to travel to an acquaintance, a female work colleague to whom he refers as 'R. W.', who was at that time holidaying on the New Jersey coast. Monroe did not know exactly where she was staying and did not inform her of his intention to travel to her in what he calls the 'second state'. At about three o'clock in the afternoon, he lay down on his bed and went into the 'relaxation pattern' he had devised for himself. Then he concentrated on the desire to go to R. W.

There was the familiar sensation of movement through a light blue blurred area, then I was in what seemed to be a kitchen. R. W. was seated in a chair to the right. She had a glass in her hand. She was looking to my left, where two girls (about seventeen or eighteen, one blond and one brunette) also were sitting, each with glasses in their hands, drinking something. The three of them were in conversation, but I could not hear what they were saying.

I first approached the two girls, directly in front of them, but I could not attract their attention. I then turned to R. W., and I asked if she knew I was there.

'Oh yes, I know you are there,' she replied (mentally, or with [a] superconscious communication, as she was still in oral conversation with the two girls).

I asked if she was sure that she would remember that I had been there.

'Oh, I will definitely remember,' the reply came.

I stated that I had to be sure she would remember, so I was going to pinch her.

'Oh, you don't need to do that, I'll remember,' R. W. said hastily.

I said I had to be sure, so I reached over and tried to pinch her, gently I thought. I pinched her in the side, just above the hips and below the rib cage. She let out a good loud 'Ow,' and I backed up, because I was somewhat surprised. I really hadn't expected to be able to actually to pinch her. Satisfied that I had made some impression, at least, I turned and left, thought of the physical, and was back almost immediately.

When they subsequently met at work, Monroe asked R. W. what she remembered about her holiday. She replied that on Saturday (the day of Monroe's astral visit), she had been in the kitchen of her cottage with her dark-haired eighteen-year-old niece and her niece's friend, who was blond and of about the same age. Monroe asked her if she remembered anything in particular about the afternoon, and she replied that she did not. Impatiently, he asked her if she remembered the pinch, a question which shocked her.

'Was that *you?*' She stared at me for a moment, then went into the privacy of my office, turned, and lifted . . . the edge of her

186

sweater where it joined her skirt on her left side. There were two brown and blue marks at exactly the spot where I had pinched her.

'I was sitting there, talking to the girls,' R. W. said, 'when all of a sudden I felt this terrible pinch. I must have jumped a foot. I thought my brother-in-law had come back and sneaked up behind me. I turned around, but there was no one there. I never had any idea it was you! It hurt!'

Monroe's experiment is fascinating for several reasons. First, he was able to influence the environment in a physical way, despite his not being there in a physical way, as testified by the painful pinch R. W. received. Second, he was able to describe the three people in the kitchen, together with their locations in the room and their activities at the time of his visit, which were later verified by R. W. Third, and perhaps most intriguing, he engaged in a brief conversation with a part of R. W.'s mind, of which she was unaware. Even while she was talking to the other young women, she was able to respond to Monroe's 'presence' on a telepathic level. Since she herself was unaware of this exchange and subsequently did not recall it (even though she had telepathically assured Monroe that she would), it seems that the communication was conducted by her subconscious, or perhaps, as Monroe suggests, a hitherto unsuspected 'superconscious' part of her mind.

Perhaps most intriguingly, Monroe has identified a number of different levels of reality to which the astral body can travel. He refers to them as 'Locales'. Locale I is the everyday world in which we all exist. Locale II is the so-called 'astral plane', to which we travel in our dreams, and which contains millions of entities of various kinds. Locale II is very similar in general appearance to the mundane material world. Locale III is a parallel universe which transcends time and space. Monroe claims that there are many other Locales beyond Locale III, but they are beyond our ability to comprehend. If these Locales exist, perhaps the higher ones are accessible only to the spirits of the dead on their journey into the infinite . . .

Whatever the true nature of the experiment described above, Robert Monroe has contributed an enormous amount to the field of parapsychology and has laid sturdy foundations on which to base future research in the field of out-of-body experiences.

ELIZABETH AND HEFIN PRITCHARD

The Revd Aelwyn Roberts, whom we met earlier, recounts a curious tale of apparent astral projection in his book *The Holy Ghostbuster*. It concerns a couple, William and Elizabeth Pritchard, who ran a post office and general store in Bangor, Wales. At the time of their experience, their son, Hefin, was working as a flight instructor with the Royal Air Force in Canada.

One night in November, Elizabeth awoke from what was apparently a dreadful nightmare. She was so disturbed by the 'dream' that she woke her husband and told him what had happened. She had been outside in the middle of a furious blizzard and had heard the sound of aircraft engines overhead. At that moment, a bomber, similar to the ones Hefin flew on his training missions, emerged from the swirling snow. In horror, Elizabeth watched as the aircraft crashed into a nearby mountain. She approached the smoking wreckage, hoping that the crew would emerge. When no one did, she opened a door in the fuselage and entered the plane.

Inside was a scene of carnage: all the crew members were dead, one man having been virtually torn in half in the impact. Elizabeth's worst fears were confirmed when she discovered Hefin lying face down among the wreckage. He had a terrible head wound and was losing a great deal of blood. One of his legs was twisted horribly, and Elizabeth assumed that he must be either dying or already dead. Elizabeth then woke up. William tried to reassure his wife that it had been only a dream and that she should not worry about their son. Nevertheless, she maintained that it had somehow felt more 'real' than a dream; that, in some strange sense, she had actually been out there in the blizzard and really had witnessed the crash of her son's aircraft.

Although Hefin was in the habit of writing home regularly, his letters suddenly stopped, and again Elizabeth felt the dread she had experienced after her dream. However, after three weeks she and William did receive a letter from their son, which explained why he had failed to write. He had been transferred to another base in Canada – a move which had prevented him writing. He also informed his parents that he had been taken off flying duties for a while, and regretfully added that the transfer meant that his leave would be postponed for six months.

On the day of his arrival, William and Elizabeth drove to Bangor station to pick up their son. When his train arrived and he climbed down to the platform, his parents saw that he was using a crutch. Otherwise, Hefin seemed in good spirits. When his parents asked him what had happened to his leg, he replied that he had been on a training flight over Alaska, when his plane had run into a blizzard and crashed into a mountain. Four of the crew had been killed, and he had sustained a serious head wound and a badly broken leg. Fortunately, there had been another aircraft behind them, which had noted their position and radioed back to base. A rescue mission had been quickly dispatched.

When his parents asked him about the letter describing his transfer, Hefin confessed that there had been no transfer, that he had invented it as a cover story to avoid worrying his parents. Since the doctors had forbidden him from travelling for several months, he needed an excuse for not returning home at the planned time. William Pritchard asked his son when the crash had occurred; but, before he could answer, Elizabeth replied for him, saying that it had happened at one o'clock on the morning of Thursday 17 November.

This event is not as clear-cut as it might seem. At first sight,

189

we might be forgiven for assuming that it is a case of astral projection, with Elizabeth Pritchard travelling out of her body to the crash site, where she discovered her badly injured son. It has been pointed out that Hefin Pritchard was unconscious at the time, which seems to rule out a telepathic contact with his mother. In other words, he had no idea of the scene inside the crashed plane, the positions of the bodies and so on; so it is unlikely that he could have transmitted his information to Elizabeth, to be received in the form of a dream. But we run into a problem here: in her 'dream', Elizabeth *opened the door* of the aircraft and stepped inside. If astral bodies *cannot* manipulate solid objects, then Elizabeth could not, literally, have been there in an astral form, since she *did* manipulate a solid object (the door of the aircraft). The out-of-body hypothesis would then become untenable. Consequently, we are forced to conclude that Hefin Pritchard *was* aware of everything that occurred immediately after the crash, perhaps making subconscious observations, which he then transmitted telepathically to his mother.

However, this does beg the question: is it really impossible for an astral body to manipulate solid objects? It will be recalled that Robert Monroe was able to pinch his friend R. W. while in his 'second state'. We are also reminded of genuine cases of poltergeist activity, in which solid objects are frequently moved by the 'entity' responsible for the disturbances. In the final analysis, we can only speculate that, since the astral body must be composed of some form of energy, it may follow that this energy is in fact capable of interacting with solid matter.

9

TRAVELLERS' TALES

ZONES OF THRESHOLD AND TRANSITION

There are hundreds of ghost reports associated with travel. Some, such as the so-called 'phantom hitchhiker', have passed into modern legend, and as such generate countless spurious 'friend-of-a-friend' stories. Precisely why such a strong connection with travel should exist is unclear; perhaps it is simply because people have always travelled, nowadays much more than ever before, and thus travel is merely one of the routine activities during which ghosts may be encountered. However, there is another point which might shed further light on such encounters. The anthropologist Victor Turner coined the term 'liminal zones' to describe places containing or characterized by 'threshold'. In *Daimonic Reality* Patrick Harpur states that these zones

> ... may be within us (between sleeping and waking, consciousness and the unconscious) or outside us – crossroads, bridges, shores. They may be at certain times, between day and night, at the witching hour, at the turn of the year. Caravan sites or trailer parks often become especially haunted by UFOs or by strange creatures, perhaps because they are liminally situated between town and country, habitat and wilderness.

In these zones of threshold and transition, the veil between the mundane and the supernatural seems to be especially thin, and many is the time when the distinction between the two is broken down, whether on lonely roads, beside running water, on the shores of oceans, on bridges or at crossroads.

Although it is far from clear why transition, in whatever form, should be so important, it might be helpful to think of the mundane everyday world as being not a continuous stream of experiential reality, but rather a series of stepping stones across which we trip, unaware of the raging torrent of the supernatural rushing past our feet. At times of transition, it may be that we are forced to make a larger jump from one stepping stone to another, during which we are more vulnerable to the influences from that alternate reality of which we are usually unaware.

For this reason, it is important to consider some of the events that have been experienced in these realms, and we must, in addition, look at the cases which follow in terms of their *source* (travellers), rather than their *type*. The reader will note that the cases display a wide variety of types, some of which were discussed earlier in this book, but which seem to be intimately connected with the very act of travelling.

THE *FLYING DUTCHMAN*

The ghost ship is a staple of supernatural lore, and few are more famous than the *Flying Dutchman*. Legend has it that the ship, built some time in the seventeenth century, was sailing from Amsterdam to Batavia (now Jakarta), when it encountered a violent storm near the Cape of Good Hope, South Africa. The ship was captained by a Dutchman named Hendrik Van der Decken, a man with a fearless – not to mention ferocious – reputation.

As the storm grew worse, his crew begged Van der Decken to admit defeat and turn the ship around, but he steadfastly refused, and challenged the Almighty to prevent him from rounding the Cape. This was evidently a serious mistake, for suddenly a glowing form appeared on the deck. Although the crew were terrified, Captain Van der Decken was unafraid, saying: 'Who wants a peaceful passage? I don't, I'm asking nothing from you. Clear out unless you want your brains blown out!' He then drew his pistol and fired at the heavenly figure, but the weapon exploded in his hand.

The figure then pronounced a curse upon the ship, adding: 'And since it is your delight to torment sailors you shall torment them, for you shall be the evil spirit of the sea. Your ship shall bring misfortune to all who sight it.'

The curse from Heaven indeed came to pass, for the sailors died in the storm and were replaced by skeletons, which continued to man the ghost ship. Captain Van der Decken himself was unable to die, and was bound to the ship and its unearthly crew, which were doomed to sail the seas for the rest of eternity.

It seems that the legend of the *Flying Dutchman* owes its existence to the exploits of a Dutch mariner named Bernard Fokke, who was so successful in guiding his ship through adverse conditions that many suspected he had supernatural aid. The legend was given further power when Fokke's ship subsequently disasppeared with all hands.

However, it seems that the *Flying Dutchman* is rather more than a legend, and there have been many sightings of the ship in the years since the seventeenth century. One witness, Helene Tydell, recalled how she was sunbathing with about sixty other people at False Bay near the Cape of Good Hope in March 1939, when they all saw the *Flying Dutchman* sailing upon the open water, in spite of the fact that the air was perfectly still. The ship then vanished.

Three years later, in September 1942, a family were sitting on the terrace of their house at Mouille Point, Cape Town, when they spotted a seventeenth-century ship sailing past, apparently heading for Table Bay. The family watched the apparition for about a quarter of an hour and noticed that it was leaving an eerie glow in its wake. It seems that on these occasions, no particular misfortune befell the witnesses.

However, on 11 July 1881, it is said that the *Flying Dutchman* was seen by none other than the then sixteen-year-old Prince George, who would be crowned George V in 1910. The sighting occurred off the Australian coast, between Melbourne and Sydney. Prince George was a midshipman on HMS *Baccante*, but was transferred to HMS *Inconstant* when his own ship suffered a rudder malfunction. While on the *Inconstant*, Prince George clearly saw the ghost ship, which was glowing red, and entered the sighting in the ship's log. In keeping with the curse, the first crewman to sight the ship from the *Inconstant* fell to his death from the rigging the very next day.

THE PHANTOM DINER

Not all ghosts associated with travel actually travel themselves: some are encountered in a particular location and their ghostly nature becomes apparent only later. One such intriguing case was reported by the main percipient, Tony Clark, in *Fortean Times* Number 69. Clark, a civil engineer, was working in Iran in 1956. He recalls that, one day, he was required to drive to Manjil in the north-west of the country, about 150 miles from Tehran, to discuss a construction project. He was making the trip with a fellow engineer, an Iranian. At that time, Manjil was somewhat isolated, with few amenities, and the two men had begun their journey back to Tehran after a meagre meal of unleavened bread and yoghurt.

When they were still 120 miles from Tehran, they both commented on how hungry they were, and Clark said that there was nothing to be done, unless they were lucky enough to stumble upon a *tchae-khana*, a kind of road-side café.

At that point, they came upon a tiny village, at which they stopped in the hope of at least buying some tea. Walking past a rather distinctive pile of rocks with a single rock balanced on top, Clark and his colleague entered a low building made of mud, where they found several lorry drivers relaxing on charpoys (beds made of rope and wood). A man hurried up to them from the rear of the building, which contained little more than the charpoys and a few wooden tables and chairs. He welcomed them in fluent English, introducing himself as 'Hovanessian', and asking them if they needed anything.

Clark replied that he and his friend were extremely hungry, and asked if the proprietor could help them. Hovanessian replied that he and his wife were excellent cooks, and ushered the two strangers to one of the tables. After his wife had put cutlery on the table, Hovanessian came out with two bowls of delicious soup, followed by wine, stuffed vine leaves, chelo kebab and, finally, Turkish coffee. When the two engineers had finished their meal, which Clark described as 'fantastic' and 'quite the best I have ever eaten', the atmosphere in the room seemed to grow hazy and 'unreal'. When Clark asked the proprietor how much they owed him, he responded with a price that Clark considered to be unbelievably cheap.

Hovanessian was extremely pleased when Clark complimented him on the quality of the meal, and said: 'I'm so glad to have served you with something you enjoyed ... It is unusual for us to see a foreigner. Do call again, and tell your friends to look in.'

When Clark returned to Tehran and told his friends about the wonderful meal he had eaten in the shabby *tchae-khana*, they refused to believe him, saying that the location was far too remote for an establishment serving food that good.

About three months later, Clark was required to make the same journey again. This time, he was with an Englishman, who had been one of the most vocal of the sceptics. In identical circumstances, they reached the plateau where the tiny village had stood. Presently, they reached the village, and passed the pile of stones with the single stone balanced on top; but there was no sign of the *tchae-khana*. When a confused Clark asked one of the villagers where it was, he replied that there had never been a *tchae-khana* in the village in all the time he had lived there, and that was forty years.

There are a number of stories of this type in the literature of the supernatural: a beautiful house or quaint hotel (or splendid restaurant) encountered on a certain day, and for ever lost afterwards, in spite of all attempts to find it again. There have been several explanations put forward to account for experiences such as this. According to one, the percipients actually enter a ghostly realm in which the building in question exists in a timeless state; another theory has it that there is nothing ghostly about the building and that the percipient is somehow drawn backwards in time to when the building existed, to interact with objects and people during the relatively brief period in which the timeslip occurs.

Although we have absolutely no reason to doubt that Tony Clark was telling the truth exactly as he remembered it, we must accept that the emphasis should be on the phrase 'as he remembered it'. With stories of this kind, one is forced to wonder exactly how accurate a person's memory can be after roughly forty years. Indeed, we already know that, contrary to what many believe, memory itself is *not* a 100-per-cent-accurate information storage and retrieval system. When we remember past events, we are not accessing the events themselves: rather, our brains are creating an artificial representation of those events. It is an unfortunate fact that, over a period of years, each successive recreation of the events will become less and less accurate, until, at a remove of decades, the memories may bear scant resemblance to the original events.

In Tony Clark's case, we must wonder if he did indeed have a splendid meal in a *tchae-khana*, but in a location other than that which he remembers. Of course, Clark himself would probably deny such a lapse in memory, and it must be admitted that neither you nor I were with him on that day, so we are ill qualified to say with any certainty precisely what happened. In the end, Tony Clark's experience will doubtless remain as unexplained for us as it is for him.

FRIEND-OF-A-FRIEND STORIES

As mentioned earlier, the 'phantom hitchhiker' has entered the realm of modern folklore. Tales of people picked up on lonely roads by good Samaritans, who turn to speak to their passengers only to find themselves alone in their vehicles, are usually known as 'friend-of-a-friend' stories: third-hand accounts that are almost certainly spurious. These amusing but apocryphal tales include the one in which a woman is driving home from work and is unnerved by a man driving close behind her, flashing his headlights. When she finally arrives home, dashes from her car and heads for her front door, the car behind screeches to a halt, as the rear door of the woman's car opens and another man runs away. The man in the car behind explains to the woman that he noticed a figure with a knife through the rear windscreen of the woman's car, which would periodically rise up from the back seat. It turns out that it was only the flashing of headlights that prevented the knifeman from killing the woman.

I have also experienced an interesting friend-of-a-friend story. A few years ago, I was working in a factory in Sheffield in the north of England. One morning, a man I worked with told me that that very morning, his friend had told him of a terrifying experience he had endured while on his way to work. It seems that his car broke down, and while he was standing with his head under the bonnet, another car pulled up, containing several young men. One of the men offered to hook up a rope between the cars and tow the man to work. Since he was already late, the man gratefully agreed. However, it turned out that the young men in the other car were joyriders who had just stolen it. They proceeded to tow the man through the city at speeds of up to 80 m.p.h., swerving in and out of traffic, and leaving the unfortunate factory worker a nervous wreck by the time they had finished.

I listened to this story with interest, assuming that it was true (which it may well have been: after all, it was supposed to have happened that very morning). For this reason, I saw no reason to ask the man's name, or to talk to him about the alleged incident. It was only when I later moved to the south of England that I realized that something was not quite right. I was having a drink with another friend of mine, when he mentioned that the very same thing had happened to someone he vaguely knew.

It seems unlikely that both incidents could actually have occurred. For one thing, the scenario has one of the essential elements in modern folklore: the twist in the tale. The stranded motorist accepts a favour, only to discover that it is offered with the intention of giving him a serious fright. (The woman motorist thinks she is being followed by a maniac, only to discover that he is trying to warn her of the real maniac in her back seat.)

Since I didn't speak to the man in Sheffield about his experience, I have no idea whether it actually happened; it could, conceivably, have been the initial, genuine occurrence that gives rise to subsequent apocryphal tales, or it could itself have been apocryphal. I may never know, as they say.

However spurious such tales may be, the idea of the motorist who encounters something strange, or terrifying, or both, has a rich provenance in the literature on ghosts and spirits. We must ask ourselves whether these apparently genuine ghostly encounters constitute the origin of the phantom hitchhiker legend or whether they are themselves another element in that legend.

THE GHOST OF BLUE BELL HILL

On Sunday 8 November 1992, Ian Sharpe was driving along the A229 towards Maidstone, Kent, in the south-east of England. It was about midnight when he passed the turn-off for Aylesford at Blue Bell Hill. Suddenly, a young woman appeared directly in front of his car and ran towards it. There was no time to stop or swerve, and in the instant before she disappeared under the front of his car, Sharpe locked eyes with the woman illuminated by his headlights.

Sharpe skidded to a halt and, with lead in his stomach, opened his door and climbed out into the pitch-black night. He said: 'I honestly thought I had killed her. You can't imagine how I felt. I was so scared to look underneath, but I knelt down and looked straight through – there was nothing there.'

Thinking that the poor woman might have crawled from under the car and on to the side of the road, Sharpe searched the bushes near by; but the woman seemed to have disappeared. Sharpe tried to flag down two cars, neither of which stopped; so, reluctantly, he climbed back into his own vehicle and drove to Maidstone police station, where he informed them that he had run over a woman but could not find the body.

The police were aware of the stories associated with Blue Bell Hill, and told Sharpe that a ghost was said to haunt the area. Understandably enough Sharpe was adamant that he had indeed run someone over, and asked the police to return with him to the spot. They did so, but none of them found the woman's body. Neither was there any damage to the front of Sharpe's car, which would have been expected, had he hit someone at speed. Ian Sharpe spent the next few days waiting for the police to turn up at his house and inform him that the woman's body had been discovered.

Two weeks later, nineteen-year-old Christopher Dawkins was driving through the area on his way to Maidstone, when he had an identical encounter with a young woman who dashed into the road directly in front of his car. Like Ian Sharpe, Dawkins could not avoid striking the girl, but once again, there was no sign of a body, in spite of a search by both Dawkins and the police.

As the police had mentioned to Ian Sharpe, his ghostly encounter near Blue Bell Hill was not without precedent. In July 1974, a bricklayer named Maurice Goodenough knocked over a young girl who appeared in the road in front of his car. Goodenough carried the injured girl, who appeared to be about ten years old, to the side of the road, wrapped her in a car blanket and rushed to the nearest police station to report what had happened. When the police accompanied him to the scene of the accident, they found the blanket, but no girl.

Goodenough described her as wearing a white blouse, white ankle socks and a skirt; she had cuts on her forehead and knees. Armed with this description, the police launched a search for the girl throughout the area, but she was never found.

It seems that one likely candidate for the ghost of Blue Bell Hill is Judith Rochester. On the evening of Friday 19 November 1965, Judith was trying on some bridesmaid's dresses, in preparation for the wedding of a friend which was to be held the following day. After they had finished trying on the dresses, she and some friends set off in their Ford Cortina to meet the bride's fiancé at a local pub. On Blue Bell Hill the Cortina collided with an oncoming Jaguar. Exactly what happened next is not quite as clear as might be expected.

Writing in *Fortean Times* Number 73, Sean Tudor gives us a brief rundown of the variations in the accident's details:

Oft-repeated variations hold that Judith was the bride-to-be, or was driving, or that she and her two passengers were killed instantly. A different story was unearthed by reporter Mike Ridley who researched it for *The Sun* (26 November 1992). According to the records he found, the driver and bride-to-be was 23-year-old Susan Browne who lived for five days after the crash. Judith, aged 22, died the day after the accident. One girl, Patricia Ferguson, also 23, died outright, and a fourth, Gillian Burchett, recovered from her injuries after months in hospital. Her father told Ridley that Gillian, now fifty, has never spoken of the crash. 'I don't reckon that what motorists see is Judith. I don't think my daughter does either.'

Tudor points out that there a number of elements common to reports of spectral jaywalkers and phantom hitchhikers, and lists them as follows:

- the ostensibly real, transport-focused apparition – often, but not exclusively a young woman in white or pale clothing
- the high incidence of lone motorists

- the nonsensical behaviour and sudden disappearance of the figure – whether an accident victim or hitchhiking passenger, the effect on the witness is the same
- the apparent conformity to the anniversary sub-motif, even in the Blue Bell Hill case of 1992 [in which the two sightings fall either side of the anniversary date, 19 November].

There is, however, a striking difference between the average tale of a phantom hitchhiker and that of a spectral jaywalker: there is almost always far more corroborative evidence in the latter than in the former. As we have seen from the Blue Bell Hill case, when a motorist thinks he or she has run over a pedestrian, the police are immediately notified, only to search the area in vain for the victim. Phantom hitchhiker reports are much more anecdotal in nature and are rarely corroborated by anyone besides the percipient. With this in mind, it is important to point to a distinction between phantom hitchhikers and spectral jaywalkers. The former seem more capable of interacting with the percipient (opening the car door, for instance), while the latter seem more passive, in that they are acted upon (being run over).

In one particularly bizarre incident, reported in the 15 July 1988 edition of *The Sun*, a French lorry driver named Didier Chassagrande accidentally ran over an elderly cyclist in his thirty-eight-ton articulated vehicle. Chassagrande claimed to have dragged the horribly injured body to the side of the road before alerting the police. When they returned to the scene, the old man was nowhere to be found. However, they did find his torch, bicycle pump and false teeth!

As Tudor points out, we must never lose sight of the fact that hoaxing is always a possibility in these and other paranormal accidents.

What, then, might these people actually be seeing? Some sceptics have claimed that so-called 'highway hypnosis' is to blame. This occurs when a person is driving along a monotonous stretch of road at night or in otherwise poor light, and enters a light trance state, in which mundane objects such as road signs can be misinterpreted as human figures. Although highway hypnosis does undoubtedly occur (and has been suggested as a possible explanation for some alleged alien abductions), it cannot account for the similarities in description of the apparitions; nor are such encounters exclusively associated with particular locations (with the exception of Blue Bell Hill), which might be expected if a particular object was to blame for a number of hallucinations.

Finally, not all such apparitions are of apparent road accident victims. A certain stretch of motorway to the north-west of Sheffield, England, which was opened on Friday 13 May 1988, seems to be the site of a particularly malevolent phantom. The stretch of road has acquired a reputation for being extremely dangerous and has claimed eight lives since it was opened. While the official explanation for this disastrous record is that the road suffers from several design flaws, local residents blame the malevolent presence of a monk who died at Hunshelf Hall near by, whose request to be buried in Stannington was ignored. According to the legend, he was buried in unhallowed ground, which was disturbed when the stretch of road was built.

According to psychic June Beevers, several of her clients had reported an 'eerie presence' in their cars while travelling along the road. She herself once felt the presence of a large, black shadow in the seat beside her.

During the road's construction in 1987, two security guards at the site were reportedly terrified by a cloaked figure that floated above the ground. Policeman Dick Ellis was sent to investigate. In an interview with the *Weekly Trader* of 15 July 1993, Ellis stated: 'I got a brief sighting of it next to the car and then something banged on the back of the vehicle . . . my partner saw it as well and felt the same eerie feeling. I can't explain it. It was scary.' As with so many other paranormal events, both the phantom hitchhiker and the spectral jay-walker show no sign of surrendering to an easy explanation.

PSYCHIC VOYAGE

The following case is especially ambiguous with regard to what the percipient actually experienced, and it carries the striking implication that apparent psychic recordings may have more to do with the nature of time than with the physical structure of the matter on which any such recordings may have been made.

It was on some date in 1973 that a coin collector named Mr Squirrel made a trip to the English town of Great Yarmouth to buy some small envelopes in which to keep his coins. An acquaintance had recommended a certain stationer's shop that would undoubtedly have what he was looking for.

When Mr Squirrel arrived at the shop, he saw that the front had recently been repainted, and was very bright and clean. The same attention had not been paid to the interior, however, which looked very old and out of date. In addition, it had suddenly become inordinately quiet: the sounds of traffic outside had completely ceased. Presently, the shop assistant came out of the rear of the place. Mr Squirrel noted that she was perhaps in her early thirties and was wearing a long, black skirt. At the neck of her blouse was a cameo brooch. He asked her if she had any of the small envelopes he was looking for; she replied that she did, and that they were usually used by fishermen to store their hooks. Mr Squirrel bought three dozen of them and left the shop.

The following week, Mr Squirrel returned to Great Yarmouth to buy some more of the envelopes. When he arrived at the shop, he realized that something was not at all right: for one thing, the cobbles that had lain on the street on his first visit were now gone and in their place were paving stones. The façade of the shop, which had been newly and brightly painted only a week before, was now extremely drab and in obvious need of smartening up.

Rather bemused, Mr Squirrel entered the shop, where he

immediately saw that the interior was likewise somewhat different from before; much of the previous stock had gone, and when the shop assistant appeared, Mr Squirrel was surprised to see a woman in her fifties. When he enquired about the young woman in her thirties who had served him last time, the assistant replied that there was no such person, and that she had worked there for years as the only assistant. Mr Squirrel decided to leave the matter aside and asked for some more of the envelopes he had purchased on his last visit. The assistant replied that the shop did not sell such envelopes, and never had done.

In her examination of the case, the researcher Joan Forman speculates that Mr Squirrel's experience might qualify as an instance of a timeslip, a temporary contact between two different zones of time. In view of the fact that material objects had been passed from a period apparently early in the century to 1973, it became obvious that the envelopes Mr Squirrel bought on his first visit to the shop were of crucial importance in the testing of this theory.

Fortunately, Mr Squirrel had one envelope left, which was sent for analysis by the manufacturers, who concluded that they had been made just ten years or so earlier. Joan Forman concluded from this, quite sensibly, that a timeslip was therefore unlikely as an explanation for Mr Squirrel's curious experience. In their *Encyclopedia of Ghosts and Spirits*, John and Anne Spencer mention another theory that was put forward: that of 'family memory'. Mr Squirrel's grandfather had also been a coin collector, and it seems that he, too, had visited Great Yarmouth. Was it possible, therefore, that he had actually visited the shop decades before and that his impression of the place had somehow been transmitted down through the years to Mr Squirrel?

The Spencers also offer the unavoidable suggestion that Mr Squirrel had unwittingly entered a different shop in another street on his first visit to Great Yarmouth, resulting in a quite genuine confusion between the two places on his part.

Be that as it may, the complete absence of sound he mentioned remains intriguing. Zones of silence and feelings of unreality are common elements in paranormal encounters, especially sightings of UFOs and alien entities. The British ufologist Jenny Randles has coined the term 'Oz Factor' to describe such feelings, in which the percipient experiences an apparent dislocation from what he or she would consider 'normal reality'. Some commentators have suggested that the Oz Factor is a sign that the percipient has entered an altered state of consciousness, which may be caused by the nature or activities of the paranormal entities encountered, or which may have a cause within the human mind itself, and which allows it access to a realm that is at once separate from, yet coterminous with our world.

Mr Squirrel's strange first visit to the stationer's in Great Yarmouth therefore contains at least one element that prevents it from being easily explained.

THE HAUNTED AIRFIELD

Bircham Newton Airfield, in Kings Lynn, Norfolk, England, was built at the beginning of the First World War, and also saw duty throughout the Second World War. At the end of that conflict, the site was purchased by a training company involved in the construction industry. The old airfield buildings were renovated and converted to a hotel, squash courts, a studio for producing management training films and various other uses.

In 1972, two men were having a game of squash, when one of them saw a man dressed in a RAF uniform looking down at them from the observation gallery above the court. The squash player pointed the figure out to his friend, and they both watched in astonishment as the airman walked along the gallery and disappeared through the doorway at the far end. The only explanation that the two men could come up with was that they had seen a ghost, and they quickly decided that it would be an interesting experiment to stay in the squash court that night, with a tape recorder.

They procured a tape recorder and were preparing to settle in for the night, when they heard loud footsteps echoing through the building. This convinced them that it might be a better idea to go home and leave the tape recorder running. Then they locked the building (apparently with the only key) and went home.

The following day, they returned to the building containing the squash courts and played the tape. Incredibly, the tape had recorded the apparent sounds of a fully functioning airfield, complete with the voices of male and female personnel, the sounds of machinery moving around and the sound of an aircraft flying low overhead, although enquiries later established that no aircraft had flown anywhere near the place at the time of the recording. As if this were not chilling enough, the tape also contained 'strange unearthly groaning noises'.

The tape was sent to the BBC for analysis, and the engineer who examined it could find no faults; neither had the tape been used before, so the likelihood of previous recordings being responsible was ruled out. It was also noted that the sounds were unlikely to have been made outside the building, since its walls were nine inches thick, and almost certainly would have completely muffled and distorted any such noises.

A reporter from the BBC television programme *Nationwide* spent a night in the squash court, armed with her own tape recorder. Although she was alone in the building, she heard doors banging and noticed a sudden drop in the temperature. She also reported that her tape recorder had stopped, for no apparent reason, at 12.30 a.m.

The next person to investigate was a medium, who went into a trance and described how an Avro Anson aircraft had crashed near by, killing its three crewmen. Apparently, the reason they were haunting the site of the airfield was that they did not realize they were dead.

This has often been suggested as an explanation for hauntings. If a person dies suddenly, he or she may enter the putative afterlife without realizing that any such transition has taken place. Indeed, it will be recalled that, according to Robert Monroe, 'Locale II' is virtually indistinguishable from our own world of mundane matter. If this is the case, and Locale II is the 'point of entry' to the afterlife, then many ghosts may be just as eager to leave the sites of their hauntings as the living are to see the back of them . . .

THE GHOST OF FLIGHT 401

Ghosts and spirits are most often associated with the distant past, with times and places long obscured by decades or even centuries of memory and history. The bearded and bedraggled ancient rattling his chains, the cowled and faceless monk forever separated from God, the soldier doomed to re-enact the battle that killed him, all emerge from the mists of a time before our own cynical, technology-worshipping, post-industrial era. And yet, in the tale of the ghost of Flight 401, we can see that an environment of high technology is just as susceptible to supernatural influences as the most ancient castle.

It was on the evening of Friday 29 December that Eastern Airlines Flight 401, *en route* from New York to Miami, ploughed into the Florida Everglades, killing 101 passengers and crew. The doomed aircraft was a Lockheed L-1011 TriStar, captained by Bob Loft who, along with flight engineer Second Officer Don Repo, was among the dead. Not long after the crash, rumours began to circulate through the civil aviation community that some strange things were happening on other planes, rumours which eventually came to the attention of investigative journalist John G. Fuller. Originally, Fuller had intended to investigate the rumours in the context of modern folklore, and the ways in which legends are created and developed through time. However, the more in-depth his research became and the more people he interviewed, the greater became his conviction that the rumours were based on actual supernatural events.

The interviews were conducted with numerous pilots, flight attendants and ground crew, who unfortunately wished to remain anonymous, for fear of reprisals from their employers. Fuller subsequently published his best-selling book *The Ghost of Flight 401*, which contained numerous admittedly anecdotal accounts of sightings of and even conversations with the apparent ghosts of Bob Loft and Don Repo.

When the wreckage of Flight 401 was retrieved, some of the components were recycled for use in other L-1011s; the plane which received the most of them was #318. On one occasion, a female passenger was sitting in the first-class section of plane #318, next to a man wearing the uniform of an Eastern Airlines flight officer. The man was pale and seemed rather unwell, which prompted the woman to ask him if he was feeling all right. When the man failed to answer her, she called a flight attendant, who asked the officer the same question. At this point, several other passengers had noticed what was happening. In full view of all, the flight officer vanished, sending the female passenger who had been sitting next to him into a panic. Later, she was shown photographs of Eastern Airlines flight officers, in an effort to identify the man she had seen. She picked out the face of Don Repo.

On another occasion, a flight engineer entered the flight deck of an L-1011 with the intention of performing a pre-flight inspection, only to discover an Eastern Airlines second officer sitting at the engineering panel. The man at the panel turned and said: 'You don't need to worry about the pre-flight. I've already done it.' He then vanished. Indeed, safety seems to have been the main reason for the hauntings, since another captain reported a conversation with Repo in which he had said that 'they' (presumably he and Bob Loft) would never let another L-1011 crash.

According to Fuller's findings, even Eastern Airlines executives had encountered the ghosts. A vice-president of the company boarded an L-1011 at John F. Kennedy Airport, bound for Miami. Upon entering the first-class section, he saw an Eastern Airlines captain and began a conversation with him. While they were talking, the president (who refused to allow his name to be revealed) realized that the officer was Bob Loft. The apparition of the dead captain then vanished.

Apart from these 'full-form' apparitions, there were a number of yet more bizarre reports of officers' faces appearing throughout the L-1011 fleet. One flight attendant was checking the first-class section and opened an overhead compartment to see Bob Loft's face staring back at her. Another attendant opened an oven door in the galley and saw Don Repo's face inside.

Back on plane #318, which was flying from New York to Mexico City, a flight attendant saw Repo's face in an oven window. She immediately called another attendant and the flight engineer, and all three then watched as the apparition said to them: 'Watch out for fire on this airplane', before vanishing. The plane landed safely at Mexico City, but when it took off again, one of the engines backfired and had to be shut down. The plane immediately returned to Mexico City and was withdrawn from service. When the malfunctioning engine was disassembled, nothing was found to be wrong with it.

In an attempt to communicate with Loft and Repo, John Fuller set up a ouija board, and received two messages from Don Repo. One was: 'Did mice leave that family closet?' The other was: 'To go into waste basket pennies sit there boys room.' These apparently nonsensical communications were later explained by Repo's family. The first seemed to refer to some mice that had been in the attic above the family room in the Repo home. Access to the attic was through the closet in the family room. The second communication apparently referred to Don Repo's collection of Indian head pennies, which were kept in a barrel in his son's room.

While the tale of the ghosts of Flight 401 is one of the most fascinating on record, many commentators have complained about the highly anecdotal nature of the evidence, not to mention the near total anonymity insisted upon by those involved. While this may have been unavoidable, it has nevertheless made it impossible for any further research into the case to be conducted by other researchers.

According to Peter Underwood (in *Guide to Ghosts & Haunted Places*), who talked extensively with Fuller about the case, the president of Eastern Airlines rejected the story,

> but liaison executive Doris Ahnstrom said that published reports of the appearance of the ghost of the flight engineer appeared in a safety bulletin in 1974, long before Fuller's book [which was published in 1976]. These followed reports received by an experienced and trustworthy pilot; the bulletin also contained the report of a stewardess who had seen the dead flight engineer.

RESURRECTION MARY

No one knows the name of the girl who died in a car accident in 1934, on her way home from a dance at the O. Henry Ballroom (now the Willowbrook) in the south-east area of Chicago, Illinois. However, she does have a nickname: 'Resurrection Mary', after Resurrection Cemetery in nearby Justice, Illinois. In the years since her death, she has appeared on numerous occasions in the area, sometimes exhibiting the attributes of a phantom hitchhiker.

Mary first began to appear in 1939, five years after her death. Motorists on their way to the O. Henry Ballroom reported that a young woman in an evening gown tried to jump on to the running boards of their cars; on other occasions she would hitch a lift and then dance with the unattached men there. She would offer vague replies when asked where she lived and those who touched her said her skin was as cold as ice.

At the end of an evening at the ballroom, the girl would be

offered lifts home and, like a phantom hitchhiker, she would vanish from the car as it passed Resurrection Cemetery. On other occasions, she would ask her escort to stop just before the cemetery, get out of the car and run towards the cemetery gates, only to vanish as she ran through them.

Mary also seemed to be possessed of colossal strength, as evidenced in one tale, in which a man passing Resurrection Cemetery noticed a girl peering out through the iron bars of the locked gates. Assuming that someone had accidentally been locked in when the cemetery closed that night, the man went to call the police. When they arrived, there was no one to be seen, but two of the bars on the gate had been bent completely out of shape. On closer inspection, two handprints, clearly belonging to a young woman, were found in the metal. (One has to wonder why the ghost would do such a thing, given that locked gates were no impediment to her.)

In 1975, Resurrection Cemetery was renovated, and this seems to have spurred Mary to greater activity. One encounter was reported in a Chicago newspaper and, perhaps because it is more recent, the report is a little more detailed than most. A cab driver was driving up Archer Avenue, not far from the cemetery, when he saw a young woman standing near the Old Willow Shopping Mall. It was January, there had been a heavy fall of snow, yet the girl had no coat. Assuming she had had car trouble, the cab driver stopped and asked if she needed help. Without a word, she climbed into the front seat beside him. She was dressed in an evening gown. She told the driver that she had to get home, and when he tried to engage her in further conversation, her responses became vague. One of her remarks was: 'The snow came early this year.'

A few miles further up Archer Avenue, the girl cried: 'Here!' The driver stopped his cab and looked out of his window in the direction she was pointing. There was nothing at the side of the road except a small, dilapidated shack. When the driver turned to ask her if this was really where she lived, he saw that his passenger had vanished. On the other side of the road from the shack stood the gates of Resurrection Cemetery.

THE OZARK SPOOK LIGHT

Mysterious balls of light have been seen on countless occasions throughout the world and are among the most puzzling of paranormal phenomena. Fortunately, they are also repetitious, as can be attested by the numerous qualified scientists who have been able to study them, as at Hessdalen in Norway, for instance. Perhaps the most famous, and frequently sighted, of these phenomena is the so-called Ozark Spook Light, which is sometimes referred to as the Hornet Spook Light or the Quapaw Spook Light.

The Spook Light was well known by native Americans, who considered it dangerous and to be avoided at all costs, and it has continued to be sighted throughout the centuries since the arrival of Europeans. The first recorded sighting was in 1836 and for the next century, travellers through south-western Missouri would see it moving through the foothills of Ozark Mountains. The first thought that came to witnesses' minds was that someone was walking the hills carying a lantern, but no one was ever able to get close enough to the light to be sure.

In the early years of the twentieth century, a couple named Dutch and Blanche were engaged to be married, and one evening were riding in Dutch's carriage towards Blanche's home in Quapaw, Oklahoma. As they were passing through a wood, they saw the Spook Light hanging in the air in front of them. Dutch moved in front of Blanche to protect her and they both watched as the light hovered for several minutes before moving off into the surrounding trees.

In their article on the Spook Light for *Fate* magazine, Wann Smith and William Equels describe a sighting made several decades later by the descendants of Dutch and Blanche Bilke:

Quapaw banker Joe Smith has seen the light on several occasions. His daughter, Josie Bilke (married to Dutch's grandson), lives in the middle of the Spook Light. 'One night she

(Josie) and her husband were in bed,' recounted Joe, 'when they thought someone had turned into their driveway. They looked out of the window and saw the light floating in their front yard.'

Since the Spook Light appears again and again with such regularity, it has been studied by various teams of researchers, including Smith and Equels, students from the University of Missouri and the US Army Corps of Engineers, who concluded (not very helpfully) that the light was of 'unknown origin'.

There have been a number of other explanations put forward to account for the Ozark Spook Light and its cousins in other parts of the world. One theory is that people are seeing car headlights which are refracted in the atmosphere, although this does not explain what Josie Bilke and her husband saw in their driveway.

Another interesting theory is that the lights are caused by mineral deposits. According to Smith and Equels:

Since the Spook Light area is rich in lead and zinc deposits, some people have speculated that the light could be caused by mineral glow. A state policeman from Quapaw said, 'The light simply is from diggings left over from the mining.' His opinion is shared by others who believe that the ghostlight is produced somehow by electrical action of these deposits.

A professor of Earth Sciences at a California university, himself an Ottawa County native, told residents of the area that the light is nothing more than minerals in the ground reflecting atmospheric conditions.

Yet it is unlikely that ground reflections could produce such a consistent and dramatic effect for well over a century and that this phenomenon could evade detection by scientific teams equipped with the knowledge and technical equipment to detect it.

Equally unlikely is the swamp gas theory, in which methane gas produced by decaying organic matter in swampy areas

213

spontaneously ignites, giving rise to the wandering light phenomena. Not only has no swamp gas ever been detected in the area frequented by the Spook Light, but the light is often seen to move against the wind.

A more interesting theory is that of ball lightning (which, like the mineral lights theory mentioned above, has been put forward as an explanation for some UFO sightings). Ball lightning is a self-contained electrical discharge which is extremely rare – so rare, in fact, that there is still some debate as to whether it exists at all. According to Keith Partain, who holds degrees in entomology and zoology, ball lightning could be linked to low sunspot activity, night-time and the spring and autumn equinoxes. However, this theory has met with opposition from other scientists, who consider it unlikely that sunspot activity could be responsible for ball lightning in a relatively small area such as that haunted by the Spook Light.

It has also been suggested that the light is a hoax perpetrated by someone holding a lantern. In view of the fact that numerous witnesses have shot at the light, this would seem a suicidally stupid prank to play.

THE PHANTOM HIGHWAYMAN

On the evening of 28 December 1967, John Watson was taking part in a rally near Denton, Lincolnshire, England. Also in the car were his mother and a navigator. The trio had just passed Belvoir Castle south of Denton, when Watson suddenly saw a shadowy figure on horseback crossing the path of the car. As Watson stamped on the brake pedal, he realized that the figure was dressed as a highwayman of the eighteenth century, with cloak and tricorn hat.

The following year, John Watson organized another rally in the same area. By that time, news of his strange encounter had spread among his friends and acquaintances, and one, Pete Shenton, claimed that he too had seen the figure of the highwayman. Shenton had also been driving with a navigator and another passenger, and like Watson, had been the only person to see the apparition. In both cases, as soon as the driver hit the brakes, the apparition vanished from the road.

It is interesting, and probably significant, that the drivers were the only people in these cases to see the highwayman; in addition, the fact that the apparition vanished when they hit the brakes also seems important. As we saw earlier in the cases of spectral jaywalkers, highway hypnosis might well provide an answer to this particular mystery. The drivers were obviously concentrating very hard on the road ahead, which might have resulted in a slightly altered state of consciousness, a state not shared by the passengers, who would have been concentrating rather less intensely on the road.

However, in *Encyclopedia of Ghosts and Spirits* John and Anne Spencer speculate intriguingly that: 'Rather than the apparition being a product of highway hypnosis, perhaps highway hypnosis itself creates a state where a genuine external event can be perceived as a result of the altered state of consciousness.' In these circumstances, it is at least conceivable that the highway hypnosis results in the percipient becoming, for want of a better expression, psychically sensitive for a brief period. This would go some way toward explaining the fact that the two percipients, Watson and Shenton, 'saw' fundamentally similar apparitions, which would seem unlikely were they the victims of straightforward highway hypnosis, in which no external event was involved.

THE HAUNTED CAR

Sometime in the 1970s or 1980s (the exact date is hard to pin down), a sixteen-year-old boy named Martin bought himself a battered old Ford Anglia car, with the intention of restoring it in time for his seventeenth birthday, the age at which he could legally begin driving lessons. He put the car in his parents' garage and devoted all his spare time to it, so that ten months later what had been an old banger was now as good as new. Martin had spent all his money on spare parts for the car and was about to begin work on repairing its electrical system.

One Saturday, Martin's friend Stephen called at the house and they went out for a ride on Stephen's motorbike. Martin's parents were always deeply worried when they did this, since they considered motorbikes dangerous; indeed, they had been immensely relieved when Martin had decided to opt for a car. Later that afternoon, their worst fears were realized when the police called at their house to inform them that there had been an accident, in which Stephen had been badly injured and Martin killed. Although utterly devastated by the tragedy, Martin's mother decided that they should not sell Martin's Anglia and that it should be kept as a memory of their son.

As they struggled to come to terms with their grief over the days that followed, Martin's parents became aware of odd sounds coming from the garage at night. Even more strangely, the bangings and shufflings would cease as soon as the couple concentrated on listening to them. Martin's mother became more and more distraught at the thought of what might be making the sounds, so one night her husband rushed into the garage to investigate. As soon as they entered the dark garage, he heard what sounded like a spanner being dropped on the concrete floor. Snapping on the light, he looked around, but could find no one there; neither were there any tools on the floor. However, the bonnet of the car was open and Martin's father was absolutely certain that it had been closed the last time he had been in the garage.

They had booked a holiday in Spain shortly before Martin's death, and had been trying to decide whether or not to go. Now it seemed like a good idea to get away from the house for a while, so they took the holiday. When they returned home, their neighbours told them that they had been concerned about the sounds coming from the garage. The lights had been on both there and in the house, and they had called the police three times to check for burglars. None was found, but the police did find the bonnet of the car open again.

Presently, the day they had been dreading arrived: Martin's seventeenth birthday, the day on which he would have finished his work on the car and started his driving lessons. That afternoon, they heard of the sound of the Anglia's engine starting and Martin's father rushed into the garage. There was still no one there, but the engine was running. When he reached in to turn the engine off, he saw that the keys were not in the ignition. He telephoned the nearest garage and asked them to send someone to check the car.

About fifteen minutes later, the engine suddenly died, although it would later be established that there was still petrol in the tank. At that moment, Martin's mother glanced towards the rear of the garage and saw her son smiling at her. He said: 'Look Mum, I've done it!'

A mechanic arrived soon after and inspected the car. He came to the conclusion that there must have been a short circuit in the wiring, which resulted in the engine starting. Strangely, though, most of the ignition wires had not yet been connected; neither had the choke cable.

The strange sounds stopped that day, perhaps because Martin's ghost had all but completed work on the restoration of the car. Martin's parents subsequently sold the car to one of his friends, who connected the ignition wires and choke cable, and found that the Anglia ran smoothly.

The case was investigated by Professor Colin Gardner of the Institute for Psychical Research, who learned from Martin's parents that the car had started up at precisely 2.15 p.m., the moment at which he was born. Professor Gardner had been alerted to the apparent haunting by one of the neighbours, who had got in touch with the Institute after seeing a young man leave Martin's house and walk through the closed garage door.

This case is an interesting variation on the so-called 'anniversary haunting', in which an apparition (in many cases a psychic recording) appears over and over again on a date which was significant to the person while alive. In Martin's case, however, the ghostly activity seemed to be occurring *in preparation* for an anniversary, and seemed also to include an interaction between the ghost and its environment – specifically, the car. Indeed, it seems to have been the opposite of a poltergeist haunting, in that an object was repaired instead of being broken or damaged.

FLIGHT INTO THE IMPOSSIBLE

In July 1941, an RAF pilot named Jimmy Corfield returned home on leave. During his stay, his seventeen-year-old brother, Bill, told him of his ambition to become a pilot just like his brother, whom he held in great esteem. Jimmy, however, was less than enthusiastic; knowing of the short life-expectancy of fighter and bomber pilots, he told his younger brother that he would be better off getting a ground job with the RAF.

On 12 August 1941, Jimmy Corfield took part in a daylight bombing raid on two factories near Cologne. In all, forty-four Blenheim bombers flew against the enemy in the surprise attack, which had been ordered by Churchill in order to undermine Hitler's movement against Russia. Their mission accomplished, the Blenheims were returning home when they were attacked both by ground forces and aircraft, and twelve Blenheims were shot down, including Jimmy Corfield's plane. The bodies of Jimmy and his crew were later washed up on an island just off the Dutch coast.

When Bill Corfield learned of his beloved brother's death, he resolved there and then to become a pilot. After completing his training, he flew Wellington and Lancaster bombers. After the war ended, he decided to stay in the RAF, and was posted to No. 1 Ferry Unit at Pershore. On 12 January 1947, Bill was assigned to fly an Anson aircraft to Singapore, a lengthy journey that would necessitate making several stops, including France, Italy and Greece.

Bill and his crew were preparing to proceed to Athens and carefully checked the weather conditions, which looked promising. The Anson was a small aircraft, which did not carry a great deal of fuel. Consequently, there was a 'point of no return' between Italy and Greece, beyond which the aircraft had just enough fuel to reach its destination (but not enough to make it back to Italy). When the Anson had passed this point, it ran into a severe thunderstorm, which forced Bill to reduce altitude to about fifty feet.

The other two crew members, the navigator and the radio operator, were with Bill in the cockpit, and together they searched for any identifiable landmarks – a hopeless task, since visibility was virtually zero. Eventually, they managed to discern the Greek coast, and Bill banked to port and flew along it. The navigator pointed out the Corinth Canal and, acting on instinct, Bill turned the plane into the opening. As they were flying through the canal, all three crew members became aware of an extraordinary peace and total silence. In addition, the aircraft was for some reason no longer buffeted by the storm and was flying in a perfectly straight line. In an interview with John and Anne Spencer reported in *Encyclopedia of Ghosts and Spirits*, Bill Corfield said: 'I knew – *absolutely and without a doubt* – that my brother was with me in the aircraft. I was as natural as I am talking to you now. There was nothing physical, but he was there.'

Bill relaxed his grip on the controls and allowed his brother to take over the flying of the Anson. In the cloying darkness of the storm, they flew down the canal for four miles, finally emerging safely at the far end, whereupon Jimmy Corfield's presence or influence left the aircraft. Their problems were far from over, however: the aircraft was almost out of fuel, visibility was still close to zero and they had now left behind their only landmark. Suddenly, Bill turned the aircraft once again, not knowing the reason, and moments later they saw the lights of Athens, their destination.

They touched down and taxied to a halt as the port engine, out of fuel, sputtered to a stop. The following day the Anson's crew found themselves in trouble with their superiors, who suspected that they had been smuggling, an activity that was frequently engaged in in the years following the war. The main reason for this suspicion was the sheer implausibility of their story regarding their flight through the Corinth Canal. The walls of the canal were only seventeen feet wider than the wingspan of the Anson, a minute clearance that would have made such a flight virtually impossible even in ideal conditions. In the midst of a violent thunderstorm, there was simply no conceivable way that the flight could have been achieved . . . at least, without supernatural aid.

BLACK DOGS AND OTHER GHOSTLY ANIMALS

The modern tales of phantom hitchhikers and spectral jay-walkers seem to have a historical provenance in the numerous legends of strange, apparently supernatural animals encountered by travellers in lonely and isolated places. Although such creatures are still occasionally reported today, the most interesting accounts originate decades or even centuries ago.

One tale from earlier this century concerns a friend of the folklorist Dermot A. MacManus, who had a terrifying encounter at Easter in 1928. Mr Martin, a student at Trinity College, Dublin, was enjoying a fishing holiday in County Londonderry, when he saw a large black dog approaching him through the shallows of the river. As he regarded the approaching animal, some intuition told him that he should not stay where he was, that the animal was somehow malevolent. Downing his fishing rod, he made for the nearest tree and clambered up into the branches.

The dog continued its leisurely approach, passing the spot at which Martin had been fishing, and finally came to a halt beneath the tree in which he had taken refuge. The creature then looked up at him and began to snarl. However, this was not what most terrified the student, for the dog's eyes were glowing bright red, like live coals. Understandably, the young man decided to stay where he was, and presently the enormous dog (if that is what it was) continued on its way, padding along through the shallow water until eventually it disappeared into the distance.

It seems that black dogs such as this one haunt the landscape right across the British Isles, as well as many countries in Europe and in the United States. In *Daimonic Reality: a Field Guide to the Otherworld*, Patrick Harpur describes the apparent ubiquity of these bizarre creatures:

> The black dogs of Lancashire and Yorkshire are known as Barguest, Trash and Striker. Trash makes a sound like heavy shoes splashing through mud; Striker screams. In Staffordshire it is called Padfoot; in Warwickshire, Hooter. But it is not only British. Reports of black dogs are also found in France, Italy, Croatia, Germany and Austria. In the USA they are seen mostly in Pennsylvania, Mississippi and Missouri – where, in Peniscot county, for instance, some hunters threw an axe at an eight-foot-long black dog. The axe passed through it and stuck in a tree. In Nova Scotia, Canada's prime black dog country, the one often seen at Rous' Brook sometimes appears only as a bright light, but can seem rather more substantial: a man who was emboldened by strong drink to face the thing that was following him was pounced on and nearly choked to death. 'It looked like a black dog,' he said, 'but when it got [me] by the throat it seemed more like a person.'

The black dogs are characterized by dreadful power and fearfulness, although this reputation is not (as we shall soon see) always deserved. An example of just how malevolent and destructive they can be is given in the record of an event which occurred in August 1577 in the village of Bungay in Suffolk, England. The village folk were attending a morning service in the church when suddenly, an enormous black dog appeared out of thin air in the aisle and set about attacking the congregation, two of whom were killed outright and a third badly burned. The creature vanished as suddenly as it had appeared, and shortly afterwards it (or another creature very like it) appeared in the church of the nearby village of Blythburgh. Apparently it chose a more orthodox way of departing, bursting out through the church doors, upon which it left scorch marks in the shape of its claws – marks that remain on the door to this day.

In addition to their antipathy towards humans, however, black dogs have also been known to offer protection, especially to women travelling alone at night. Patrick Harpur gives an example:

> Early this century, a woman walking home from Scunthorpe to Crosby in Lincolnshire 'found herself accompanied by a strange dog as she passed a group of [so-called] Irish labourers who were saying what they would have done to her if the dog weren't with her'. In the same county, in the thirties, a schoolmistress who often cycled at night along a lonely lane near Manton was frequently accompanied by a very large dog trotting along the grass verge. Its presence reassured her.

Harpur goes on to make some interesting speculations on what the black dogs might actually be:

> They are the ghosts of dogs, some say, or ghosts of the dead taking animal form. In earlier times ... they were thought of as a manifestation of the Devil or, at least, as witches' familiars. They certainly possess ... an archetypal resonance which echoes the black dogs that guard treasure in fairy tales, and extends all the way back to such mythical dogs as triple-headed Cerberos who guards the Underworld. In Celtic cultures they fit naturally into the usual fairy framework, whether as the Isle of Man's Buggane or Moddy Dhoe, or as the Scottish Highlands' *cu sith*. In Ireland, black dogs are only one of many fairy creatures.

Black dogs are not the only 'mystery animals' to have been encountered over the years. There have been numerous sightings of large puma-like cats in many parts of the British Isles, although few of these seem to have supernatural attributes, and it is more than likely that escapes from zoos and private collections account for the vast majority of sightings. Altogether more puzzling are the 'creatures' described by investigator Jonathan Downes as 'zooform phenomena', meaning entities that have the appearance of animals, but which seem to have a supernatural origin.

For instance, on the eve of the battle of Culloden in 1746, a terrifying monster appeared in the sky above the field. The shrieking thing (which came to be known as the 'Skree') had a human head with glowing red eyes and enormous, leathery wings. In his book *The Unexplained*, cryptozoologist Dr Karl Shuker gives another example of the kind of monster travellers may encounter:

> . . . a monstrous horse-like beast with the face of an evil, leering man . . . blocked the path of John Farrell and Margaret Johnson for almost two minutes as they drove along a lonely road near Drogheda in County Louth, Eire, one spring evening in 1966. Only when it suddenly disappeared were its two terrified witnesses able to continue their journey. Irish tradition tells of a fearful supernatural creature called the pooka, which often assumes the guise of a malevolent horse.

As Shuker says, it may be that there are certain areas in Britain – not to mention the rest of the world – where myths are able to become reality. On the other hand, perhaps the myths of the world are based on real events involving real entities, which even now have the power to manifest themselves in lonely places, far from our comfortable urban environment.

GHOST PILOTS ON THE ISLE OF WIGHT

The aviation journalist and historian Alexander McKee investigated several ghostly sightings on the Isle of Wight, off the southern coast of England, which he included in his fascinating book of air mysteries, *Into the Blue*. McKee and his wife visited Mrs Violet Brown and her husband Hubert on the island, and were told some intriguing tales of a ghostly pilot which had been seen a number of times in the area.

McKee reports that as soon as he and his wife were shown into the Browns' drawing room, they both felt compelled to stand at a window in the adjoining sunlounge, which looked on to the garden. As the Browns began to tell of their experiences, it became clear that the window in the sunlounge was significant, which may have accounted for the McKees' having been drawn to it, although they felt no sense of the supernatural at the time. The Browns' first encounter with the unexplained in their house occurred in late 1975 or early 1976. Mrs Brown said that between 9.30 and 10.30 p.m., she became aware of what she called a 'loud silence', followed by the sound of a large prop-driven aircraft, perhaps a bomber, flying overhead. She then felt her attention drawn to the window in the sunlounge, through which she could see a figure, 'six feet tall, curly hair. Wearing bomber jacket and dark tie.' After standing there for fifteen minutes, the figure disappeared. Although the figure appeared to be perfectly solid (as with the vast majority of ghost sightings), Mrs Brown had the impression that he was somehow 'insubstantial'. When McKee asked her if she had been able to sense anything of the figure's emotions, she replied that she had not, but had the feeling that he wanted to impart some information. She then added: 'What struck me most was his face. The curly hair was distinct, but the face was blank, there was no expression at all.'

Hubert Brown was at that time working the Cunard shipping line, and so spent a fair time away from home, but he also saw the figure on several occasions and also commented that the pilot's head was somehow obscured. He described it as being 'foggy'. Interestingly, this attribute has often been described by ghost percipients; for some reason, the ghost's face is never as distinct as the rest of the figure.

McKee also spoke to the Browns' son, Garry, who said that although he had never heard the bomber or seen the pilot, he had occasionally felt the presence of his grandmother in the house. Hubert reported several impressions of an evil entity following him around the house, a sensation he had also experienced at a place called Dame Anthony's Common on the island. There seemed to be some kind of connection between the appearance of the pilot, Hubert Brown's feelings of an evil presence and the evil atmosphere on Dame Anthony's Common, although McKee was uncertain as to precisely how they were connected.

He then recalled an incident that had occurred during the war, in which two Hawker Hurricane aircraft had collided in mid-air. Apparently, in November 1941, two Hurricanes had been called up from the airfield at Tangmere and had then been recalled. While one pilot received the message and turned back, the other had not, and kept to his flight path, with the tragic result that the two aircraft collided. One of the pilots parachuted to safety, although when local residents found him, he was wandering around in a state of shock. The other pilot died in his machine when it crashed to earth.

McKee speculates that perhaps the surviving pilot was killed later in the war and subsequently returned to search for his lost friend. However, this seemed unlikely to account for the presence of evil in the area, so McKee turned his attention to another report from the Second World War, in which a German Messerschmitt Me 110 was forced by British fighters to crash-land on Dame Anthony's Common. According to the story, both crew members survived the impact, but one was shot dead by members of the Channel Islands Militia and his body was left out for a week before being picked up. According to local resident Brian Warne, who was twelve at the time:

The Jersey and Guernsey Regiment were billeted 200 yards away at West Ashey Farm. One German got out. The other German was still in the plane, fiddling about. They thought he was going to fire it, so they shot him. Practically blew his head off. I don't know how many fired. I did not see this – it was the story they told. Of course, Jersey and Guernsey were occupied then.

It therefore seems at least conceivable that the German airman, who had been shot dead while his colleague was surrendering, was unable to rest in peace, and continued to haunt the scene of his death. Perhaps the sensation of evil for which Dame Anthony's Common has become notorious arises from the airman's anger at the manner of his death; and, the figure seen by the Browns outside their window is the spectre of the Hurricane pilot who was so distraught at the death of his friend, for which he perhaps felt responsible.

10

CASES YET MORE STRANGE

THE DEVIL'S FOOTPRINTS

The 'Devil's Footprints' were discovered in Devon, England, on the morning of 8 February 1855. It seems that during the night, something visited several towns in the area and left its footprints in the newly fallen snow. The London *Times* of 16 February reported:

Considerable sensation has been evoked in the towns of Topsham, Lympstone, Exmouth, Teignmouth, and Dawlish, in the south of Devon, in consequence of the discovery of a vast number of foot-tracks of a most strange and mysterious description. The superstitious go so far as to believe that they are the marks of Satan himself; and that great excitement has been produced among all classes may be judged from the fact that the subject has been descanted on from the pulpit.

It appears that on Thursday night last there was a heavy fall of snow in the neighbourhood of Exeter and the south of Devon. On the following morning, the inhabitants of the above towns were surprised at discovering the tracks of some strange and mysterious animal, endowed with the power of ubiquity, as the foot-prints were to be seen in all kinds of inaccessible places – on the tops of houses and narrow walls, in gardens and courtyards enclosed by high walls and palings, as well as in open fields. There was hardly a garden in Lympstone where the foot-prints were not observed.

The track appeared more like that of a biped than a quadruped, and the steps were generally eight inches in advance of each other. The impressions of the feet closely resembled that of a donkey's shoe, and measured from an inch and a half to (in some instances) two and a half inches across. Here and there it appeared as if cloven, but in the generality of the steps the shoe was continuous, and, from the snow in the centre remaining entire, merely showing the outer crest of the foot, it must have been convex.

The creature seems to have approached the doors of several houses and then to have retreated, but no one has been able to discover the standing or resting point of this mysterious visitor. On Sunday last the Rev. Mr Musgrave alluded to the subject in his sermon, and suggested the possibility of the foot-prints being those of a kangaroo; but this could scarcely have been the case, as they were found on both sides of the estuary of the [River] Exe.

At present it remains a mystery, and many superstitious people in the above towns are actually afraid to go outside their doors at night.

Perhaps wisely, *The Times* left it at that, and there was no follow-up on the subject from that paper. Although many theories were put forward to account for the bizarre set of footprints, which extended for roughly 100 miles through towns and countryside, none was entirely satisfactory.

The appearance of the Devil's Footprints remains virtually unique in the literature on the paranormal, with the single exception of a report made by Captain Sir James Clark Ross, who commanded two ships on a voyage of exploration in the Antarctic Circle in 1840. Captain Ross's comments on what he discovered on Kerguelen Island are cited by Jerome Clark in his book *Unexplained!*

Of land animals we saw none; and the only traces we could discover of their being any on this island were the singular foot-steps of a pony or ass, found by the party detached for surveying purposes, under the command of Lieutenant Bird, and described by Dr Robertson as 'being 3 inches in length and

$2\frac{1}{2}$ in breadth, having a small and deeper depression on each side, and shaped like a horseshoe'.

It is by no means improbable that the animal has been cast on shore from some wrecked vessel. They traced its footsteps for some distance in the recently fallen snow, in hopes of getting a sight of it, but lost the tracks on reaching a large space of rocky ground which was free from snow.

We can only speculate as to what caused the strange footprints in these two cases. Were they caused by some escaped animal, unlikely as that sounds (especially in the case of the remote Kerguelen Island)? Perhaps a hitherto unknown (but entirely natural) creature left them, although this is equally unlikely in the view of the belief that they had been caused by a biped, as opposed to quadruped. Perhaps a supernatural entity was to blame . . . even the Devil himself.

THOUGHT-FORMS

So far in this book we have, for the most part, examined ghosts and spirits in the context of deceased humans who, for various reasons, have returned to the physical world, to be perceived by those still living. At this point it is worth turning our attention to ghosts, spirits and other entities that have been 'raised' or otherwise created by human beings. Of course, the most obvious and well-known example of this is the religion of spiritualism, which was dealt with earlier in the book; but there are a number of other occult methods by which this has been achieved.

We can begin by examining what are known as 'thought-forms' or *tulpas*. These strange entites, while appearing solid and physically real, are actually created by the minds of those with sufficient knowledge and discipline to do so, hence the name. Although they are said by some to be visible only to clairvoyants, and are sensed intuitively by others who are less 'sensitive' to psychic manifestations, there is evidence to suggest that they may be directly perceived by anyone coming into contact with them.

According to the theories of the Theosophists (more of whom later), there are three types of thought-forms: first, there are those which are actually the three-dimensional image of the person thinking about them (which might account for some of the 'spirit doubles' we encountered earlier); second, there are images of inanimate objects created by the thinker; and third, and most interestingly, there are those thought-forms that exhibit an independent intelligence.

Within these categories, there are thought-forms which are differentiated by the emotions the thinker was experiencing at the time of their creation: thus base thoughts such as anger, lust and hatred produce forms that are characterized by dark, heavy colours and an appearance of great density, while those arising from a higher, spiritual cast of mind are the opposite, possessing great purity and clarity.

According to occult lore, thought-forms have the ability to interact with their environment, and thus can be used as powerful weapons against one's enemies in so-called 'psychic attacks'. However, if the form cannot attach itself to the psychic field or 'aura' generated by its target, it will return to victimize its creator. This is one reason why black magic is said to be so dangerous: the forces invoked can easily rebound on the magician, causing exactly the problems intended for the target of the attack.

The duration of thought-forms depends entirely on the strength and clarity of the mind that created them. Sometimes they may begin to draw energy from other sources, and may become entirely independent, developing their own intelligence and will. In these cases, they can exist for years, and it is interesting to speculate that some 'ghosts' may actually be independent thought-forms – especially the ghastly elemental creature said to have haunted 50 Berkeley Square (see p. 241). When a thought-form achieves independence from its creator, it can usually be destroyed only by thought of a comparable power to that which produced it. For the most part, however, they fade away once their purpose has been fulfilled.

In Tibetan occultism, thought-forms are known as *tulpas*. They are created for various purposes and are usually human in form. A striking report of a *tulpa* is that provided by the French author and Tibetan scholar, Alexandra David-Neel, who travelled widely in the East in the late nineteenth century, in her book *Magic and Mystery in Tibet*.

Having engaged in intense study with the lamas of Tibet, David-Neel decided to attempt the creation of a *tulpa*, despite the warning from a lama that the 'children of our mind' can become hard to control and thus dangerous. Mindful of this warning, she decided that it would be wise to create a character that was inherently harmless, and so she visualized a short, fat, jolly monk. It took her several months of both intense concentration and the practice of certain rituals before she was able to create the monk, who appeared exactly as she had visualized him and became a guest in her apartment.

When David-Neel decided to go on a trip, she took the monk, along with her servants and tents. While travelling, she would watch her *tulpa* with interest, and would see him performing 'various actions of the kind that are natural to travellers, and that I had not commanded'.

Eventually, however, the lama's warnings proved well founded, for the monk indeed began to wrest himself free of her control. A subtle physical alteration became apparent: he grew leaner, and his hitherto jolly face became malignant and mocking. He also developed the unsavoury habit of touching her and rubbing himself against her. Not surprisingly, David-Neel decided that enough was enough, and set about dispersing the *tulpa*, a process that proved much harder than she had anticipated. In fact, the monk's resistance to her plan meant that it took her six months of concentration and ritual to destroy him.

It has been suggested by some researchers that thought-forms might be externalizations of material existing within the human collective unconscious, and thus might be responsible for the appearance not only of ghosts, but of UFOs, 'aliens' and other non-human creatures. This explanation may not be as outlandish as it seems, especially when we turn our attention to the following case.

THE CASE OF 'PHILIP', THE INVENTED GHOST

In 1972, the fundamental question 'are ghosts products of our mind?' was addressed by a research group based in Toronto, under the leadership of Dr and Mrs George Owen. Since ghosts are notoriously disinclined to reveal themselves to researchers who turn up at the sites of hauntings, it seemed an eminently sensible idea for the group to attempt the creation of their own 'ghost', whom they decided to call Philip. Acting on the assumption that only total belief by every member of the group would result in the creation of Philip, they set about inventing a detailed life history for him.

They decided that he had been an English aristocrat living in the seventeenth century. He had been married, but had had an affair with a gypsy girl, who was tried and found guilty of witchcraft. Although Philip could have intervened on her behalf, he failed to do so and she was burned at the stake. Driven to distraction by remorse, Philip killed himself, and his anguished ghost could thenceforth be seen on his estate. In their book *Ghostwatching*, John Spencer and Tony Wells make the interesting observation that Philip's life and background were not particularly historically accurate, but were considered plausible by the research group, which seems to have been more important to the experiment.

The group then tried to 'raise' Philip in a series of seances. Although they tried for months, they met with no success. Eventually, however, in the summer of 1973 it was decided to introduce a more relaxed and light-hearted atmosphere to the proceedings, whereupon there was a rap on the table they were using for the seances. Using the standard code (one rap for 'yes', two for 'no'), the group were able to establish contact

232

with the 'spirit' of Philip, whose answers to their questions conformed to the life history they had created for him.

In later sessions, Philip made a table move around the room, sometimes at a great speed. In 1974, the group took the table they were using for the seances to the studios of Toronto City Television. Philip continued to manifest via raps and the movement of the table in front of the television cameras, and responded to various questions put to him.

Perhaps the most interesting aspect of the whole case concerns Philip's response when one of the group said to him: 'We only made you up, you know.' Instantly, the rappings stopped and Philip could not be contacted again. He only 'returned' when the process of belief reinforcement had once again been completed, that is, when the group as a whole had learned once again to believe in his existence.

The Philip case offers some intriguing insights into the nature of ghosts in general and spirit communications in particular. It is perhaps not too glib to suggest that the case inverts the traditional maxim that 'seeing is believing'; it would seem to suggest that 'believing is seeing'. A sceptic would doubtless endorse this view wholeheartedly; yet we are still left with the question: what *was* Philip? He certainly wasn't a ghost or spirit in the accepted sense of those terms; yet he definitely was able to manifest his presence in the form of table-tilting and rapping, and was also able to answer the questions put to him by the research group.

According to Colin Wilson in *The Directory of Possibilities*:

We may, of course, prefer to believe that the being who called himself Philip was an alien entity with nothing better to do; but a less far-fetched hypothesis is that the unconscious mind of the group had finally obliged them and created a 'ghost'.

All this suggests another tempting hypothesis: that all para-normal occurrences are evidence not of 'the dark side of nature', but of 'the dark side of the human mind'. Such an hypothesis can be made to fit most, but not all, cases of hauntings or apparitions ... It seems more probable that the real answer may lie in a far wider and more comprehensive theory of the paranormal.

THE BLACK ART OF NECROMANCY

While attempts to communicate with the dead found their modern expression in spiritualism, with its table-tilting, rapping codes and disembodied voices, the practice has an altogether darker provenance in the terrible practice of necromancy, or 'divination by the dead'. The British author Richard Cavendish calls necromancy one of the ugliest and most dangerous of magical operations, with good reason. Necromancy has been performed in numerous cultures, both primitive and modern, throughout the world, and is regarded as the province only of the most powerful, courageous and disciplined magicians. The perils involved are manifold; for instance, it is believed by practitioners that, once summoned, the 'astral corpse' will do anything in its power to live again, including sucking the life-energy from the magician himself.

In his book *The Magical Arts*, Richard Cavendish provides a detailed account of what is required of the magician if he is to communicate with the souls of the dead and compel them to answer his questions. The account is quite comprehensive, and is worth quoting at length:

> For nine days before the ceremony the necromancer and his assistants prepare for it by surrounding themselves with the aura of death. They dress in musty grave-clothes, filched from corpses, and these must not be taken off until the operation is finished. When they first put these on they recite the funeral service over themselves. They abstain from even the mere sight of a woman. They eat dog's flesh and black bread, baked without salt or leaven, and they drink unfermented grape-juice. The dog is the creature of Hecate, the goddess of ghosts and death and sterility, the terrible and inexorable one, the

234

dweller in the void, who is invoked with averted head because no man can see her and remain sane. The absence of salt is a symbol of putrefaction after death, because salt is a preservative. The bread has no leaven and the grape-juice is unfermented to stand for matter without spirit, the physical clay without the spark of life. The bread and the grape-juice are also the necromantic equivalents of the bread and wine of communion, unleavened and unfermented as a sacrament of emptiness and despair.

Through these preparations the magician puts himself in touch with death, into a corpse-like state in which he is in rapport with the real corpse he intends to disturb. When everything is ready he goes to the grave, either between midnight and one in the morning – the first hour of the new day, a suitable time for raising the corpse to life – or at sunset, the first hour of the new day in the older tradition. A magic circle is drawn round the grave. The assistants carry torches and burn a mixture of henbane, hemlock, aloes, wood, saffron, opium and mandrake.

They open the grave and the coffin, exposing the corpse. The magician touches it three times with the magic wand, commanding it to rise . . .

They take the body and arrange it with its head to the east, the direction of the rising sun, and with its arms and legs in the position of the crucified Christ, so that it will rise from the dead. At its right hand they place a dish containing a little wine, mastic [an aromatic resin] and sweet oil, which they set alight. The magician conjures the spirit to enter its old body again and to speak, 'by the virtue of the Holy Resurrection and the bodily posture of the Saviour of the world' and 'on pain of torment and wandering thrice seven years, which by the force of sacred magic rites I have power to inflict on thee'.

When this incantation has been repeated three times, the spirit returns to its old body, which slowly rises until it stands upright. It answers the magician's questions in a faint, hollow voice. Then the magician rewards the spirit by giving it rest.

He destroys its body – burning it or burying it in quicklime – so that it can never again be troubled and called back by sorcery.

It can readily be seen that necromancy is a somewhat more extreme way of contacting the dead than the genteel drawing-room seances favoured by the spiritualists, yet the ultimate objective is virtually the same. Each practice is an expression of the desire on the part of the living to gain information from the spirits of the dead. However, the motives do differ in character somewhat: in the case of necromancy, the information sought usually refers to future events, knowledge of which can be turned to the magician's advantage, or the location of buried treasure; whereas the information sought by spiritualists is usually more in the nature of reassurances that friends and loved ones continue to exist in some blissful post-mortem state, and that we have nothing to fear from death.

SPIRIT GUIDES

Another belief common to many cultures worldwide is that everyone has a spirit guide, which arrives the moment they are born and stays with them throughout their lives, finally appearing to them at the moment of death in order to guide them over the great threshold to the afterlife. It is said that the primary function of the spirit guide is to aid and protect the individual throughout life and to assist in spiritual development. It must be said that, in view of the bloody history of the world, few spirit guides could be described as particularly competent. Nevertheless, they occupy a prominent position in the field of the supernatural. They are divided into primary guides and other guides who arrive to perform various minor functions, before departing once again.

To some people, the presence of a spirit guide is easily discernible, whether visually, or through dreams or disembodied voices. It has also been suggested that children who have invisible playmates may be interacting with their spirit guides, while some artists have claimed that their inspiration comes from the same source.

In fact, the notion that spirit guides offer inspiration is a clue to the origin of the Western belief in these entities, in the civilization of ancient Greece. The Greeks believed in the existence of entities known as 'daimons', which offered guidance to their charges, usually by whispering in the ear. Socrates claimed that his own daimon warned him against making bad decisions and that it was more trustworthy than other forms of divination favoured at the time.

In view of the main function of spirit guides – that is, to guide the individual through his or her life – it has been suggested (by the psychical researcher F. W. H. Myers, among others) that they are actually manifestations of the 'subliminal self', which we would call the unconscious mind. The (frequently unreliable) ability of spirit guides to warn us of danger or unwise decisions could be compared to the concept of intuition.

In tribal and shamanic cultures, the spirit guide is rarely the spirit of a human being: while it fulfils similar functions, the traditional guardian spirit usually takes the form of an animal possessing magical powers, which can be called upon at various times. In some cultures, the presence of a guardian spirit is absolutely essential to a successful life, and even to life itself: if the spirit is not present, the person will die before reaching adulthood. Guardian spirits are inextricably linked to the interaction between the culture and its environment, especially as regards the search for food. For instance, it is these spirits which are called upon to make a hunt successful and whose permission is asked before any of the animals which they represent are killed. In native North American cultures, the totem animal of a tribe may not be killed at all.

In shamanic cultures, shamans (or medicine men) have the capacity to enter an altered state of consciousness, wherein they may communicate with their own totem animals, having been initiated into the shamanic way of life through serious illness or injury. Unlike his counterparts in modern cultures, who may spend their entire lives with no idea that they have a guardian spirit, the shaman actively searches for his and embarks on what is known as a 'vision quest', which may be initiated through the taking of hallucinogenic drugs or through ecstatic dancing. Once in contact with his guardian spirit, the shaman both sees and converses with it, and enlists its aid in a variety of ways, which include ensuring the success of hunts and the treatment of members of the tribe who have fallen ill or been injured.

THE TERRIBLE SECRET OF GLAMIS CASTLE

Magnificent, vast and brooding, Glamis Castle in Scotland is where the British Queen Mother, née Elizabeth Bowes-Lyon, was brought up. The seat of the Earls of Strathmore has the unenviable reputation as the most haunted building in Britain, with nine ghosts identified by various researchers. Even a cursory glance at the history of the place is enough to explain why. In 1034, Malcolm II was murdered there; according to legend, the bloodstain in his room could not be removed by any amount of scrubbing, and eventually the entire floor was replaced. In 1372, Sir John Lyon inherited the house from his father-in-law, Robert II, and was killed in a duel eleven years later. In 1533 Janet Douglas, Lady Glamis, was convicted of witchcraft and burned at the stake in Edinburgh.

Apart from the ghosts that have been seen and heard in the castle, which include the phantom Janet Douglas (known as the 'Grey Lady') and a skeletal ghost known as 'Jack the Runner', there are two legends of a curse that was visited upon Glamis in the dim past. The first concerns Patrick, the 3rd Earl of Strathmore, who was by all accounts something of a hellraiser. Legend has it that one Saturday evening, he was playing dice with the Earl of Crawford. When midnight passed, a servant came into the room to remind him that gambling was forbidden on the Sabbath, by order of the chaplain. Patrick threw him out of the room, saying that the Devil himself could join for all he cared. Sure enough, the Devil promptly knocked on the door and entered the room in the guise of a tall, dark man. Patrick and the Earl of Crawford played dice with the Devil and, of course, lost everything, including their souls. The Devil then informed them that they were doomed to play dice in the room until Judgement Day. And indeed, many people have heard the rattling of dice coming from that room over the years.

The other legend on which the evil reputation of Glamis Castle is based concerns the fabled 'beast', a truly hideous, half-human creature said to have been sired by Patrick, and which was imprisoned in a secret chamber within the castle's fifteen-feet-thick walls. Charles G. Harper has this to say in *Haunted Houses* about the legend:

> The one absolutely secret chamber is never known to more than three persons at one time: to the Earl of Strathmore for the time being, to his eldest son (or to the next heir), and to the factor, or steward, of the estate. The solemn initiation ceremony takes place upon the coming of age of the heir, on the night of his twenty-first birthday, when the three are supposed to be armed with crowbars to break down the masonry which walls up the mystic recess. This rite duly performed and the wall again built up, the factor invariably leaves the castle and rides for home, no matter how stormy the night or late the hour. The Lyon family is wealthy ... and could easily reside elsewhere, but on the night that witnesses the coming of age of the heir, its members will be all gathered together at Glamis.
>
> The theories as to what this terrible secret may be embrace every possibility and impossibility. An often-repeated story is that which narrates how the unhappy Lady Glamis, 'the witch', who was burnt on Castle Hill, Edinburgh, was really in league with the Devil, and that her familiar demon, an embodied and visible fiend, inhabits the spot!

239

With other people, greedy of the horrible, a favourite theory is that there exists, in this dungeon, a hideous half-human monster, of fearful aspect and fabulous age. Another variety would have us believe that a monster of the vampire type is born every generation into the family, to represent the embodiment of a terrible curse upon the house of Lyon.

Although there have been many suggestions as to what the terrible secret of Glamis Castle actually is, that there is (or was) indeed a secret seems to be borne out by a comment made by the 13th Earl, who died in 1904, to a friend: 'If you could guess the nature of the secret, you would go down on your knees and thank God it were not yours.'

There is some very interesting (albeit tenuous) evidence that some strange event indeed befell the Strathmores, in the form of a painting in the drawing room of Glamis Castle. The portrait is of the 3rd Earl, who is seated and pointing across a landscape towards the castle. Two figures, one a child dressed in green, stand to the earl's left, while to his right, stared at by two greyhounds, stands an unknown man who wears a strangely misshapen breastplate, and whose left hand is apparently crippled. Some commentators have speculated that this is the earl's deformed son, and Harper's comment about a generational curse is rather interesting when taken in conjunction with some questions asked by Brian Innes in his *Catalogue of Ghost Sightings*: 'Was some genetic defect transmitted down the generations, another, even more hideous, child being born at a later date? Was this child kept hidden from the world in a distant chamber of the castle? And have the Strathmores always feared that the defect would surface again?'

The rumours of a secret chamber in the castle have always been popular, and a number of people have attempted to discover its exact location. Harper describes one such attempt:

Once, in the temporary absence of a former Earl of Strathmore, a party of guests, headed by the Countess herself, made an ingenious effort to discover the secret chamber. Starting on the supposition that it must have a window (but why?) they hung towels out of every casement, concluding that any window which displayed no towel would be the mystic chamber. The attempt failed, and while it was in progress my lord returned, with unpleasant results. It was even said that Earl and Countess parted, never to meet again.

Innes tells a virtually identical story set in the 1920s, with the 14th Earl coming upon the search for the secret chamber and being similarly enraged. Whatever its ultimate origin, the legends associated with the haunted Glamis Castle are bound to continue to seduce the imagination, especially since discussion of the secret by modern visitors is regarded with stern disapproval.

SOMETHING UNSPEAKABLE IN BERKELEY SQUARE

Number 50 Berkeley Square is an extremely prestigious London address, and the tales of what dwelt within the house have a comparable pedigree in the history of the unexplained. Indeed, if the reports are to be believed, 50 Berkeley Square must have been a most terrifying and dangerous place indeed.

Today, this attractive late-Georgian house is occupied by the antiquarian booksellers Maggs Bros Ltd.; in the nineteenth century, few took up residence there and for many years it lay empty. In 1872, the magazine *Notes & Queries* received a letter enquiring whether the place was haunted, thus accounting for the scarcity of tenants. After a multiple correspondence in the magazine lasting some seven years, W. E. Howlett wrote a letter directing attention to an article in the *Mayfair* magazine in May 1878, which, among other things, noted: 'The house contains at least one room of which the atmosphere is supernaturally fatal to body and mind. A girl saw, heard, or felt such horror in it that she went mad and never recovered sanity enough to tell how or why.'

241

In his book *Haunted Houses*, Charles G. Harper describes a similar tragedy:

> There is quite a literature accumulated around No. 50, and even in the staid pages of *Notes & Queries* the questions of 'Haunted or not haunted?' and if so, 'By what or whom?' have been debated. It seems that a Something or Other, very terrible indeed, haunts, or did haunt, a particular room. This unnamed Raw Head and Bloody Bones, or whatever it is, has been sufficiently awful to have caused the death, in convulsions, of at least two foolhardy persons who have dared to sleep in that chamber. The story is told of one who was not to be deterred by the fate of an earlier victim. He was sceptical and practical as well. Before retiring to bed he gave some parting instructions to those who occupied the rest of the house. 'If I ring once,' said he, 'take no notice, for I might perhaps be only nervous, without due cause; but if I ring twice, come to me.'
>
> They bade him good night. When the clock struck twelve they heard a faint ring, followed by a tremendous peal, and on opening the door they found the unfortunate man in a fit. He died, without ever being able to reveal what It was. A shuddery pendant to this story is that which tells how, a dance being given at a house next door, a lady leaned against the wall dividing the Haunted House from its neighbour, and distinctly felt an inexplicably dreadful shock.

Additional testimony came from a well-to-do family who had hired the house for the London season, during which their daughters were to be presented to society. One of the daughters was engaged, and her fiancé was invited to stay with the family for the period they would be in London. One of the maids was instructed to make up a room for the fiancé, a task that kept her occupied well into the night on the eve of his arrival. At midnight, the family were shaken from their beds by a series of terrified shrieks from the room. Upon opening the door, they were greeted with the dreadful sight of the maid lying on the floor in convulsions. She was staring in abject horror at a particular corner of the room. The family took her to St George's Hospital, where the unfortunate girl died the following morning. She had been unable to tell them what she had seen, saying only that it was horrible beyond imagining.

When the fiancé arrived, the family told him what had happened to the maid and assured him that he would not be sleeping in that room. However, he refused to believe that something awful was lurking in the house and insisted on being allowed to stay in the room. The family eventually relented, on condition that he wait up until midnight, with a bell which he might ring if anything untoward happened.

Sure enough, at midnight the bell sounded loudly and frantically, and when the family rushed upstairs, they found the fiancé stretched out upon the floor, in convulsions. Like the maid, he was staring in terror at one corner. Unlike the maid, however, he survived, but would not speak of what he had seen.

This sounds like a variation on the tale related earlier, and it has to be admitted that testimony of this kind, at a remove of more than a century, must be treated with a dose of healthy scepticism. However, there are other stories of a terrible 'something' residing at 50 Berkeley Square. One relates how two sailors, at a loss for somewhere to stay for the night, broke into the empty house. They saw something that so terrified them that one jumped from the top-floor window and was impaled on the railings in front of the house. The police were called to the scene and discovered his friend, still in the room on the top floor. The hapless sailor was quite insane, and babbled about a figure with enormous talons instead of arms.

The article in the May 1878 issue of the *Mayfair* magazine, referred to earlier, provided a little more information, which is yet more intriguing:

The very party walls of the house, when touched, are found saturated with electric horror. It is uninhabited save by an

243

elderly man and woman who act as caretakers, but even they have no access to that room. This is kept locked, the key being in the hands of a mysterious and seemingly nameless person, who comes to the house every six months, locks up the elderly couple in the basement, and then unlocks the room, and occupies himself in it for hours.

Who was this strange person? Why did he alone have keys to the room of terror? Why did he lock himself away in it for hours at a time? And for that matter, how was he able to do so without succumbing to whatever the room contained? Of course, rumours are the food of speculation and it is hard to resist the temptation to speculate wildly on what might have lived in the upper room at 50 Berkeley Square, especially given that the puzzle will almost certainly never be solved. Perhaps the nameless man who held the keys to the room was unafraid of the thing that lay within because he had created it, allowing it to feed on some unfathomable psychic energy that might already have existed in the place, infusing the very walls with 'electric horror'. Or perhaps that energy had attracted a ravenous discarnate entity from some Lovecraftian outer realm, which was being studied by the mysterious stranger . . .

At any rate, the evil influences that so plagued the house in the last century seem to have disappeared. Representatives of Maggs Bros. Ltd. say that they have had no trouble of a supernatural kind whatsoever at the house, although they still occasionally receive enquiries from those interested in the house's macabre history.

THE GIRL WITHOUT A BODY

In the 1950s, the Manila *Times* carried a most peculiar report concerning a girl named Mayakoa, who was a member of the Southeast Asian Negrito race, and whose body apparently disappeared in 1948, leaving her consciousness intact. On 9

November 1955, Miss Marion Walker, an American Method-ist missionary, arrived in Capas Town on the island of Tarlac in the company of her travelling companion, Carlos Nacpil, and two Negritos, Saria Molina and Francisca Ignacio. As they had approached the town, Miss Walker had been some-what bemused to hear the voice of a fifth person singing in the station wagon.

When she asked who the person was, Saria Molina replied: 'That is my sister, Mayakoa,' and went on to relate the girl's astonishing fate.

Upon arriving in Capas, Miss Walker took her companions to the Methodist Church, where she spoke with the Revd Dr Fidel P. Galang, and related the strange story she had been told. To her surprise, Dr Galang confirmed that he, too, had spoken with Mayakoa on several occasions.

Presently, word reached the Manila *Times*, and two report-ers were dispatched to cover the story and interview the witnesses. Dr Galang told them that Mayakoa 'has the small voice of a Negrito and [speaks] Pampango'. Not surprisingly, the reporters were unsure whether they were the victims of some jape, and wondered if the story were worth printing; nevertheless, they asked the missionaries to pose for a photo-graph. One of the reporters then asked: 'Where is Mayakoa now?'

'Here I am, sir,' replied a disembodied voice behind him. The reporters were shocked: the last thing they had expected was for the missionaries' strange tale to be verified by the disembodied voice itself. They went back to Manila and printed the story.

THE HEADLESS SOLDIER

The war in Vietnam has spawned a number of strange tales, from UFOs to winged female entities and giant glowing humanoids. Amongst these bizarre reports, however, it seems that there was still room for more traditional supernatural activity. One such tale concerns the US Air Force airfield at Ton Son Nhut. The US personnel could not understand why their Vietnamese colleagues refused to stand nightwatch in the battlements at the end of the runway.

One night in October 1965, Staff Sergeant James Hinton was on night patrol near the ammunition dump, when something triggered one of the flares. Assuming an attack was under way, the captain in charge began to fire in the direction of the flare. According to Hinton: 'He thought he saw someone in black pyjamas drop into a ditch, but when he got there, the ditch was empty. The next thing we knew another flare went off and there seemed to be someone up in a tree just beyond the old French tower. The captain opened up again and so did the rest of us. Nothing fell down.'

From then on, the mysterious, pyjama-clad figure returned many times, and was frequently seen wandering around the old French watchtower near the ammunition dump at the end of the runway. It seemed that the Vietnamese personnel had not been suffering from superstitious delusions after all, and when they refused to allow the French tower to be pulled down, even when the runway was extended, the Americans acquiesced to their wishes.

When the Americans finally took the situation seriously, they asked their Vietnamese counterparts about the possible origin of the sightings of the man in black pyjamas. The Vietnamese replied that it was the ghost of a French captain who was on duty in the tower when the airfield was attacked by Vietminh. Although he fought valiantly, he was eventually captured. So frustrated had they been by his staunch defence of his post that the Vietminh decided to subject him to the ultimate humiliation of being beheaded, rather than shot. According to their beliefs, one who is beheaded can never find rest in the spirit world. Despite his pleas for the final dignity of being shot, the Frenchman was dressed in black pyjamas, and his head was cut off.

His head and body were then buried in different places, the body, apparently, in a nearby Buddhist cemetery, and the head somewhere near the watchtower. Since the day of his death, according to the Vietnamese soldiers, the unfortunate had been doomed to wander around the watchtower. Since it must be extremely difficult to look for anything without a head, we can only assume that the hapless soldier is searching there still . . .

THE GHOST ISLAND OF THE SOUTH ATLANTIC

The September 1960 issue of *Fate* magazine carried what must be one of the strangest ghostly tales on record, a tale that is oddly reminiscent of H. P. Lovecraft's short story 'The Call of Cthulhu'. The main witness, Carlo Bel Moro, was a cadet on the Argentina Navy cutter *Benito Grande*, which was on patrol in the South Atlantic in September 1955. The ship was on its way to the southern Shetland Islands, when it came upon a large, natural harbour between two enormous, jagged mountains. Although these mountains were covered with snow, the beaches were bare. When Moro asked why there was no snow on the beaches, the bos'n, Rojez, replied that they were covered with still-hot volcanic ash.

In the *Fate* article, Moro stated: 'There was something so eerie and mysterious about the island. When we entered the harbour, there was drift ice there. Two hours later every piece of ice had gone.'

On one of the beaches, the sailors saw a battered, derelict pier. Rojez pointed to it and explained to the younger man: 'Whalers use that pier sometimes, but they never stay here long. No one does. They say it would take only the slightest earth tremor or noise to collapse those mountains. The gap between them would close, and anyone caught inside would stay there for ever.' Rojez added that the island had been named Deception Island by the whalers, who maintained that it was capable of vanishing and reappearing without warning.

The *Benito Grande* stopped at the island to take advantage of the large number of seals there, and while a hunting party was dispatched to the shore, Moro, along with Raphael Gomprez and Francisco Ruiz, was sent in a small boat back through the harbour entrance and into the open sea to fish for cod. So intense was their concentration on their task that the three cadets did not realize how far they were drifting from Deception Island and the *Benito Grande*. When they had finally filled their boat with cod, Gomprez and Moro took the oars, while Ruiz manned the tiller.

It was then that Moro heard Ruiz's mystified whisper. 'The island ... the island is gone!' The three men stood up in the boat and desperately searched the horizon for any sign of Deception Island, but it seemed to have vanished without trace. Gomprez sat down again and began to mutter about being in the hands of the Devil. He muttered the same thing over and over, and his shipmates began to worry that he might end up succumbing to panic.

To add to their problems, the sun set, and it became even colder than the bitter temperature during the day. As night fell upon them and the fish they had caught gradually froze solid, Moro and Ruiz discussed the limited options open to them. They agreed that their only hope of survival lay in making for Tierra Del Fuego, and perhaps making landfall on one of the myriad islands scattered throughout the area.

Gomprez took no part in this discussion: he was fighting a losing battle with the terror rising within him. Presently, he broke down and started to sob uncontrollably. Ruiz tried to calm him down, even slapping him across the face at one point, but it was useless: Gomprez had lost his grip on rationality. Just before morning, he stood up and screamed something about the 'curse of the sea', before losing his balance and falling overboard. His companions could do nothing to save him, for to jump into those waters would have meant swift death for them also. Gomprez disappeared beneath the icy waters and was not seen again.

At sunrise, Moro and Ruiz searched once again for Deception Island, but the morning revealed nothing but the endless ocean. After a meagre breakfast of emergency rations, the two surviving cadets sat down and began to row towards the south-west. They had been rowing for some time, when Ruiz turned to Moro to say something, and glimpsed something out of the corner of his eye. Turning around fully towards the bow of the boat, he gasped and cried: 'Look ahead of us!' Together they watched as the form of a ship gradually took shape in the distance, despite the fact that the atmosphere was perfectly clear. It was the *Benito Grande*, coming into view as if from out of nowhere.

Moro and Ruiz screamed frantically and waved their arms at the ship, which quickly sighted them. Once aboard and recovering from the ordeal, the two cadets told the captain of what had happened. The captain found their tale hard to believe, and took his men up on deck to show them the island, which was still clearly visible from the stern quarter of the ship.

Later, Moro spoke again to Rojez. The bos'n said: 'Don't think you have lost your mind. I have heard it said that if you approach the island from a certain side you won't see a thing. The horizon just seems to continue and there is no island visible.'

Suddenly, a terrifying loud rumbling sound assaulted their ears, which Moro likened to a mixture of thunder and bomb explosions. In the article in *Fate*, he recalled: 'Rojez came running aft and soon the rest of the crew stood there, too, watching with staring eyes. The perfect visibility had deteriorated into a disturbed, shimmering haze. Through it we could see the two pinnacles lean drunkenly together as the deafening thunder clap rolled out over the ocean. Slowly, before our eyes, the distant island sank into the sea.'

YOU ONLY DIE TWICE

The Heinz family had lived happily in their small, two-storey farmhouse in Portage, Wisconsin, for ten years. In the summer and autumn of 1925, however, August and Patricia Heinz and their three children – Freddy, seven, Elizabeth, eleven, and nine-year-old Charles – were plagued by a mischievous and perhaps even dangerous spirit. The prelude to the haunting seems to have begun in February, when one of their barns was destroyed by fire. In June, another barn went up in flames; no cause for either of the blazes could be discovered. Later that month, as the family were eating supper, footsteps sounded on the stairs leading to the first floor. Fearing that an intruder had managed to get in, August Heinz took Charles and searched the house, but found no one. When they returned to their supper, the footsteps began again. For the next three months, the family would hear the same sounds from time to time.

Not content with stomping up and down the stairs, the ghost developed a fascination with Patricia Heinz's broom, which would go missing every morning, to be found later elsewhere in the house, or even in other parts of the farm. Mr and Mrs Heinz naturally assumed that their children were to blame, but Freddy, Elizabeth and Charles steadfastly maintained their innocence.

Eventually, August Heinz decided to chain the broom to the kitchen wall, but discovered the following morning that the chain had been broken and the broom, once again, was missing.

One day in late autumn, Heinz went hunting with a family friend, whom he invited to stay for supper after their trip. They had barely started the meal when the familiar footsteps sounded on the staircase. The friend was naturally curious as to who was making the racket, and August reluctantly told him about the mischievous spirit.

Not having any experience of such things, the friend was at a loss as to what to do about the ghost. Eventually, he had the idea of frightening the ghost away by threatening it with his unloaded shotgun. He got up from the table, took his shotgun, and slowly and quietly moved towards the foot of the staircase. Suddenly lunging into the hallway, he screamed at the top of his voice and pulled the trigger.

Unfortunately, he had forgotten that he had reloaded the gun earlier, and the blast blew away part of the wall. As the plaster dust slowly cleared, they heard a low moan, as of someone badly injured. In the days that followed, the moans and cries continued, apparently coming from the cellar. Eventually, the pain-racked sounds faded away, and the family were disturbed no more.

It seems preposterous to suggest that the shotgun blast had 'killed' the ghost; however, as we have already seen, some ghosts seem not to realize that they are dead, and continue to frequent the places they knew in life. It is just possible that this unfortunate spirit had been suffering from such a misapprehension, and had perhaps been trying, in frustration, to attract the family's attention through childish antics. Perhaps the manner of its death had been so sudden and unexpected that it assumed it was still alive. In that case, the man screaming wildly, pointing a shotgun at it and firing would surely have informed it, unequivocally, that its time on Earth was most definitely up! In its confused state, the spirit may have assumed that *this* was the time of its passing, and, after some imagined death throes, departed for the spirit world.

11

THEORIES ON THE ORIGIN OF GHOSTS AND SPIRITS

No survey of the realm of ghosts and spirits would be complete (and this one is all too brief) without some speculations on the possible origin and nature of these fascinating, ubiquitous yet elusive entities. Of course, the most often cited explanation put forward by those who do not dismiss the phenomena out of hand is that ghosts and spirits are indeed the discarnate souls of human beings and animals who have died and been some- how translated into a higher realm of existence. Although in this chapter we will look at the various theories to account for the existence of ghosts, it will become clear that they are actually elements in a single theory, since each, as we observed earlier, contains subtle strands of meaning that reach out towards the others, and thus none can be taken in isolation.

LIFE AFTER DEATH?

The concept of life after death has been one of humanity's abiding interests since our species rose to self-awareness and we became cognisant of our own mortality. The likeliest explanation for this is that the alternative is, quite literally, unthinkable. It is impossible to comprehend oblivion from the point of view of a thinking being. If the reader should suspect that I am being a little dramatic here, he or she should take a moment to consider the temporary oblivion of dreamless sleep, in which self-awareness is annihilated for a few hours, and then imagine that stateless state extrapolated into the rest of eternity. Like the apprehension without mathematical aids of

252

four-dimensional space-time, it is beyond the abilities of our senses, and this is the reason for the terror inspired by any lengthy contemplation of the death of awareness.

Although a sceptic might say that this is in itself enough to kick-start a species-wide belief in an afterlife, with all the self-delusion such a fervent belief might engender, there is an alternative interpretation: that the annihilation of self-awareness after death is impossible to comprehend because it *cannot occur* – it is simply not the way things are in this universe. This is, of course, a rather sweeping statement to make, and I certainly have little evidence to back up the assertion. However, if we accept the assertion of physics, that energy can neither be created nor destroyed – only transferred from one form to another – then we are left with the question of what happens to the energy fields of which consciousness seems to be composed, when a human being dies.

With nothing to maintain them, with the heart, brain and central nervous system permanently inactive, it would seem that there is no longer any mechanism by which these energy fields can be maintained. The apparently inescapable conclusion is that when this happens, they are simply converted to other, less coherent forms of energy which are incapable of carrying the information which constitutes consciousness.

But is this necessarily so? The evidence we have examined in this book, although in many instances anecdotal and lacking in the exactitudes of date, time and location that would ideally be present in a qualitative database, is at any rate compelling in its quantity. And its principal value lies in its prompting us to consider a progression of ideas, beginning with the notion that the brain is not only the location of consciousness, but also its engine, without which our self-awareness is doomed to fade away into nothingness.

OUT-OF-BODY EXPERIENCES

The starting point of this progression has to be the out-of-body experiences described earlier, most notably those of Robert Monroe. The information he gathered during his journeys, largely confirmed as accurate later, militates heavily in favour of some aspect of his consciousness actually leaving his physical body, journeying to other locations (sometimes quite distant), gathering information and retaining it for later recollection. If we accept that this really is what happens in such OBE cases, we nevertheless encounter a problem with the claim that they prove the existence of post-mortem consciousness. Although this disembodied intelligence is capable of existing apart from the body, just how independent is this existence? In other words, how much does it depend on the body's living systems for its maintenance? Were the body suddenly to die during an OBE, would the person's 'astral consciousness' be instantly annihilated, like a bursting soap-bubble? Relevant here is the peculiar element (which we saw earlier) in many (but by no means all) out-of-body experiences: that people who have undergone OBEs report the presence of a slender, silvery cord connecting the head of the astral body with that of the physical body. This cord is apparently infinitely long, allowing the astral body to roam where it will, and people claiming the experience feel that the cord is extremely important in some way. This begs the question: what is the function of the silver cord? The implication is that it is a conduit, a kind of power cable allowing the astral body to exist (temporarily) in locations other than the physical body.

However, this interpretation also has its problems. For one, it seems a little 'Heath Robinson' to have such a power cable connecting the physical and astral bodies, a little too 'material'. Why should such a contraption be required, given the 'ethereal' nature of the OBE in the first place? Perhaps it is not a power conduit, but is rather simply a safety tether, whose function is to prevent the astral body from becoming lost during its wanderings. The experiences of Robert Monroe would suggest otherwise, however: he claims that all that is needed to return to the physical body is the *thought* of returning, whereupon one is home once again. The true nature and purpose of the silver cord remains, therefore, as mysterious as the experiences during which it has been reported, although it does highlight the interesting question of the 'power source' for the consciousness.

An experience which is comparable to the OBE – perhaps directly so – is the so-called near death experience (NDE), in which a person on the point of death, and occasionally pronounced clinically dead, reports the continued activity of the personality, of consciousness. The most commonly reported experience, is that of proceeding through a long, dark tunnel, which leads to a bright light in the far distance. When this light is reached, the percipient frequently encounters the spirits of dead relatives and loved ones, and senses the presence of a 'being', an immensely powerful force of love and compassion. At this stage, a review of the person's life is sometimes conducted, and he or she is then asked if they consider their work on earth to be completed. Compelled to answer honestly, they reply 'No', and are informed that they therefore must return to life to fulfil their destiny. Alternatively, they may be informed that it is not yet 'their time', and are sent back to the world of the living.

Sceptics have an impressive argument against the literal interpretation of such experiences, saying that they are no more than hallucinations of a wish-fulfilling nature, occurring within the dying brain. The cause is oxygen starvation. In addition, there have been numerous experiments conducted, in which the temporal lobes of the brain have been stimulated by physical means, resulting in hallucinations remarkably similar to NDEs. It has therefore been claimed that there is no such thing as a 'genuine' near death experience; that the visions experienced have their origin exclusively in the mind of the individual.

It is puzzling, however, that percipients suffering from oxygen starvation should experience such *coherent* visions, especially when oxygen starvation usually results in bizarre and heterogeneous hallucinations. It is also interesting that near death experiencers report intelligent and cogent conversations with entities residing in the light at the end of the tunnel. In addition, people who report out-of-body experiences can apparently make observations of their surroundings from locations outside the physical body, observations that were later verified. To say that they are receiving such information subconsciously (that they are not 'outside the body' at all) at these moments is surely stretching things somewhat, especially in view of the fact that the dying brain is supposed to be in a state of utter chaos at the time.

What we are left with, then, is the strong possibility that the consciousness of human beings is capable of existing outside the body, at least while the brain is functioning (even if erratically). Yet, unsurprisingly, we once again find ourselves coming up against a brick wall with 'DEATH' scrawled across it. The evidence for out-of-body experiences is compelling, but the fact that the body and brain are alive when they happen is of unavoidable significance. If the idea that human consciousness continues after death is to be retained as a distinct possibility, it seems that we desperately need to come up with some mechanism by which the energy fields of which it is composed are maintained indefinitely, perhaps eternally.

As an illustration of this problem, let us turn to a ghost report from 1964. The incident happened in a car factory in Detroit. A fitter was standing next to a body press, which was supposed to have been switched off during lunchtime. However, through some oversight it had been left on, and the man's co-workers watched as he suddenly lurched out of its path. The fitter later said that he had been pushed out of the way by a tall black man with a scarred face. From his description of the man, the older workers recognized him as a worker who had been decapitated in the factory in 1944. The fitter said: 'The coloured guy was real enough to me. He had enormous strength, and just pushed me out of the way like I was a feather-weight. I never believed in spooks before, but if this was a spook I take my hat off to him.' It is possible that one of the fitter's colleagues unconsciously registered the danger and exerted a psychokinetic force to push him out of the way of the press, but this does not explain the fitter's description of a real person who had died two decades earlier in that part of the factory. Was his life saved by a ghost, a genuine spirit able to interact with the physical environment? The problem then, is finding some mechanism by which the energy constituting a person's mind might be coherently maintained, so that it could not only function within the earthly environment, but could also influence that environment to the extent that another person's life was saved through direct intervention.

I hesitate to begin a sentence in a book on the paranormal with the words 'Could it be . . .?', since the answer to such questions is frequently: 'Maybe yes, but probably no.' However, it is worth noting that theoretical physicists have postulated the existence of a truly immense energy source contained within the very fabric of spacetime itself, locked away in the vacuum between the atoms and particles that constitute physical matter. It has been suggested that, if we could ever access this vacuum energy, we could power our civilization for ever, at zero cost. Could it be, therefore, that this hidden energy, which is said to pervade the entire universe, is actually the same energy that maintains the individual consciousness of an intelligent being after death? Does some arcane 'translation' occur, whereby our essence of being switches from the energy provided by the body's living systems to an energy supplied by spacetime itself? Indeed, this may even be the secret of out-of-body travel by the living, with the switching mechanism being a two-way system. After all, at the deepest level, at the smallest scale, our brains are quantum mechanical systems, and the processes occurring within them do so near the level at which the vacuum energy is said to exist.

FANTASY-PRONE PERSONALITIES

We must also consider a concept that is quite new and has been suggested as a possible explanation for many UFO encounters, but which can be extended to cover various paranormal events, including ghost sightings. The concept is that of the 'fantasy-prone personality', which was first proposed by Sheryl Wilson and Theodore Barber, who suggest that approximately four per cent of the adult population experience extremely vivid fantasies – so vivid, in fact, that they are indistinguishable from reality. According to Wilson and Barber, fantasy proneness results from a profound immersion in fantasy during childhood, which some adults are unable to leave behind when they enter maturity. They also provide some evidence that this attribute may result from childhood abuse, with the child creating elaborate fantasies either to escape from its tormentor, or to simulate the exercise of control of its environment. As the child grows into an adult, this defence mechanism is extremely difficult to abandon.

In his book *Borderlands*, the anomalist Mike Dash summarizes the characteristics of an adult fantasy-prone personality, according to Wilson and Barber:

> Wilson and Barber compared a small sample of apparently fantasy-prone people to a control group, and concluded that they spent much of their time attending to fantasies in which they could 'see', 'hear', 'smell' and 'touch' the things they were imagining. Not only were they sometimes able to orgasm without physical stimulation; they were more likely to experience vivid dreams and waking hallucinations, *including visions of ghosts* [emphasis added] and monsters. Half believed that they were receiving special messages from some higher intelligence. Others underwent apparently psychic experiences, and almost all of them tended to be susceptible to hypnosis. Indeed, the psychologist Robert Baker has observed that 'the behaviour

we commonly call "hypnotic" is exhibited by these fantasy-prone types all the time'. Wilson and Barber stressed that although the fantasy-prone may have low self-esteem and cope poorly with stress, they are not disturbed or mentally ill and are capable of living perfectly happy and apparently normal lives.

Dash also cites an interesting point made by another highly regarded anomalist, Hilary Evans, who notes that people who encounter the paranormal are often going through some difficulty or trauma, for instance, adolescence. It will be remembered that teenagers are frequently the apparent foci for poltergeist manifestations. In addition, other difficulties such as poverty or unemployment may prompt certain individuals to retreat into a fantasy-prone state to cope with unpleasant situations.

The individual has a need (not necessarily one that he is aware of) which can be either an immediate crisis, usually of a personal nature, or a temporary awkward phase in his development which he finds it difficult to surmount, such as adolescence or menopause, which may well be accompanied by an identity crisis; or a long term uncertainty, such as a religious doubt, or a chronic frustration, such as a boring or humiliating existence. Unable to resolve this by normal means, his subconscious mind devises and projects to his conscious mind as simulated reality a dramatic episode in which he seems to encounter an otherworldly being which, to him, represents authority together with whatever other attributes are required.

To make the incident effective, it must be believable; to be believable, it must be lifelike. So it is presented in such a way that the conscious mind accepts it as a reality.

Since the concept of the fantasy-prone personality is a relatively new one, much work needs to be done before we can submit it as anything more than a possible explanation for paranormal encounters in general, and ghostly ones in particular.

Dash also mentions that many spiritualist mediums seem to have exhibited fantasy-proneness in childhood, notably Leonora Piper, who felt a sudden, sharp blow on her left ear when she was eight years old. She then heard a sibilant sound, which presently resolved itself into the audible message: 'Aunt Sarah not dead, but with you still.' Not long after, the girl experienced a bright light, containing numerous faces, in her room. In addition, it doesn't seem such a terribly long step from spiritualist mediums to people who claim no such talent, but who are nevertheless psychically sensitive and therefore able to detect the presence of supernatural phenomena.

ANIMAL PERCIPIENTS

Not only human beings are capable of perceiving apparent ghosts. Anyone who owns a dog or cat will surely recall their animals watching things that 'aren't there'. I have had cats all my life and, at one time or another, every single one has done this. Typically, the cat will be doing some cat thing, such as licking its paws. Suddenly, it will stop, as if its attention has been caught by something; it will sit up, and its eyes – wide open and with pupils dilated – will move across the room very steadily. At times like this, it is clear, beyond any conceivable doubt, that the cat is *watching* something. Then, a few moments later and apparently none the worse for its experience, the cat will settle down and return to its paw-washing. To observe an animal following the movement across the room of something that cannot be seen is a rather unnerving experience; but it is also a fascinating and thought-provoking one. (I must remember to photograph the room the next time my cat does this. One never knows!)

The reactions of animals to apparent ghost phenomena

have been documented, notably by a psychiatrist, Dr Robert Morris, who on one occasion reported on an investigation conducted by a colleague in a haunted house in Kentucky. It was alleged that one room in particular was the site of ghostly activity, due to a tragedy that had occurred there. Dr Morris's colleague took a dog, a cat, a rat and a rattlesnake with him into the haunted room. The case is reported in Colin Wilson's and Christopher Evans's *World Famous Strange But True*.

> The animals were brought into ... the haunted [room] one at a time. 'The dog upon being taken about two or three feet into the room immediately snarled at its owner and backed out the door. No amount of cajoling could prevent the dog from struggling to get out and it refused to reenter. The cat was brought into the room carried in its owner's arms. When the cat got a similar distance into the room, it immediately leaped upon the owner's shoulders, dug in, then leaped to the ground, orienting itself toward a chair. It spent several minutes hissing and spitting and staring at the unoccupied chair in a corner of the room until it was finally removed ...'
>
> The rat showed no reaction to whatever had disturbed the dog and cat, but the rattlesnake 'immediately assumed an attack posture focusing on the same chair that had been of interest to the cat. After a couple of minutes it slowly moved its head toward a widow, then moved back and receded into its alert posture about five minutes after ...'
>
> The four animals were tested separately in a control room in which no tragedy had occurred. In this room they behaved normally. Apparently, the animals were reacting to some invisible presence in the first room.

Assuming that these animals were indeed reacting to someone or something that the investigators could not see, what was it? The ghost of someone who had died in that room? The Revd Christopher Neil-Smith, a writer and exorcist, is of the opinion that this is the case. 'For the most part, I believe that the soul of a person who dies a "natural" death leaves the body for another place. The soul, or spirit, of one who dies violently may not immediately do so; it is bewildered by the sudden transition, and remains earthbound. If you examine cases of haunting which are well authenticated, you generally find that a sudden or unnatural death lies behind these events.'

TIMESLIPS

When a person encounters a ghost, the initial and understandable assumption is that the ghost is intruding into the frame of reference of the percipient. In other words, everything is as it should be, both with the percipient and with his or her environment, and the appearance of the ghost marks the arrival of something extraordinary from 'elsewhere' – from beyond the grave or wherever. But it is equally possible that everything is most certainly not 'as it should be' when an apparition is perceived: that the percipient has, in a sense, left 'normal reality', and is in a new state, one that is the result of a 'timeslip'.

Timeslips have been proposed to explain certain ghost encounters in which the immediate environment undergoes an alteration. When this happens, people and objects in the vicinity of the percipient are profoundly changed or disappear entirely, to be replaced by an environment that differs in numerous respects from the percipient's own. For a very good example of this, we can turn to a case examined by Ian Wilson in his book *In Search of Ghosts*.

At 8.50 a.m. on 3 October 1963, Mrs Coleen Buterbaugh, who worked as a secretary at the Nebraska Wesleyan University in Lincoln, Nebraska, took a message from Dean Sam Dahl to a professor in the C. C. White Building. As she entered the professor's suite, her eyes were drawn to a cabinet along a wall, at which she saw the figure of a woman.

In a letter to the psychical researcher Dr Gardner Murphy,

quoted in Vol. 60 of the *Journal of the American Society for Psychical Research*, Mrs Buterbaugh writes:

> She had her back to me, reaching up into one of the shelves of the cabinet with her right hand, and standing perfectly still. She wasn't at all aware of my presence. While I was watching her she never moved. She was not transparent and yet I knew she wasn't real. While I was looking at her she just faded away – not parts of her body one at a time, but her whole body all at once.

Ian Wilson continues:

> ... Mrs Buterbaugh was able to give a clear and convincing-sounding description of the figure she had seen. The woman was very tall, probably six feet to Mrs Buterbaugh's own diminutive five. The cabinet she was reaching into was an old music one with high shelves, and whatever she was looking for was on one of the topmost shelves, way beyond Mrs Buterbaugh's own reach. She had a 'bushy bouffant' hairstyle, the sort that was fashionable around the time of the First World War. Again consistent with this period she was wearing a long-sleeved white blouse and a long dark brown or black skirt reaching to her ankles.
>
> ... this ghost also proved identifiable. From enquiries made among older members of staff, Mrs Buterbaugh's description seemed to correspond with a spinster music teacher, Clarissa Mills, who worked at the university between 1912 and her death in 1936. In a photograph of Miss Mills in an old yearbook she was wearing a bouffant hairstyle ... Significantly, the filing cabinet which Mrs Buterbaugh saw Miss Mills reaching into contained choral group arrangements dating mostly from Miss Mills's time at the university.

The most intriguing element in this encounter was the alteration in the environment as Mrs Buterbaugh noticed the apparition of Clarissa Mills.

Up until the time [the apparition] faded away I was not aware of anyone else being in the suite of rooms, but just about the time of her fading out I felt as though I still was not alone. To my left was a desk, and I had a feeling there was a man sitting at that desk. I turned around and saw no one, but I still felt his presence. When that feeling of his presence left I have no idea, because it was then, when I looked out of the window behind that desk, that I got frightened ... when I looked out of that window there wasn't one modern thing out there. The street (Madison Street) which is less than a half-block away from the building, was not even there and neither was the new Willard House. That was when I realised that these people were not in my time, but that I was back in their time ...

The window was open. Even though it was fairly early in the morning it appeared as though it were a very warm, summer afternoon. It was very still. There were a few scattered trees – about two on my right (east) and about three on my left (west). It seems to me there were more, but these are the only ones I can be definite about. The rest was open field; the new Willard sorority house and also Madison Street was not there. I remember seeing a very vague outline of some sort of building to my right and that is about all. Nothing else but open field ...

It was not until I was back out in the hall that I again heard the familiar noises ... The girls that were going into the orientation class as I entered the rooms were still going in and someone was still playing the marimba.

It is clear from Mrs Buterbaugh's account of her experience that what, at first sight, was an encounter with an apparition, was actually something far more complex. It seems that, for the few moments of her experience, she had direct access to a period decades in the past. Her description of the scene outside the window corresponded to an old photograph from the period. In addition, the extreme quietness she reported is interesting (and was touched upon earlier in this book), since it implies that her native environment was somehow muted, as if the apparitional surroundings had been superimposed over it. It is also interesting that Mrs Buterbaugh reported sensing a presence at the nearby desk, even though when she turned towards it she saw no one there. This could imply that her access to the past was not quite complete: that there were other people in the vicinity (together with the normal sounds of that time), but they did not enter her awareness.

Is it possible that people such as Mrs Buterbaugh can involuntarily travel backwards through time, to apprehend with their senses people and scenes from the past? In considering this question, we find ourselves entering one of those fascinating areas in which various aspects of the paranormal begin to merge, linking up with each other and forming a network containing an astonishing diversity of anomalous events. Most notable among these is the mysterious disappearance of people who apparently vanish from the face of the earth, some of whom never return. An extremely interesting case of this kind is that of Benjamin Bathurst, who in 1809 stopped at an inn to rest. Preparing to continue his journey, he walked out to the courtyard of the inn to check on his horse and carriage ... and was never seen again. Both his family and the British government conducted an intensive investigation (with the aid of Napoleon himself), but nothing was ever seen or heard of him.

Another astonishing incident occurred in the winter of 1975. A couple named Jackson and Martha Wright were driving to New York, and had entered the Lincoln Tunnel, when Jackson stopped the car so that they could clear snow from the windows. Jackson went to the front of the car, Martha to the rear, where she vanished, never to be seen or heard from again.

There have also been numerous reports of people who have disappeared and then later reappeared, sometimes far from the scene of their vanishing. Unfortunately, no such report has ever been established as absolutely reliable to everyone's satisfaction; but of course, in the world of the paranormal, that is hardly unusual. On 25 April 1977, a Chilean army corporal named Armando Valdes vanished in front of six of his men. His disappearance was short-lived, for he reappeared fifteen minutes later. However, as his men noted with disbelief, the calendar on his watch was five days ahead, and he also had acquired a five-day growth of beard. For his part, Valdes was as mystified as his men, and could remember nothing of what had happened while he was 'away'.

The American author Whitley Strieber is noted for his work on the subject of encounters with non-human beings. In his latest book *The Secret School: Preparation for Contact* he gives us a fascinating account of an apparent timeslip he experienced in March 1983, in New York. He was about to cross a busy street, when he quite distinctly heard the sound of a horse and cart moving past, directly in front of him, although he could not see them. Almost immediately, the scene changed radically: the street was full of horse-drawn traffic and the Silver Towers (a double-block of condominiums) were no longer there, having been replaced by a row of brownstone houses.

When he tried to move, Strieber felt icy waves crashing through his body, a terrifying sensation which made him wonder whether they actually represented the hold of this past time upon him, and whether, if he moved too suddenly, he would be forever locked into this alien era. At this point, Strieber noticed a small woman looking at him in utter shock, before hurrying away. A man began shouting at him, 'his voice taut with fear and questioning', apparently because of Strieber's twentieth-century clothes. Then, everything returned to normal; Strieber was back in the present, quickly realizing that only a few seconds had passed, whereas he had apparently spent between five and ten minutes in the past.

In view of Whitley Strieber's testimony, one can't help but wonder if, had she turned away from the cabinet, Clarissa Mills would have seen Mrs Buterbaugh staring at her in astonishment, an involuntary visitor from the future. It is also worth noting at this stage that the idea of rifts in time (whether natural or artificially induced) has been suggested as a possible explanation for a number of paranormal events. Some researchers have suggested that UFOs might be time machines from the distant future, while others have wondered whether the sightings of apparent dinosaurs in various parts of the world, such as the Congo, can be accounted for by those long-extinct beasts blundering momentarily through rifts in the spacetime continuum.

With regard to certain ghost encounters, it could be that, under obscure conditions, a pathway might be opened between time zones, allowing the percipient to experience the sights and sounds of the past – including people who were alive then. However, in considering this suggestion, we are obliged to ask if these events occur exclusively in the physical world – that is, in the environment external to the percipient.

In his book *The Paranormal*, Brian Inglis addresses this question:

> If ... we can have precognitive glimpses of the future, it would seem logical for us occasionally to have retrocognitive glimpses of the past: scenes, that is, which we could not have known about, or inferred, in the ordinary way from books or other sources. But as the main function of those who can induce psychic experiences – shamans, seers, diviners – has been to give guidance about the future, the ability to peer back into the past has not been highly regarded.
>
> Perhaps for this reason, although there have always been indications that information may flow through psychics about past events, it has seldom been considered significant, except in so far as it seems to provide evidence for [life after death] or for reincarnation. The spirits who 'control' or 'possess' mediums have often identified themselves as having previously lived on earth; but the tendency has been to regard the spirits as still living in the spirit, rather than to assume that the medium is shifting back in time in order to allow them to communicate.

This illustrates what might be a serious misconception with regard to ghostly encounters, which was mentioned earlier:

that all such experiences are grounded in the present, with the percipient encountering something that has intruded upon the environment from some outside source. It seems at least feasible that, on the contrary, it is the percipient who is intruding (albeit involuntarily) upon events that happened long ago. Inglis continues:

> Glimpses of the past [have] been reported in the *SPR Journal*, some relating to specific events. In 1950 Miss F. E. Smith of Letham in Angus was driving home when her car skidded off the road; walking back for the rest of the way, in the rain, her dog began to growl and she saw men carrying torches, wearing clothes which were strange to her. They struck her as looking like men searching for their dead, after a battle, to bury them. There had indeed been a battle there, in A.D. 685, accounts of which fitted reasonably well with what Miss Smith had 'seen' which could not be attributed to anything that was actually happening at the time she was walking home.

Is it necessary to suppose that Miss Smith was physically transmitted more than 1,200 years into the past, to witness the aftermath of an ancient battle? Or might a preferable alternative explanation for such experiences lie within the percipient's brain? This seems to be implied in other, less extreme experiences, such as one related by the writer John Buchan in his book *Memory Hold the Door*, which Brian Inglis summarizes:

> ... [Buchan] was on his way out to a yacht in Scotland when he 'was switched back two centuries'. He was sure that something fateful had happened, and was about to happen again when he went on board (all that happened was a welcome with a glass of Scotch). [In another experience] while serving as Lord High Commissioner in Edinburgh, he was sitting in the garden of Holyrood House when he was suddenly transported to 'some Château of Touraine' in the Ronsard era, where he knew the stage had been set for some high drama in

268

which he was to play a part; but before he could be summoned to play it, an ADC appeared to remind him that 'seventy provosts and bailies were invited to luncheon'.

This seems to imply that human awareness can occasionally become displaced in time, observing events that happened in the past. In Miss Smith's case (in addition to others), her dog was also able to sense the presence of the seventh-century warriors. Since this faculty is apparently shared by some animals, we can infer that it does not represent activity in the higher brain, but rather occurs on a deeper, more instinctive level.

But what is actually *happening* in the brain to give rise to these experiences? If they are no more than hallucinations, as the sceptics would maintain, how can they be historically accurate, as in many instances they are? Perhaps the answer lies in the quantum mechanical processes that are occurring at the smallest scale within the brain, and which may have a direct bearing on how the brain perceives and processes information. It is quite a long (not to mention fashionable) leap to make, but the possibility exists that the brain is capable of utilizing the properties of fundamental particles.

According to the physicist and philosopher Danah Zohar in *Through the Time Barrier: a Study in Precognition and Modern Physics*:

It has been known for decades that the visual cortex of the human brain is sensitive enough to register a single photon [or 'particle'] of light, and that is equivalent to saying that it is registering a single quantum process – the passage of one electron from a higher energy state within an atom to a lower energy state. Such single quantum processes are, of course, subject to the Uncertainty Principle ... Before settling finally into its most stable state (and thereby emitting a photon), the electron is spread out through space and time in a myriad virtual transitions, interfering with itself and with other electrons in flagrant disregard of causality or temporality.

Zohar goes on to explain the 'Uncertainty Principle', with reference to an interesting observation by Professor David Bohm:

> The central tenet of the Uncertainty Principle is that it is impossible ever to pin down a quantum event with great precision, because the mere act of looking at it (attempting to measure its position and its momentum) changes what one was hoping to see. Bohm points out that the same is true of thought. 'If a person tries to observe what he is thinking about at the very moment that he is reflecting on a particular subject, it is generally agreed that he introduces unpredictable and uncontrollable changes in the way his thoughts proceed thereafter.'

If the brain has the ability to react to quantum-level processes (and in truth the evidence for this is somewhat tenuous), might not their spreading out through time and space result, occasionally, in the transmission of information through time, to be detected by the mind of the percipient? As Albert Einstein himself once said, 'the separation between past, present and future has the value of mere illusion, however tenacious'.

CRISIS APPARITIONS

This is all well and good, but we are nevertheless left with the $64,000 question: does the appearance of an apparition in any way signify the survival of some aspect of the human personality after physical death? We are still a long way from formulating any convincing answer. For instance, take the case of crisis apparitions, which appear to a percipient when the agent (the person whom the apparition represents) is undergoing some intense – and usually unpleasant – experience, such as injury, illness, or death itself. According to the Census of Hallucinations, conducted by the Society for Psychical Research in 1889, it is most likely that such crisis apparitions represent telepathic activity on the part of the agent, who may have been thinking of the percipient at the time of the crisis, and who may thus have generated an image of him- or herself, which was transmitted to the percipient via telepathy. (The reader will doubtless appreciate that we are unavoidably on terribly shaky ground here, as elsewhere in this Chapter, as a result of the necessity of using one disputed phenomenon to explain another disputed phenomenon.)

Just how telepathy in general is achieved, and how such telepathic signals might take the form of apparently solid, three-dimensional images, are of course beyond the bounds of our understanding. However, we do know that the mind can experience images of an apparently visual nature when the eyes are not in use, as in vivid dreams. This is especially true in the case of hypnagogic hallucinations (the hypnagogic state being that lying between wakefulness and sleep). During the hypnagogic state, when the eyes are closed and are not seeing anything except the dark insides of the eyelids, images may spring into the awareness, usually in the form of faces. I sometimes see such faces in my own hypnagogic states – unfortunately for me, they are usually so horrific as to shock me back to full wakefulness.

We can also look to hypnosis as an example of how the eye can be made to 'see' things that are apparently three-dimensional and capable of interacting with the immediate environment, but which aren't actually 'there' at all. Through post-hypnotic suggestion, a suggestible person can be brought out of a trance and see people or things that are not present, or not see people and things that are. It can thus be appreciated that apparitions are at least fundamentally poss-ible, even if the exact mechanisms by which they are created remain ill understood. The main problem, of course, is that a post-hypnotic suggestion is implanted in the mind of a subject by the hypnotist, who is in direct contact with him or her through the audible communication of ideas and instructions. In the case of apparitions, there is apparently no such direct contact, since the agent may be many miles away from the percipient. The problem is compounded in cases of severe crisis, where the agent is actually unconscious, or even dead, at the time the apparition is 'seen'. In addition, in such cases the apparition is not 'seen' in the physical condition of the agent. If a person is on his or her deathbed, for instance, the crisis apparition will not appear as such to the percipient; rather, it will appear as the agent was when in good health, wearing the clothes the agent usually wore.

For this reason, it seems likely that the mind of the agent cannot be the sole factor in the appearance of apparitions; there must in some way be an unwitting co-operation on the part of the percipient. At such times, the apparition is apparently well grounded in the percipient's environment, as illustrated by the case of Lieutenant McConnell, described in Chapter 6, who opened the door of his room before saying hello to his room-mate, while his body lay mangled in his crashed aircraft miles away. Crisis apparitions almost always relate to the *percipient*'s environment, rather than that of the *agent*.

How can this be so? In his book *Apparitions*, the psychical researcher G. N. M. Tyrrell has this to say on this curious attribute:

> ... [Apparitions] adapt themselves almost miraculously to the physical conditions of the percipient's surroundings, of which the agent as a rule can know little or nothing. These facts reveal the apparition to be a piece of stage machinery which the percipient must have a large hand in creating and some of the details for which he must supply – that is to say, an apparition cannot be merely a direct expression of the agent's *idea*; it must be a drama worked out with that idea as its *motif*.

So, in a crisis apparition, what seems to happen is that the mind of the agent creates a fundamental idea of himself, perhaps comparable to a blueprint, which is then transmitted to the percipient. Once installed in the percipient's mind, this 'blueprint' is realized in three dimensions, with the realization process taking account of the nature of the environment into which it is to be projected. In addition, the percipient's mind also supplies the initial idea with accessories, such as clothes, borrowed from its own memories of the agent. The process might be compared with the transmission of television pictures: the events occurring in a studio are captured by a camera (the initial idea), which are then transmitted in the form of waves of electromagnetic energy to a receiver, a television set. Once there, they are decoded by the set, and appear as 'apparitions' on the screen. This is, of course, a rather imperfect analogy, since what we see on our screens is pretty much the same as what happens in front of the studio cameras; and television images cannot interact with the environment of our homes. But the idea of encoding, transmission and decoding in a receiver is nevertheless a useful one.

In the book he edited with Christopher Evans, *World Famous Strange But True*, Colin Wilson cites a case in which the interaction between the agent and the percipients was not the result of a crisis, and did not have an entirely 'lifelike' quality:

Such fidelity to natural laws is not a feature of all apparitions. Tyrrell mentions a case in which an apparition close to a mirror did not have a reflection. Another case collected by the SPR illustrates the unrealistic features of some of these apparitional dramas. One day about a hundred years ago, an English clergyman, Canon Bourne, went out fox hunting with his two daughters. After a time the daughters decided to return home with their coachman while their father continued hunting, but they were delayed for several minutes when a friend rode up to talk to them. 'As we were turning to go home,' reported Lousia Bourne in an account confirmed by her sister, 'we distinctly saw my father, waving his hat to us and signing us to follow him. He was on the side of a small hill, and there was a dip between him and us. My sister, the coachman, and myself all recognized my father, and also the horse [the only white horse in the field that day]. The horse looked so dirty and shaken that the coachman remarked he thought there had been a nasty accident. As my father waved his hat I clearly saw the Lincoln and Bennett [hatter's] mark inside, though from the distance we were apart it ought to have been utterly impossible for me to have seen it . . .'

The girls and the coachman quickly rode toward Canon Bourne, losing sight of him as they rode into the dip in the terrain. When they emerged from the dip and approached the place where he had been, he was nowhere to be seen. After riding around looking for him, they finally went home. Later Canon Bourne – who arrived home shortly after them – told them that he had not even been near the place they had seen him.

One peculiarity of this case, apart from the odd feature of the clarity of the hatter's mark, is that no crisis occurred. Canon Bourne suffered no accident, as his daughters and coachman feared, nor, apparently, did he even narrowly escape having one – which might have triggered an unconscious telepathic call for help. There is a slim possibility that the hallucination was a subjective one, created by the percipients themselves, who may have had some fear that he might have met with an accident.

Of course, this hypothesis is far from satisfactory, in view of the fact that three people saw the apparition of Canon Bourne, which would have been most unlikely, had his appearance been merely a subjective hallucination. Tyrrell acknowledged this problem of the collective perception of apparitions by multiple witnesses, made worse by the unlikelihood of an image being transmitted to several percipients simultaneously, and suggested that once an agent has transmitted the initial idea of himself (for whatever reason), and it has been received by the mind of the percipient, the latter then involuntarily retransmits the information to his companions, acting, in effect, as a kind of 'relay station' for the telepathic signal.

At this point, an obvious problem presents itself: if telepathy can be made to account for crisis apparitions of the badly injured or nearly dead, and other apparitions of the living, then how do we account for the apparitions of people who have been dead for hours, weeks or years? Who, then, is the agent, the source of the signal, whatever its true nature?

In their book *Phantasms of the Living*, the psychical research-ers F. W. H. Myers, Frank Podmore and Edmund Gurney concluded from their investigation of numerous cases that it was possible for a crisis apparition to be generated up to twelve hours after an agent's death. They suggested that one reason for the time lag could be that a percipient might be concentrating on other matters at the time of transmission, and that the idea of the agent might be somehow stored in the mind for later retrieval, when it was more open to such perceptions.

Another possible reason for delayed visualization might be furtive, fluctuating but nevertheless continuing activity in a brain that otherwise gives every indication of being dead. Indeed, a faculty such as telepathy, which is little understood and whose very existence is hotly disputed, might very well continue undetected by doctors for some time after a patient has been pronounced dead.

PSYCHOKINESIS

A related attribute (no less controversial than telepathy) which might account for many apparently ghostly occur-rences is psychokinesis, or the movement of objects through the action of the mind alone. We have seen that many poltergeist cases involve the movement and destruction of objects, frequently in the presence of an adolescent, which has led many researchers to speculate that some psychokinetic (PK) events may be a result of the action of a burgeoning sexual energy.

Ghost researcher Andrew Green investigated a poltergeist

case in an English bakery, which had been owned and run by the same family for many years, before being sold to another family. One of the new owners, a woman, immediately had the feeling that something was not quite right with the place, that 'someone' was there, even though it was empty apart from herself and her husband and son. There followed the usual poltergeist manifestations, such as doors opening and closing, and various objects being moved around by unseen hands. On several occasions, the woman felt someone push past her.

The family, husband, wife and son, went to see the family from whom they had bought the bakery, in an attempt to find out if the place really was haunted, and if so, by whom. The other family assured them that there was no ghost in the bakery, and that they had never experienced anything untoward in all the years they had owned and run the place. While they were having this conversation, the new owners noticed that one of the family, an old man, was dozing throughout ... Still puzzled and disturbed by their experiences, the new owners returned to the bakery, in which they continued to experience the manifestations for the next two years.

It was on a Tuesday that they got up to begin what they assumed would be another day of strange, disturbing goings-on. But it soon became evident to them that the atmosphere in the bakery was subtly different: there were no more uneasy feelings of an unseen presence, and indeed, from that day onward, the apparent poltergeist manifestations ceased completely and the family were at last left in peace.

It later emerged that on that very same day, the old man whose family had previously owned the bakery had died. It seems that the old man had been haunting the bakery while still alive. After his retirement, he did little but sit and doze in an armchair, doubtless remembering the past events of his life, much of which was taken up with working in the bakery. While doing so, he seems to have projected some aspect of himself into the environment in which he had spent so much of his life, with the result that its presence could be felt by the new owners. In addition, its activities in the bakery were played out physically, with the movement of various utensils, the opening and closing of doors, and so on.

In short, the apparent poltergeist activity was actually caused by psychokinesis, which was conducted at a considerable distance from the actual site of the disturbances. This sounds absurd, even more outrageous than the idea of a person moving objects with the mind while only a few inches away from them. But the correlation between the date of the old man's death and that of the cessation of the disturbances seems more than coincidence. It has to be admitted that one possible (even likely) explanation for the events in the bakery is that the old man was haunting the place before he had died! (Incidentally, there were no reports of him returning to the place after his death.) And yet, if it is possible for a person to move objects with the power of the mind alone (and there is a certain amount of evidence in support of this), then should we expect physical distance, be it inches or miles, to be a relevant factor? Perhaps not.

PSYCHOMETRY

As the chapter arrangement of this book shows, there is an important distinction to be made between apparitions of those in crisis, which frequently interact with their percipients, and ghosts which merely haunt a certain place, and which seem to ignore – or be unaware of – the presence of living people. As mentioned in Chapter 3, the latter cases imply an absence of consciousness on the part of the haunting ghosts, which has led many researchers to suspect that they are no more than psychic recordings, moving images imprinted on the very atmosphere in a house or other locale.

How could this be so? What processes might be at work, which would allow such a recording to be made and retrieved by the percipient? A clue to a possible answer lies in the word 'retrieved', for once again, as with crisis apparitions, it seems that the percipient plays an important part in the perception of haunting ghosts. One interesting theory was proposed early this century by Eleanor Sidgwick of the SPR, and is based on the concept of psychometry. Psychometry is a psychic ability which allows a person to access information about the history of an object simply by coming into physical contact with it. For example, if a psychometrist holds a wristwatch, he or she is able to relate events in the life of its owner, or if it is an old wristwatch, all of its owners. The word 'psychometry' was coined by Professor Buchanan of the Eclectic Medical Institute in Covington, Kentucky, in 1842. Buchanan began to research the ability when an acquaintance mentioned to him that he was able to detect brass in the dark by touching it and experiencing a metallic taste in his mouth. Later experiments proved that he was able to identify a number of substances exclusively through the sense of touch.

Eleanor Sidgwick suggested that certain people may have the ability to unwittingly psychometrize a building or a particular location, and thus access the historical information associated with it, including the lives of the people who lived there in the past. This information may take the form of visual images of these past lives and events, which the percipient sees as 'ghosts'. However, the reader may detect a flaw in this theory, in that such a person, upon psychometrizing a building, would surely be expected to 'see' much more than an occasional phantom flitting past. He or she would surely access the whole – or at least a substantial part – of the history of the house, including all the people who ever lived there. In view of the great age of countless 'haunted' buildings around the world, percipients who unwittingly used their psychometric abilities would be expected to be literally surrounded by image upon image from the past. This is clearly not the case.

So, if psychometry is a factor in such experiences, why is only one ghost (or a mere handful of ghosts) encountered? The answer may lie in a factor that has been said to account for psychic recordings in general: that they almost invariably occur as a result of violent or traumatic events. In other words, if a person has died violently, or there has been great suffering of another kind, a psychometrist (especially one who doesn't even realize he or she possesses the ability) might pick up only on this, by virtue of its much greater emotional intensity, and be unable to access the rest of a house's history, including that which involved people who did not suffer in such extreme ways.

PSYCHIC REMNANTS

The behaviour of the majority of haunting ghosts – as opposed to crisis apparitions – strongly implies that there is no 'mind' behind the manifestations. They merely wander around, ignoring anyone who happens to be near by, drifting up and down corridors or in and out of rooms in a generally pointless fashion. They indeed appear to be little more than moving images on an ethereal tape recorder that goes on and on playing, *ad infinitum*. However, questions remain as to what powers these recordings.

We have already looked at the theory that certain events in the long-extinct lives of certain people have the capacity to become imprinted in certain locations. Another related theory as to the processes by which haunting ghosts can continue to appear is that of 'psychic remnants'. According to this theory, the energy required to sustain a ghost is actually supplied by the person while still alive, as explained in Wilson's and Evans's *World Famous Strange But True*.

The Oxford philosopher H. H. Price suggested the existence of a 'psychic ether' permeating all matter and space. This ether could be impressed with certain mental images. Such an impression would be most likely to occur in traumatic circum-stances [as with the psychic recording theory] – violent death, or great emotional suffering. Thus the correlation often noted between unnatural death and subsequent haunting need not be attributed to a trapped soul [the traditional reason for ghostly manifestations]. The thing trapped in the haunted place would be a kind of recording made on the medium of psychic ether, capable of being perceived in the form of an image, sound, or touch by a sensitive person.

Such a theory has the advantage of bringing the haunting apparition under the same umbrella with the telepathic apparition. If a person is capable of sending a psychic impulse telepathically to a particular person, it seems equally possible that he could project a psychic impulse with no particular receiver in mind, and that that impulse might remain free-floating in the area where the person is at the time he projects the impulse.

This link between psychic remnants, psychic recordings and telepathic apparitions illustrates my earlier point, that the various theories regarding ghosts tend to merge into one another, providing a tantalizing glimpse of a complete, unifying theory of all apparitions (perhaps all paranormal phenomena) which might one day be developed.

APPARITIONS OF INANIMATE OBJECTS

If certain apparitions can be explained through recourse to one of the above theories, how may we account for apparitions of inanimate objects, such as the Dakota aircraft we encountered in Chapter 3? They obviously have no mind with which to project images of themselves, yet they have been perceived many times, and are just as (apparently) solid and three-dimensional as apparitions of people.

G. N. M. Tyrrell pondered this question also, and came up with the concept of the 'idea-pattern'. With reference to the legends of the god Pan, he writes in *Apparitions* of the belief in this semi-human, supernatural creature, whose habitat is isolated tracts of woodland and upland regions.

280

The widely spread idea that this happened might conceivably sink into the [perception] of . . . a whole community, and there form a telepathic idea-pattern, having a multiple agency. Anyone (suitably sensitive) going to the places which, according to the idea pattern, Pan was especially supposed to inhabit would then see and hear Pan with the same reality that a person going into a haunted house sees and hears a ghost.

There is a clear correlation between Tyrrell's idea-pattern and another great favourite of paranormal theorists, Jung's collective unconscious. According to Jung, the human species possesses an unconscious quite apart from that of the individual. The collective unconscious consists of thoughts and memories common to all humanity, the principal components of which are the 'archetypes', which correspond to the defining characteristics of human experience, such as death, procreation and so on. The archetypes find their expression in the most profound activities of human intelligence, such as religion and mythology, and Jung theorized that they can be externalized in various forms. Probably the most well known of these (especially to those with an interest in the paranormal) is the mandala, a circular archetype denoting balance, continuity and harmony, which he suggested formed the basis of UFO sightings, as an external expression of humanity's universal longing for this balance and harmony.

If the consciousness of each human being is really an island rising up out of a vast ocean of collective memory and emotion, it is conceivable that the impressions of inanimate objects would also be available for access by the mind. In addition, it may be that the very events that, because of their violence or trauma, result in the imprinting of psychic energy upon the environment contain elements that are 'downloaded' into the collective unconscious and stored there, for later retrieval by percipients who possess the requisite psychic sensitivity. These would, of course, include every inanimate object, from Second World War aircraft to phantom coaches.

As far as the postulated psychic energy is concerned, by which apparitions are 'powered', there is a certain amount of support in the form of a case cited by Colin Wilson and Christopher Evans, which was reported by researcher Andrew Green. In a certain mansion in England in the eighteenth century, the ghost of a woman was seen. She was wearing red shoes, a red gown and a black headdress. A number of years later, the apparition was seen again, but this time, she was wearing pink shoes, a pink gown and a grey headdress. The third time she was seen, in the mid-nineteenth century, the shoes and gown had become white. In the years just prior to the Second World War, the sounds of footsteps and a swishing dress were reported. By 1971, when the house was to be demolished, several workmen reported feeling a presence. Did this lady's apparition gradually run out of the psychic energy required to maintain it? Perhaps, although this doesn't explain how other apparitions can appear again and again for hundreds of years . . .

Although, in some respects, we are a little closer to understanding the subject of ghosts and spirits than we were a century and a half ago, when spiritualism first arose, bringing the supposed power to communicate with the dead within the reach of anyone with a table or an ouija board, we are nevertheless not much closer to proving that human personality survives the death of the physical body. It has always been assumed that the presence in our midst of ghosts and other apparitions was itself proof of survival, but as we have just seen, it is incredibly hard to establish any such thing without the activities of the living brain intruding into our hopeful speculations.

Some cases are impressive as evidence of life after death, such as the case of the Detroit factory worker shoved out of the way of the body press by (apparently) the ghost of a previous victim; or that of Friederike Hauffe, the Seeress of Prevorst, whose contact with the ghost of an embezzler resulted in the proof of another man's innocence. To this we might add a case described by Lyall Watson in his book *The Romeo Error*, in which a man named James Chaffin died in North Carolina in 1921.

> ... [Chaffin left] all his property to one of his four sons who himself died intestate a year later. In 1925, the second son was visited by his dead father dressed in a black overcoat, who said: 'You will find my will in my overcoat pocket.' When the real coat was examined, a roll of paper was found sewn into the lining with instructions to read the 27th chapter of Genesis in the family Bible. Folded into the relevant pages was a later will than the first one, dividing the property equally between all four sons.

When we are confronted with cases like this, it seems altogether simpler just to accept that they represent the activities of discarnate human beings who have died, that there is life after death. The alternatives to this interpretation are so clumsy as to become untenable in comparison. However, cases such as this are frequently anecdotal, and the fact that they occurred decades or even centuries ago is a serious disadvantage to their being accepted at face value.

In the final analysis, there is, of course, no absolute proof. But the question of whether there really is an afterlife is one to which we will all find an answer, sooner or later.

BIBLIOGRAPHY AND
SUGGESTED FURTHER READING

Cavendish, Richard: *The Magical Arts* (originally published as *The Black Arts*). London: Arkana, 1984.

Clark, Jerome: *Unexplained!* Detroit, Michigan: Visible Ink Press, 1993.

Cohen, Daniel: *Encyclopedia of Ghosts*. Waltham Abbey, Essex: Fraser Stewart, 1991.

Dane, Christopher: *The Occult in the Orient*. New York: Popular Library, 1974.

Dash, Mike: *Borderlands*. London: William Heinemann, 1997.

Denning, Hazel M.: *True Hauntings: Spirits With a Purpose*. St Paul, Minnesota: Llewellyn Publications, 1996.

Evans, Hilary: *Gods, Spirits, Cosmic Guardians*. Wellingborough: Aquarian Press, 1986.

Fuller, John G.: *The Ghost of 29 Megacycles*. London: Grafton, 1987.

Guiley, Rosemary Ellen: *Harper's Encyclopedia of Mystical & Paranormal Experience*. Edison, New Jersey: Castle Books, 1991.

Harper, Charles G.: *Haunted Houses*. London: Senate, 1996.

Harpur, Patrick: *Daimonic Reality: a Field Guide to the Otherworld*. London: Arkana, 1995.

Inglis, Brian: *The Paranormal*. London: Paladin, 1985.

Inglis, Brian: *The Hidden Power*. London: Jonathan Cape, 1986.

Innes, Brian: *The Catalogue of Ghost Sightings*. London: Blandford, 1996.

McKee, Alexander: *Into the Blue*. London: Granada, 1983.

Monroe, Robert A.: *Journeys Out of the Body*. London: Souvenir Press, 1972.

Myers, F. W. H., Podmore, Frank, and Gurney, Edmund: *Phantasms of the Living*. London: Kegan Paul, Trench, Trubner & Co., 1918.

Roberts, Aelwyn J.: *The Holy Ghostbuster*. London: Robert Hale Ltd., 1990.

Scott, Beth, and Norman, Michael: *Haunted Heartland*. New York: Warner Books, 1985.

Shuker, Karl P. N.: *The Unexplained*. London: Carlton Books, 1996.

Spencer, John and Anne: *The Encyclopedia of Ghosts and Spirits*. London: Headline, 1993.

Spencer, John, and Wells, Tony: *Ghostwatching*. London: Virgin Books, 1994.

Steiger, Brad: *The Unknown*. Toronto: Popular Library, 1966.

Strieber, Whitley: *The Secret School: Preparation for Contact*. London: Simon & Schuster, 1997.

Townshend, Marchioness, and ffoulkes, Maude: *True Ghost Stories*. London: Senate, 1996.

Tyrrell, G. N. M.: *Apparitions*. London: Duckworth, 1953.

Underwood, Peter: *A Gazetteer of British Ghosts*. London: Pan Books, 1973.

Underwood, Peter: *Dictionary of the Supernatural*. London: Harrap, 1978.

Underwood, Peter: *Nights in Haunted Houses*. London: Headline 1994.

Underwood, Peter: *Guide to Ghosts & Haunted Places*. London: Judy Piatkus, 1996.

Wilson, Colin: *Poltergeist: a Study in Destructive Haunting*. St Paul, Minnesota: Llewellyn Publications, 1993.

Wilson, Colin, and Evans, Christopher (eds): *World Famous Strange But True*. Bristol: Parragon, 1995.

Wilson, Colin, and Grant, John (eds): *The Directory of Possibilities*. Exeter: Webb & Bower, 1981.

Wilson, Ian: *In Search of Ghosts*. London: Headline, 1996.

Zohar, Danah: *Through the Time Barrier: a Study in Precognition and Modern Physics*. London: Paladin, 1982.

JOURNALS

Fortean Times, various issues.
Fate, various issues.

INDEX

USA Networks' *Sci-Fi Channel* is available in millions of homes worldwide and features a mix of original and classic science fiction, science fact, fantasy and horror. For further information, visit the *Sci-Fi Channel*'s web site – The Dominion – at http://www.scifi.com.